Adventures in Criminal Justice Research

3RD EDITION

Adventures in Criminal Justice Research

Data Analysis for Windows® Using SPSS™ Versions 11.0, 11.5, or Higher

3RD EDITION

George W. Dowdall
St. Joseph's University

Kim A. Logio
St. Joseph's University

Earl Babbie
Chapman University

Fred Halley
State University of New York, Brockport

SAGE Publications
International Educational and Professional Publisher
Thousand Oaks ▪ London ▪ New Delhi

For information:

Sage Publications, Inc.
2455 Teller Road
Thousand Oaks, California 91320
E-mail: order@sagepub.com

Sage Publications Ltd.
6 Bonhill Street
London EC2A 4PU
United Kingdom

Sage Publications India Pvt. Ltd.
B-42, Panchsheel Enclave
Post Box 4109
New Delhi 110 017 India

Printed in the United States of America

Library of Congress Cataloging-in-Publication Data

Adventures in criminal justice research: Data analysis for Windows®
using SPSS™ versions 11.0, 11.5, or higher / George W. Dowdall . . . [et al.]— 3rd ed.
    p. cm.
Includes bibliographical references and index.
ISBN 0-7619-8808-4 (pbk)
   1. Criminal justice, Administration of—Data processing. 2. Criminal justice, Administration of—Statistical methods. 3. Information storage and retrieval systems—Criminal justice, Administration of. 4. SPSS (Computer file)
I. Dowdall, George W.
HV7412.4.A38 2004
364´.07'27—dc21

                                   2003005184

03   04   10   9   8   7   6   5   4   3   2   1

Acquiring Editor:	Jerry Westby
Editorial Assistant:	Vonessa Vondera
Production Editor:	Diana E. Axelsen
Copy Editor:	Linda Gray
Typesetter:	C&M Digitals (P) Ltd.
Indexer:	Jeanne Busemeyer
Cover Designer:	Michelle Kenny

CONTENTS

To our students, past, present, and future; and to Nathan, Olivia, Nina, and Rob;
Jim, Nolan, and Owen; Aaron, Ara, and Evie; and Matthew, Mark, Meghan, Mitchell, and Karris.

ABOUT THE AUTHORS

George W. Dowdall is Professor of Sociology at Saint Joseph's University in Philadelphia, where he teaches undergraduate and graduate criminal justice and sociology. He is chair-elect of the American Sociological Association's Section on Communication and Information Technologies. He has taught methods, statistics, and data analysis courses at Saint Joseph's University, the Harvard School of Public Health, and the Brown University School of Medicine.

Kim A. Logio is Assistant Professor of Sociology at Saint Joseph's University in Philadelphia. She teaches research methods for sociology and criminal justice students. She is actively involved in research on victims of juvenile crime and on adolescent body image.

Earl Babbie is Professor of Sociology at Chapman University. He is best known for his many texts in research methods as well as introductory sociology that have been widely adopted throughout the United States and the world.

Fred Halley is Associate Professor of Sociology at the State University of New York College at Brockport and has been developing computer-based tools for teaching social science since 1970. He has served as a collegewide social science computer consultant, directed Brockport's Institute for Social Research, and now directs the college's Data Analysis Laboratory.

PREFACE FOR INSTRUCTORS

This book is offered to you with a number of aims in mind. To begin, we want to introduce students to the logic of criminal justice research, particularly survey research. Furthermore, we present the essentials of using SPSS™ as a vehicle for putting that logic into practice. As we pursue these twin goals, however, there are a number of agendas in the background of this book. For example, students who complete the book will have learned a very useful, employable skill. Increasingly, job applicants are asked about their facility with various computer programs: word processing, spreadsheets, and data analysis. SPSS is the most popular professional program available for criminal justice data analysis—hence our choice of it as a vehicle for teaching criminal justice research.

A Focus on Developing Professional and Intellectual Skills

What sets this book apart from others that teach SPSS or similar programs is that we cast that particular skill within the context of criminal justice research as a logical enterprise. Thus in addition to learning the use of SPSS, students are learning the intellectual "skills" of conceptualization, measurement, and association. Whereas those who know only SPSS can assist in data analysis, our intention is that our students will also be able to think for themselves, mapping out analytic paths into the understanding of criminal justice data. As they polish these intellectual skills, they should be able to progress to higher levels of research and to the administration of research enterprises.

Increasingly, educators are being challenged to demonstrate the practical value of instruction, in criminal justice and the social sciences no less than in other fields. Too often, overreaction to this demand results in superficial vocational courses that offer no intellectual meaning or courses hastily contrived as a vehicle for current buzzwords, whose popularity is often short-lived. We are excited to be able to offer an educational experience that is genuinely practical for students and that also represents an intellectual adventure.

Educators who have taught methods or statistics courses typically find themselves with the daunting task of igniting their often unwilling students with the fire of enthusiasm they themselves feel for the detective work of criminal justice research at its best. In this book, we seek to engage students' curiosity by setting them about the task of understanding issues that are already points of interest for them, topics such as college student drug and alcohol abuse, criminal and juvenile justice systems across the American states, international crime survey data, and abortion. For many of our readers, we imagine that mathematical analysis still smacks of trains leaving point A and point B at different speeds and the like. Now they are going to learn that a familiarity with the logic and mathematics of criminal justice research can let them focus the light of understanding on some of the dark turbulence of opinion and hysteria. We do not tell students about opinions on abortion as much as we show them how to find out for themselves. We think that will get students to point C ahead of either of the trains.

A Focus on Active Learning

Because we are teaching students to learn for themselves, this book offers a good example of what educators call "active learning." We have set up all the exercises so that students should be executing the same SPSS operations we are discussing at any given point. Although we may give them the "answers" to assure them that they are on the right track, we leave them on their own often enough to require that they do the work rather than simply read about it. Finally, the culture of personal computers has been one of "collaborative learning" from its very beginning. More than people in any other field of activity, perhaps, computer users have always delighted in sharing what they know with others. There is probably no better context in which to ask for help: Those who know the answer are quick to respond, and those who don't often turn their attention to finding an answer, delighting in the challenge.

We would imagine that students will often want to work together as they progress through this book. That has been our experience in student testing and in courses we've taught involving computers. We suggest that you encourage cooperation among students; we are certain that they will learn more that way and will enjoy the course more. In fact, those who are initially intimidated by computers should especially be encouraged to find buddies to work with.

We've designed this book to support students' first "hands-on" course in criminal justice research. If they have had earlier introductory methods or statistics courses, they will probably come to this book at full speed; but those who have never taken a methods or statistics course can easily make it through this book. At the same time, it is not too elementary for graduate students who are having their first direct experience with criminal justice research.

Appendix C contains quizzes and independent projects to go with each chapter. These can be used as assignments for class, in lab, as homework, or simply as study aids for students.

The Book and the CD: What's Included?

This book and its accompanying CD-ROM contain everything students need, except for SPSS for Windows itself. The data on the CD are for use with SPSS version 11.0 or higher (including the student version) for Windows 95, 98, or XP. Among the data sets we've included on the CD is one with 43 variables from the 2000 General Social Survey. Another includes a sample ($n = 1,400$) from the 1993 Harvard School of Public Health College Alcohol Study. Others include criminal and juvenile justice data from across the 50 states and crime data from around the world. Other data sets and supplemental learning materials are also on the CD.

As you will see, the data sets cover a broad terrain, although we've provided for some in-depth analysis in a few instances. In addition to working their way through the exercises presented in the book, students will be able to find original lines of inquiry that grow out of their own interests and insights.

Using the General Social Survey or any of the other data sets on your CD is easy. After starting SPSS for Windows, click the sequence

File → Open → Data

to display the Open File window. Click on the "Drives" dialog box and select the drive that contains your CD. Next, move the mouse to the "File Type" dialog box and click on the suffix for SPSS for Windows data files, "SPSS(*.SAV)." Now you should see the name of the General Social Survey system file, "GSS.SAV," in the dialog box and a field labeled "File Name." Select "GSS.SAV" by placing the mouse on it and clicking. Click on "OK" in the upper right corner of the Open File window. In a few seconds, SPSS will display the GSS data in its data window. Specific instructions on using SPSS with these data are provided in later chapters, as well as suggestions for using the other data sets we've included on the CD. In Chapter 3, we instruct the students to back up GSS.SAV to another storage source.

SPSS for Windows comes with extensive help screens. They are almost like having a coach built into your computer! To use them, simply click on "Help" when you get stuck. You will notice that some key words are green in the help screens. If you click your mouse on a green word, SPSS will take you to a screen that gives you more information related to your problem.

At the top of most help screens is the option "Search." Clicking on it will give you a menu of SPSS commands and topics. Clicking on any one of them will display help screens specific to that particular command or topic. Also, at the top of most help screens is the option "Back." Clicking on "Back" takes you to the previous help screen you selected. Using "Back" allows you to back out of a series of help screens if you find that your choices have led you to a dead end.

The World Wide Web Site

Finally, we've developed a World Wide Web site for this book, and we invite you to visit it. You'll find links to criminal justice data and information all over the world. We think you will find some of the site's links particularly exciting. You'll be able to find links to a source of the entire General Social Survey, including the ability to download whatever data you want, completely free of charge. You'll also find links to SPSS and to other statistical programs. Point your browser to www.sju.edu/~gdowdall.

Among the many sites easily accessed are these:

- *General Social Survey Data.* Data from the entire set of General Social Surveys since 1972 can be extracted easily and downloaded to your own computer. Maintained by the Queens College Sociology Department, this site also allows you to search through a complete bibliography of all published uses of GSS data.
- *Bureau of Justice Statistics.* The home page of the most important source of criminal justice statistics for the United States.
- *United Nations Crime and Justice Information Network.* Visit this Web site for the latest developments in international criminal justice research and statistics.

- *National Criminal Justice Information Service.* This site will help you learn about the many data sets and publications you can download from federal and other criminal justice agencies.
- *SPSS, Inc.* The latest information and support for SPSS are available at this site.

Software Support and Service

If you or your students run into any problems using this package, several sources of support should serve your needs. Frequently, college and university computing centers have student assistants who are very helpful to new computer users. In fact, most academic computing centers employ a user services coordinator who can help faculty plan student use of the school's computers and provide aid when problems arise. If you can't find local help to solve a problem, you can call Fred Halley at Socware, Inc., in Brockport, New York, at (716) 352-1986. Or you can send e-mail to Kim Logio at logio@sju.edu or call her at St. Joseph's University in Philadelphia at (610) 660-1685. If you get the answering machine, please leave a time and phone number where you can be reached. And as a last resort, you can call SPSS, Inc., in Chicago for technical support at (312) 329-2400. Be forewarned that SPSS can't give assistance with pedagogical or substantive problems and that you may have a long wait in a telephone queue for your turn to talk to a technical support person. It has been our experience that the best help comes from local resources.

Acknowledgments

We would like to acknowledge a number of people who have been instrumental in making this book a reality. First and foremost, Jerry Westby and Vonessa Vondera of Pine Forge Press have been full partners from start to finish. And we are once again grateful for Steve Rutter's work in getting this book started. The criminal justice students, faculty, and staff at Saint Joseph's University were very helpful in supporting this project, with particular thanks extended to Marybeth Ayella, Raquel Kennedy Bergen, Dan Curran, Rick Malloy, Rob Moore, Claire Renzetti, Denise Shaw, Darren Stocker, Thad McKenna, Carrie Maloney, and Kevin Clapano. A special word of thanks to Bernie Hall, who prepared the screen shots for this edition, and to Larry Walsh for his many suggestions. The book could not have been completed without Jean Dowdall and Jim Rau.

We would also like to thank the many reviewers who helped us along the way, including Karen F. Parker, University of Florida; Jeffrey D. Monroe, Pennsylvania State University–Abington; Darryl Wood, University of Alaska–Anchorage; and Debra S. Kelley, Longwood College.

We reserve our final acknowledgment for our students, to whom this book is dedicated, with special thanks to the undergraduate and graduate students in criminal justice at Saint Joseph's University. We recognize that we've often asked them to think and do things they sometimes felt were beyond their abilities. We have admired their courage for trying anyway, and we have shared in their growth.

Part I Preparing for Criminal Justice Research

Chapter 1 **Theory and Measurement**

Chapter 2 **Criminal Justice Data Sets**

Chapter 3 **Using SPSS**

In the opening chapters of this book, we address its two main purposes: (a) to introduce you to the logic of theory, research, and practice in criminal justice and (b) to give you some practical experience through the use of the SPSS for Windows computer program.

In Chapter 1, you will discover that criminal justice research (like other forms of scientific inquiry) is based on two pillars: logic and observation. You will see how theory (the logic component) informs our investigations, making sense of our observations, and, sometimes, offers predictions about what we'll find. A particularly important step is formulating a hypothesis that becomes the center of our research. The other aspect of research on which we'll focus in this book is the collection and analysis of data. In criminal justice today, an important way of collecting data is the survey, and this book presents data from several completed surveys. A major way to explore criminal justice is to design and carry out your own survey. This book also helps you plan and carry out your own survey. Finally, using official criminal justice system data is often particularly important in our field, so we talk about how to gather data about crime and justice that's already been collected or published. We will enter data on how much each of the 50 states spends on its criminal justice system and create a file to which we can add other important data later on.

This chapter also delves more deeply into one central component of scientific inquiry: measurement. We look at some of the criteria for measurement quality and start examining the kinds of measurements represented by the data at hand.

Chapter 2 describes several data sets. One is the General Social Survey, conducted among a national sample of American adults. The CD that accompanies this book has a GSS data set, and the book's World Wide Web page explains how to get any (or all) of the data collected by this important national poll since it began in 1972. Another data set is the Harvard School of Public Health College Alcohol Survey, in which thousands of college students at 140 American campuses completed detailed questionnaires about their use of alcohol, their lifestyles, and their experience of crime, among other topics. We also present data about criminal justice and juvenile justice issues and activities across the 50 American states.

This book comes with a CD that contains data sets that you can use immediately in your exploration of crime and society—usually, all the data you'll need to begin that exploration. But in case you have special research interests, both book and CD also explain how to enter and analyze your own survey data.

The computer program we will be using, SPSS, is introduced in Chapter 3, where you will learn that there are several different versions of SPSS. Chapter 3 provides you with some initial familiarization with the version you'll be using, and you'll see how it differs from the others available.

By the time you've gone through the chapters in Part I, you should be amply prepared to undertake your adventure in criminal justice research. Welcome! Now let's get started!

Chapter 1 **Theory and Measurement**

Criminal justice research is the detective work of big questions. Whereas a conventional detective tries to find out who committed a specific crime, the criminal justice researcher or criminologist looks for the causes of crime in general. And the logic of criminal justice investigation extends far beyond criminology to include many issues surrounding crime and justice: criminal justice occupations, systems of criminal justice, patterns of crime and correction, juvenile delinquency, the courts, interpersonal violence, mental illness and crime, drug and alcohol use—the list goes on and on.

Many other issues help us understand crime and justice—social class, race, gender, the state of the economy; in fact, anything that is likely to concern you as an individual is the subject of criminal justice research because so many things are affected by, or play a role in shaping, crime and justice. Criminal justice is a truly multidisciplinary and interdisciplinary field: Although many early researchers in this field were drawn from social science areas such as sociology, today's criminal justice research employs approaches from all the social sciences as well as from fields such as management.

1.1 The Purpose of This Book

The purpose of this book is to lead you through a series of investigative adventures in criminal justice research. We can't predict exactly where these adventures will lead because you are going to be the detective. Our purpose is to show you some simple tools (and some that are truly amazing) that you can use in your investigations. We'll also provide you with several bodies of data—collected in national surveys or by criminal justice agencies throughout the country and, in one case, all over the world—that are so rich you will have the opportunity to undertake investigations that no one else has ever pursued.

If you have access to a personal computer and SPSS for Windows, this book and the computer CD included with it contain everything you need for a wide range of social investigations. This material also works with SPSS for Macintosh.

This tool is designed specifically for "messing around." If you are already comfortable with computers, you can jump right in, and very quickly you will find yourself in the midst of a fascinating computer game. Instead of fighting off alien attacks or escaping from dank dungeons, you'll be pitting your abilities and imagination against real life—but you'll be looking at a side of life that you may not now be aware of.

This tool is also well designed for the creation of college term papers. Throughout, we suggest ways to present the data you discover in the context of a typical term paper in criminal justice or the social sciences. Whereas most students are limited in their term papers to reporting what other investigators have learned about crime and the justice system, you will be able to offer your own insights and discoveries.

Finally, the data sets included here are being analyzed by professional criminologists and other social scientists today. Moreover, the analytical tools we've provided you with are as powerful as those used by many professional researchers. Frankly, there's no reason you can't use these materials for original research worthy of publication in a research journal. All it takes is curiosity, imagination, practice, and a healthy obsession with knowing the answers to things. In our experience, what sets professional researchers apart from others is that they have much greater curiosity about the world around them, are able to bring powerful imagination to bear on understanding it, are willing to put in the time required of effective investigation, and are passionately driven to understand.

Today, the two statistical packages most widely used by social scientists are **SPSS**[1] (the Statistical Package for the Social Sciences) and **SAS** (the Statistical Analysis System). Until the mid-1980s, these large, generalized statistical packages were available only for large mainframe computers.

The advent of personal computers set off a revolution in how social science data analysis was done. By the mid-1980s, personal computers had become powerful enough to run statistical packages and cheap enough for individuals to purchase. This made it feasible for statistical package producers to rewrite their packages for personal computers. Although personal computers do not have the storage capacity to work with extremely large amounts of data, they are very appropriate for moderate data analysis needs.

1.2   Why Use SPSS?

We have selected SPSS for your use in these exercises for four reasons. First, early versions of SPSS date back to 1968. The package is well-known, and there is hardly a criminologist who has earned a graduate degree in the past 30 years who has not had some contact with SPSS. At a recent national meeting of criminal justice statistics experts, it wasn't at all surprising that there was a special training session in using SPSS—and it was the only statistical package that had such a session devoted to it. If you are or will be a graduate student in criminal justice, you're almost certain to want to use SPSS. Second, SPSS takes you through all the basic issues of using a statistical package. This knowledge will give you a head start if you learn some other package later on. (In fact, data sets saved within SPSS can be translated into other statistical packages quite easily.) Third, SPSS lets you access literally a world of data. The General Social Survey (GSS) is one of the best sources of data for understanding crime and justice trends in our society, and we'll show you how all its data, and the SPSS instructions necessary to use them, can be accessed through the Internet. We'll also introduce some of the most important criminal justice databases available from the National Institute of Justice (NIJ). NIJ data sets all come with instructions prepared in SPSS, so learning SPSS allows you to investigate important American criminal justice data. Moreover, the World

---

[1]Terms that appear in boldface in the text are important, and you should be able to define them.

Crime Survey data comes complete with SPSS instructions, so you can access an entire world of crime and justice data!

Finally, SPSS comes in several versions. The mainframe version is available for all the major mainframe computers. The most recent version of SPSS is designed for use with Windows, and many people have found it to be by far the easiest version to use, thanks in part to the Windows user interface. The present book is designed specifically for that version and was specially written for criminal justice researchers and students. SPSS also now has a version for Macintosh users.

SPSS is a professional tool used across the social and behavioral sciences. Mainframe versions are not sold but are leased to organizations on a yearly basis. The costs range from $1,000 to tens of thousands of dollars, depending on the type and size of the organization. The Base System of SPSS for Windows can be purchased for far less. Optional features, including graphics, data entry, advanced statistics, and specialized statistics, can be added to the Base System for Windows. But graduate students may be able to get the Base System and all the options for a fraction of that list price—check with your instructor or campus bookstore.

The SPSS for Windows Student Version can be purchased only through college and university bookstores. SPSS offers substantial discounts for courses using its products. For up-to-date information, call SPSS's sales and marketing office at (800) 543-2185. The Student Version is available from Prentice Hall. (Check the Web page for this book at www.sju.edu/~gdowdall for links to SPSS.) The Student Version can handle up to 50 variables and 1,500 cases; this is more than enough for many important criminal justice investigations. Not surprisingly, several of the statistical approaches available in the full version of SPSS for Windows are not available in the Student Version, but you will be impressed by how many of the most important techniques are available. The computer requirements for each version of SPSS are presented clearly on each product; call SPSS if you have any questions about these requirements.

The SPSS programmers have made an effort to keep the structure and syntax of all the SPSS versions very similar. If you learn any version, you should have little difficulty using the other versions. You may notice a slight difference in what you see onscreen when you move from version to version.

The exercises included on the CD have been specifically designed for both the professional and student versions of SPSS for Windows. We think you are going to enjoy the book. If you have half as much fun working with the exercises as we had creating them, you're in for a treat. The determining factor is probably your level of enjoyment in solving an engaging puzzle. If you like figuring out how the pieces fit, you're ready to set out on your search for understanding crime and criminal justice! We should note that learning how to use SPSS for Windows will provide you with a marketable skill in today's competitive job market. Many criminal justice agencies can make use of a person who knows how to use software such as SPSS in understanding the huge amount of data they are required to collect.

1.3   Research in Criminal Justice

This book addresses primarily the techniques of criminal justice data analysis. Thus we're going to spend most of our time analyzing data and reaching conclusions about the people who answered questions about crime, justice, substance use, and other issues in two surveys—the GSS and the College Alcohol

Survey—which are described in more detail below. Moreover, we'll discuss how to do your own survey and how to use SPSS to analyze it. We'll also examine an equally important set of sources of data for criminal justice research—official data about crime and the justice system gathered by local, state, and federal agencies and by criminal justice agencies throughout the world.

Data analysis doesn't occur in a vacuum, however. Scientific inquiry is a matter of both observing and reasoning. Before getting into the techniques of data analysis, then, let's take a minute to consider the role of theory in conjunction with research and practice.

Given the variety of topics examined in criminal justice research, no single, established set of procedures is always followed in inquiry. Nevertheless, data analysis almost always has a bigger purpose than the simple manipulation of numbers. Our larger aim is to learn something of general value about crime and society. To understand those larger issues, we will first discuss the national agenda for research on crime and then discuss criminological and criminal justice theory.

The federal agency committed to understanding crime is the NIJ, the research and development agency of the U.S. Department of Justice. Created by Congress in 1968, the NIJ is authorized to "improve and strengthen the Nation's system of justice with a balanced program of basic and applied research." **Basic research** means scientific research designed to test and extend a theoretical understanding of crime and its consequences for society. **Applied research** means research that helps improve the operation of criminal justice agencies by studying what works and what doesn't in areas such as crime prevention, punishment and corrections, or juvenile justice. Examples of basic research might include attempts to study the basic causes of violent crime, the impact that the criminal justice system has on rates of crime, and the ways in which organizations such as prisons change over time. By contrast, applied research might look at how a particular program designed to lower the risk of drug abuse actually changes (or doesn't change) people's behavior.

We have noted that basic research tests and extends a theoretical understanding of crime and its consequences. But what is **theory**? Schutt (2001) explores theories of crime, defining theory as "a logically interrelated set of propositions about empirical reality" (p. 36). So theories of crime might turn out to be interconnected statements that explain why criminal behavior is related to other events in a person's life or why certain kinds of communities or societies have specific rates of crime.

Some theorists think that biological and physiological factors play a causal role. Others link personality type to crime. Yet others see crime as the product of special subcultures or of the gap between cultural goals and the opportunities (or lack of opportunities) with which to reach those goals. Finally, some theorists look to very basic parts of society—the development of capitalism, the persistence of patriarchy—to understand crime. In fact, there are many theories of crime. Curran and Renzetti (1994) discuss several broad paradigms or schools of thought that have shaped contemporary theories of crime.

Social scientific **research** (including research in criminal justice) involves a bringing together of concepts and data—ideas and observations about human social life. Ultimately, we seek to establish a correspondence between what we observe and our conceptual understanding of the way things are. Some of the criminal justice concepts you are familiar with might include crime, victimization, social class, deviance, political orientation, racial prejudice, and alienation.

Many concepts, such as those just mentioned, distinguish variations among people. Gender, for example, distinguishes "men" and "women." Social class might distinguish "upper class," "middle class," and "working class." Binge drinking might differentiate between students who drink heavily on occasion ("binge drinkers") from students who don't drink heavily ("nonbinge drinkers" or "nonbingers"). When social scientists actually measure concepts that capture variations among people, we shift terminology from concepts to variables. As an idea, then, gender is a concept; when actually measured, in a questionnaire, for example, it becomes a variable for analysis. Explanatory social inquiry is a matter of discovering which attributes of different variables are associated with one another and then trying to figure out whether that association reflects a cause-and-effect relationship. Are men or women more likely to binge drink? Does maleness in some way determine that men will be heavier drinkers than women? Which ethnic groups are likely to support gun control? Are members of the upper and middle social classes less likely to support capital punishment than members of the working and lower classes? Is social class somehow related to punishment philosophy? These are the kinds of questions that criminal justice researchers address.

Criminal justice researchers also examine a variety of very practical questions. Are crime rates in a particular jurisdiction rising or falling? Is the use of police or other criminal justice personnel changing? Do local trends reflect national trends? These and other practical questions are often at the center of research in criminal justice.

1.4   Theory in Criminal Justice: Routine Activity Theory

A theory is a statement or set of statements pertaining to the relationships variables. A theory, therefore, is a set of logical explanations about patterns of human social life, patterns among the variables that describe people. For example, one of the most influential recent theories in understanding crime has been termed **routine activity theory** by its creators, the American criminologists Cohen and Felson (1979). This theory shifts attention away from the motivation of criminals toward three factors that might account for the location and amount of crime: (a) the presence or physical proximity of likely offenders, (b) the absence or physical removal of capable guardians, and (c) the availability of suitable targets. This very broad theoretical approach was initially developed to shed light on why, during the period after World War II when affluence was rising in the United States, crime was also rising. Cohen and Felson argued that the changing patterns of offenders, guardians, and targets could better account for the rise in crime than any motivational shift could.

Many years after the original formulation of routine activity theory, Schwartz and Pitts (1995) published an article in the important criminal justice journal *Justice Quarterly* that used the theory to examine sexual assault on college campuses by noting that certain college women are viewed as "suitable targets" by potential offenders. They theorized that the routine activity approach suggested that women who go out drinking often and women who are friends of motivated offenders might be more likely to be sexually victimized. Schwartz and Pitts used survey data to examine these two variables—frequency of drinking and friendship with motivated offenders. The theory explains why these variables are related to each other in a particular way.

1.5   Hypotheses in Criminal Justice Research

Looked at only a little differently, the theory offers expectations about the ways variables would be found to relate to one another in life. In scientific language, these expectations are called hypotheses.

Schutt (2001) defines a **hypothesis** as "a tentative statement about empirical reality, involving the relation between two or more variables" (p. 38). Sometimes the hypotheses are specific implications drawn from a theory. In the case of research on campus sexual assault, the researchers drew out the implications of routine activity theory to formulate two hypotheses: (a) Women who drink more, and more often, than other women are more likely to be victims of sexual assault; (b) women who have male friends who use alcohol to get women drunk in order to have sex are more likely to be victims.

Sometimes the hypotheses are expectations that a person develops because of direct experience. Those of us who have been participants in the criminal justice system often develop ideas based on our experiences in the system that tell us what we expect to happen in given situations. One of the authors of this book worked on a criminal defense team some years ago. Based on their experience in the courts, the defense lawyers believed that women, young people, and members of minority groups were more likely to be skeptical of police witnesses in criminal trials than were men, older people, or members of majority groups.

And sometimes hypotheses are statements about what we expect to see happen when a new policy or program is put into place. For example, many in the criminal justice system think that students who participate in the Project D.A.R.E. (Drug Abuse Resistance Education) program should have lower drug and alcohol use than students who don't participate.

So in criminal justice research, factors such as criminological theory, practical experience in the criminal justice system, or experience with a new prevention program or intervention might lead one to formulate a testable hypothesis.

It is important to recognize that relationships predicted in a particular hypothesis are often **probabilistic relationships**. Not every college woman who drinks heavily will be the target of sexual assault, but the hypothesis predicts that such women will on the average have higher rates of sexual assault victimization. Not every woman or young person or minority group member will be skeptical of police witnesses, but on average such a person might be more skeptical than the average man, older person, or member of the majority group. That is the nature of probabilistic relationships.

Sometimes theories and the hypotheses derived from them are the result of largely intellectual procedures—that is, thinking about and reasoning what the relationships in some set of variables should be. Other times, researchers build theories later, to explain the relationships they've already observed in their analysis of data. Much of the research about binge drinking is of this type: The researchers suspect that binge drinking is related in some way to crime perpetration and victimization and to some other behavioral and health problems. The data analysis occurred first, and the researchers then faced the task of making sense of the several relationships they uncovered.

Stepping back a pace for a larger perspective on the process of social scientific inquiry, we find an alternation between the two approaches just described. Understandings and expectations are reached; they are tested through the collection and analysis of data; the findings arrived at in the data analysis are then subjected to further evaluation and understanding, producing a modified theory.

Often the phase that involves moving from theoretical understandings and the derivation of specific hypotheses to the collection and analysis of data is called deduction, and the process that proceeds from data back to theory is called induction. More simply, **deduction** can be seen as reasoning from general understandings to specific expectations, whereas **induction** can be seen as reasoning from specific observations to general explanations. Although criminal justice researchers might disagree about the role of each in actual investigation, both deduction and induction are essential parts of any scientific inquiry.

1.6   Should Abortion Be Legal?

One of the most dramatic and controversial issues in American society is abortion. For much of the past century, abortion was illegal. But during the 1960s and 1970s, a broad movement for its legalization began to have a big impact on state laws. In 1973, in the case of *Roe v. Wade,* the U.S. Supreme Court struck down a state's ability to restrict a woman's access to abortion. As a social issue, it has figured importantly in religious and political debate ever since.

Abortion is an important issue for crime and justice: If abortion were made illegal again, it would classify as criminal offenses specific behaviors that tens of millions of American women have engaged in. Moreover, it would criminalize behavior that is unusually difficult to monitor, let alone police effectively. But many people believe that abortion is murder and as such constitutes the most common form of loss of human life in our society. No matter which side you feel is correct, you will probably agree that understanding attitudes about abortion is an important research topic for students of criminal justice.

The GSS contains several variables dealing with attitudes toward abortion. Each asks whether a woman should be allowed to have an abortion for a variety of reasons. The following list shows these reasons, along with the abbreviated variable names you'll be using for them in your analyses later on. (Most data analysis software such as SPSS makes use of short names for variables such as these.)

ABDEFECT	Because there is a strong chance of a serious defect
ABNOMORE	Because a family wants no more children
ABHLTH	Because the woman's health would be seriously endangered
ABPOOR	Because a family is too poor to afford more children
ABRAPE	Because the pregnancy resulted from rape
ABSINGLE	Because the woman is unmarried
ABANY	Because the woman wants it, for any reason

Before we begin examining answers to the abortion attitude questions, it is worth taking a moment to reflect on their logical implications. Which of these items do you suppose would receive the least support? That is, which will have the smallest percentage of respondents agreeing with it? Think about that before continuing.

Logically, we should expect the smallest percentage to support ABANY, because it "contains" all the others. For example, those who would support abortion in the case of rape might not support it for other reasons, such as the family's poverty. Those who support ABANY, however, would have to agree with both of those more specific items.

Three of the items tap into reasons that would seem to excuse the pregnant woman from responsibility:

ABDEFECT   Because there is a strong chance of a serious defect

ABHLTH   Because the woman's health would be seriously endangered

ABRAPE   Because the pregnancy resulted from rape

We might expect the highest percentages to agree with these items. We'll see if our expectations are correct.

When we analyze this topic with data, we'll begin by finding useful ways of measuring overall attitudes toward abortion. Once we've done that, we'll be in a position to find out why some people are generally supportive and others generally opposed.

1.7   Crime, Punishment, and Violence

The GSS also contains some other questions that Americans were asked about crime and justice topics. Among the most important is this question dealing with capital punishment: "Do you favor or oppose the death penalty for persons convicted of murder?" Would you expect more Americans to favor the death penalty or to oppose it? A little later in this book, we'll discuss the fact that the United States is unique among the developed nations of the world in still having a death penalty for murder. The United States is also unique in that some of its states allow the death penalty and others do not.

Why would some people support the death penalty while others oppose it? Would you expect their general attitudes about politics—whether they think of themselves as conservatives or liberals—to predict their attitudes about capital punishment? How about their attitudes about abortion—do you think those who oppose abortion would also oppose the death penalty? Why? You're about to learn how to use SPSS to test your own hypotheses.

Another important question for the criminal justice system was asked of respondents to the GSS: "Would you favor or oppose a law which would require a person to obtain a police permit before he or she could buy a gun?" The responses to this question make up the variable we will come to know as GUNLAW. What percentage of respondents would you think favored or opposed GUNLAW? Do you believe the percentage has been increasing or decreasing over time?

In addition to issues of crime and justice, the GSS also asked about how respondents viewed sexual behavior. The variable PREMARSX began with a somewhat longer introduction: "There's been a lot of discussion about the way morals and attitudes about sex are changing in this country. If a man and woman have sex relations before marriage, do you think it is always wrong, almost always wrong, wrong only sometimes, or not wrong at all?" The variable HOMOSEX was based on the question, "What about sexual relations between two adults of the same sex—do you think it is always wrong, almost always wrong, wrong only sometimes, or not wrong at all?" Another question was used to construct the variable XMOVIE: "Have you seen an X-rated movie in the last year?"

1.8   The Logic of Measurement

Measurement is one of the most fundamental elements of science. In the case of criminal justice research, the task is typically one of characterizing individuals in terms of the issues under study. Thus a crime victimization study will characterize respondents in terms of which criminal victimizations (if any) they have experienced during a particular period of time. A study of abortion attitudes will describe people in terms of their attitudes on that topic. A study of substance abuse will indicate what illegal or legal substances the respondents have used and perhaps how frequently they have used or abused each substance.

1.9   Validity Problems

Validity is a term used casually in everyday language, but it has a more precise meaning in social research. It describes an indicator of a concept. Most simply, the indicator is said to be valid if it really measures what it is intended to measure and invalid if it doesn't.

As a simple example, let's consider political orientation, ranging from very liberal to very conservative. For an example of a valid measure of this concept, here's the way the GSS asked about it:

We hear a lot of talk these days about liberals and conservatives. I'm going to show you a seven-point scale on which political views that people might hold are arranged from extremely liberal to extremely conservative. Where would you place yourself on this scale?

1. Extremely liberal
2. Liberal
3. Slightly liberal
4. Moderate, middle of the road
5. Slightly conservative
6. Conservative
7. Extremely conservative

At the opposite extreme, a simple question about the respondent's gender would obviously not be a valid measure of political orientation. It has nothing to do with politics. But now let's consider another questionnaire item that lies somewhere in between these two extremes of validity with regard to measuring political orientation.

Which of these two political parties do you most identify with?

1. Democratic Party
2. Republican Party
3. Neither

This second item is another reasonable measure of political orientation. Moreover, it is related to the first, because Democrats are, on the whole, more liberal than Republicans. But conservative Democrats and liberal Republicans do exist. If our purpose is to tap into the liberal-conservative dimension, the initial item that asks directly about political orientation is obviously a more valid indicator of the concept than the item about political party.

This particular example offers us a clear choice as to the most valid indicator of the concept at hand, but matters are not always that clear. If we were measuring levels of prejudice, for example, we could not simply ask, "How prejudiced are you?" because no one is likely to admit being prejudiced. As we search for workable indicators of a concept such as prejudice, the matter of validity becomes something to which we must pay more attention. Similarly, a lot of denial surrounds the use of drugs and alcohol, with the result that people who abuse these substances often won't admit it. So it might make more sense to ask in a non-threatening way how many alcoholic drinks a person has in a given time period and then try to categorize that person's drinking. This is usually better than asking a person to judge whether he or she "abuses alcohol."

Validity is also a problem whenever you are reanalyzing someone else's data—as you are doing in this book. Even if you can think of a survey question that would have captured your concept perfectly, the original researchers might not have asked it. Hence you often need to use ingenuity in constructing measures that nonetheless tap the quality in which you are interested. In the case of political orientation, for example, you might combine the responses to several questions, asking for attitudes about civil liberties, past voting behavior, political party identification, and so forth. We'll return to the use of multiple indicators shortly.

In large part, the question of validity is settled on prima facie grounds: We judge an indicator to be relatively valid or invalid "on its face." (Not surprisingly, this approach to validation is called **face validity**.) It was on this basis that you had no trouble seeing that asking directly about political orientation was a valid indicator of that concept, whereas asking a person's gender was definitely not a valid measure of political orientation. Later in the book, we'll explore some simple methodological techniques that are also used to test the validity of measures.

1.10   Reliability Problems

Reliability is a different but equally important quality of measurements. In the context of survey research, reliability refers to the question of whether we can trust the answers that people give us, even when their misstatements are honest ones.

Years ago, one of us was asked to assist on a survey of teenage drivers in California. Over researcher objections, the client insisted on asking the question "How many miles have you driven?" and providing a space for the teenager to write in a response. Perhaps you can recognize the problem in this question by attempting to answer it yourself. If you have ever driven an automobile, we doubt that you can report how many miles you have driven with any accuracy. In the survey mentioned, some teenagers reported driving hundreds of thousands of miles.

A better technique in that situation, by the way, would be to provide respondents with a set of categories reflecting realistically the number of miles respondents are likely to have driven—for example: fewer than 1,000 miles, 1,000–4,999 miles, 5,000–9,999 miles, and so on. Such a set of categories gives respondents a framework within which to place their own situations. Even though they still may not know exactly how much they had driven, there would be a fair likelihood that the categories they chose would actually contain their correct answers. The success of this technique, of course, would depend on our having a good idea in advance of what constitutes reasonable categories, determined by previous research, perhaps. As an alternative, we might ask respondents to volunteer the number of miles they have driven but limit the time period to something they are likely to remember. Thus we might ask how many miles they drove during the preceding week or month, for example.

Conceptually, the test of reliability is whether respondents would give the same answers repeatedly if the measurement could be made in such a way that (a) their situations had not changed (they hadn't driven any more miles) and (b) they couldn't remember the answer they gave before.

Perhaps the difference between validity and reliability can be seen most clearly in reference to a simple bathroom scale. If you step on a scale repeatedly (scales don't remember) and it gives you a different weight each time, the scale has a reliability problem. Conversely, if the scale tells you that you weigh 125 pounds every time you step on it, it's pretty reliable, but if you actually weigh 225, the scale has a problem in the validity department: It doesn't indicate your weight accurately.

Both validity and reliability are important in the analysis of data. If you are interested in learning what causes some people to have deeply held religious beliefs while others do not hold those beliefs, asking people how often they attend church would be problematic. This question doesn't really provide a valid measure of the concept that interests you, and anything you learn will explain the causes of church attendance, not religious belief. And suppose that you asked people how many times they had attended church in the past year. Any answers you received would probably not be reliable, so anything you might think you learned about the causes of church attendance might be only a function of the errors people made in answering the question. (It would be better to give them categories to choose from.) You would have no assurance that another study would yield the same result.

1.11   Multiple Indicators

Often the solution to the problems discussed lies in the creation of composite measures, using multiple indicators. Later in this book, we will examine whether college students who binge drink experience any of a series of alcohol-related problems, such as getting into arguments or getting into trouble with campus or community police. If we create an overall index that measures how many of these alcohol-related problems a student has, we may be in a better position to understand the overall impact of alcohol abuse on student behavior.

As a simple example, to measure the degree to which a sample of Christian church members held the beliefs associated with Christianity, you might ask them questions about several issues, each dealing with a particular belief, such as the following:

- Belief in God
- Belief that Jesus was divine
- Belief in the existence of the devil
- Belief in an afterlife: heaven and hell
- Belief in the literal truth of the Bible

The several answers given to these questions could be used to create an overall measure of religious belief among the respondents. In the simplest procedure, you could give respondents 1 point for each belief they agreed to, allowing you to score them from 0 to 5 on the index. Notice that this is the same logic by which you may earn 1 point for each correct answer on an exam, with the total scores being taken as an indication of how well you know the material.

Some social science concepts are implicitly multidimensional. Consider the concept of social class, for example. Typically, the term *class* is used in reference to a combination of education, income, occupation, and sometimes dimensions such as social stratum identification and prestige. This would be measured for data analysis compositely through the use of multiple indicators.

When it becomes appropriate in the analyses we will undertake together, we'll show you how to create and use some simple composite measures.

1.12   Levels of Measurement

As we convert the concepts in our minds into empirical measurements in the form of variables, we sometimes can choose their statistical sophistication, the levels at which the variables are measured. Researchers usually distinguish between four levels of measurement.

Nominal Variables

Some variables simply distinguish different kinds of people. Gender is a good example of this, simply distinguishing men from women. Another example: Has a person been arrested or not? Political party distinguishes Democrats from Republicans and from other parties. Religious affiliation distinguishes Protestants, Catholics, Jews, and so forth. We refer to these measurements as nominal because they "name." **Nominal variables** simply name the different categories constituting them.

Ordinal Variables

Many social scientific variables go a step beyond simply naming the different categories constituting a variable. **Ordinal variables** arrange those categories in some order: from low to high, from more to less, and so on. Whereas the nominal variable "religious affiliation" classifies people into different religious groups, "religiosity" might order them in groups, such as very religious, somewhat religious, and not at all religious. And whereas the nominal variable "political party identification" simply distinguishes different groups (e.g., Democrats and Republicans), an ordinal measure of "political philosophy" might rank the very liberal, the somewhat liberal, the middle-of-the-road, the somewhat conservative, and the very conservative. Similarly, one can imagine a variable that ranges from no support to total support of the death penalty.

Ordinal variables share the nominal-variable quality of distinguishing differences between people and add the quality of ranking those differences. At the same time, it is not meaningful to talk about the distances separating the categories that make up an ordinal variable. For example, we have no basis for talking about the "amount of liberalism" separating the very liberal from the somewhat liberal or the somewhat liberal from the middle-of-the-road. We can say that the first group in each comparison is more liberal than the second, but we can't say by how much.

Ratio Variables

Some variables allow us to speak more precisely about the distances between the categories constituting a variable. Consider age for a moment. The distance between 10 years old and 20 years old is exactly the same as that between 60 years old and 70 years old. Similarly, the time served in a prison is a ratio variable: 30 months and 20 months are separated by the same amount of time as 40 months and 50 months. Moreover, **ratio variables** such as age have the additional quality of containing a genuine zero point. This is what allows us to examine ratios between the categories constituting such variables. Thus we can say that a 20-year-old is twice as old as a 10-year-old. A prisoner who has served 40 months has been in prison exactly twice as long as one serving 20 months. By comparison, notice that we would have no grounds for saying one person is twice as religious as another. Ratio variables, then, share all the qualities associated with nominal and ordinal variables but have additional qualities not applicable to the lower-level measures. Other examples of ratio measures include income, years of schooling, and number of delinquent acts.

Interval Variables

Rarer in social research are variables that have the quality of standard intervals of measurement but that lack a genuine zero point: **interval variables**. One example is the intelligence quotient (IQ). Although it is calculated in such a way as to allow for a score of zero, that would not indicate a complete lack of intelligence because the person would have at least been able to take the test.

Moving outside the social sciences, consider temperature. The Celsius and Fahrenheit measures of temperature both have zero-degree marks, but neither represents a total lack of heat, given that it is possible to have temperatures below zero. The Kelvin scale, by contrast, is based on an absolute zero, which does represent a total lack of heat (measured in terms of molecular motion); it is therefore a ratio variable.

A great deal of recent effort in social science research methodology has gone into developing ways of measuring attitudes and behaviors at higher and higher levels of measurement. Although well beyond what can be discussed in detail in this book, you should be aware of efforts to use "scaling" or "multidimensional scaling" to measure at the interval level issues such as social or psychological attitudes, until recently measurable only at the nominal or ordinal level. It will constitute a fascinating additional chapter in the recent advances in social science methodology.

As a way of summarizing the levels of measurement, we suggest that you inspect the following table, which lays out very clearly how each succeeding level of measurement adds even more information to what you know about a variable.

	Nominal Variables	Ordinal Variables	Interval Variables	Ratio Variables
Mutually exclusive	Yes	Yes	Yes	Yes
Exhaustive	Yes	Yes	Yes	Yes
Ranking		Yes	Yes	Yes
Intervals			Yes	Yes
Zero point				Yes

Measurement Options

Sometimes you will have options regarding the levels of measurement to be created in variables. For instance, although age qualifies as a ratio variable, it could be measured as an ordinal (e.g., young, middle-aged, old) or even as a nominal (baby boomer, not baby boomer) variable. Similarly, the amount of time served in prison might be considered a ratio variable, but it could be measured as an ordinal (e.g., greater than average for a particular prison, less than or equal to that average) variable.

The significance of these levels of measurement will become more apparent when we begin to analyze the variables in our data set. As you'll discover, some graphical and statistical techniques are appropriate to nominal variables, some to ordinal variables, and some to ratio variables. The most basic statistical techniques depend on the level of measurement, such as whether to use the arithmetic mean, the median or middle case, or the mode or most typical value as a measure of the center of a distribution of scores. This is a very important issue, and we'll discuss it at several points later in the text.

On the one hand, to determine which analytic techniques are appropriate, you will need to know a variable's level of measurement. On the other hand, when you have options for measurement, your choice of measurement level may be determined by the techniques you want to employ.

1.13   Units of Analysis

Another important part of the process of measurement is the specification of the **units of analysis**—exactly who or what is being studied? Often in survey research, the unit of analysis is clearly an individual person or respondent. Thus in the GSS, the unit of analysis is the individual person asked to respond to the interviewer's questions. And in the College Alcohol Study, the unit of analysis is usually each of the college students who completed the self-administered questionnaire; the CD for this book includes 1,400 students from the more than 17,000 who completed the questionnaire. But some surveys use individuals as informants about entire organizations or groups. For example, the College Alcohol Study had three specialized questionnaires, filled out by three kinds of college administrators—deans of students, directors of public safety or security, and directors of student health services. Each of these administrators on each campus answered for the college as a whole, describing or analyzing what was taking place at that college. And so the unit of analysis for this part of the study is the individual college (one of 140 in the study).

Other units of analysis in criminal justice are often political jurisdictions. Several of the data sets on your CD contain evidence about each of the individual U.S. states, so the unit of analysis in our study of imprisonment is the state. Cities, police departments or districts, or even whole countries or societies could be units of analysis as well.

It is important to specify correctly what the unit of analysis is in a study. Sometimes individual responses within a broader unit are aggregated (added together) to make up the values of that broader unit. So the data for each student on a campus might be aggregated to come up with a single measure of the entire campus—what proportion of students were binge drinkers; such a proportion refers to the entire campus as the unit of analysis, not to the many individual students but to their aggregation. Similarly, data about how many individuals were murdered in a society might be added together to give the number of murders. When this number is divided by a base population (approximating the population at risk of murder), the result is a murder rate. That rate refers to the unit of analysis—in this case, an entire society.

1.14   Summary

This book has two educational aims. First, we want to share with you the excitement of criminal justice and other social scientific research. You are going to learn that a table of numerical data—pretty boring on the face of it—can hold the answers to many questions about why people think and act as they do. Finding those answers requires that you learn some skills of logical inquiry.

Second, we will show you how to use a computer program that is very popular among criminologists and criminal justice researchers. SPSS is the tool you will use to unlock the mysteries of crime and society, just as a biologist might use a microscope or an astronomer a telescope.

You may have seen prepared foods with the instruction: "Just add water and heat." Well, the package in your hands is something like that, but the instructions read, "Just add you, and let's get cooking."

This chapter also has given you an initial impression of the relationship between theory and research in criminal justice and in the social sciences. This examination will continue throughout the book. Although our most direct attention will focus on the skills of analyzing data, we will always want to make logical sense out of what we learn from our manipulations of the numbers.

Measurement is a fundamental aspect of social science research. It may be seen as the transition from concepts to variables—from sometimes ambiguous mental images to precise, empirical measures. Whereas we often speak casually about concepts such as prejudice, social class, and liberalism in everyday conversation, social scientists must be more precise in their uses of these terms.

This chapter has given you some of the logical grounding of social scientific measurement. Chapters to follow will continue this discussion, showing you the concrete techniques that allow you to act on that logic.

Key Terms

applied research	probabilistic relationships
basic research	ratio variables
deduction	reliability
face validity	research
hypothesis	routine activity theory
induction	SAS
interval variables	SPSS
measurement	theory
nominal variables	units of analysis
ordinal variables	validity

Chapter 2 **Criminal Justice Data Sets**

To explore a diverse field such as criminal justice, you need to have easy access to a variety of different data sets that have already been created. In this chapter, we'll explain several of them. You'll want to familiarize yourself with how each was collected, and you can always return to this chapter to see what kinds of variables are available on each of the data sets. They have been selected to provide you with a wide variety of variables, units of analysis, and types of data collection. Several of the data sets are about general attitudes toward crime and justice issues, one concerns college student binge drinking and its correlates (including crime perpetration and victimization), and two deal with the criminal justice and juvenile justice systems across the American states. That should be more than enough data for you to explore criminal justice research—but don't forget to check out this text's Web page on the Internet (www.sju. edu/ ~gdowdall), where you will find even more information about the world of criminal justice research.

But for many students and researchers in the field of criminal justice, the real adventure involves collecting one's own data, so we'll begin by examining the differences between primary and secondary data analysis.

2.1   Primary and Secondary Data Analysis

Primary data analysis is the term used to describe a researcher's analysis of data that he or she has collected. So if you create your own questionnaire or interview schedule, draw a sample of respondents, have them respond to your questions, code and enter the data into a computer, and then use a statistical package such as SPSS to complete your analysis, you're doing primary data analysis. If you are working on a senior research seminar or a master's or doctoral thesis that requires you to do original data collection, you will end up doing primary data analysis. This text will help you figure out how to plan the development of a questionnaire, draw samples, create codes, enter data, and do statistical analyses.

If you bring together data that other people or organizations originally collected and then use SPSS to complete the analysis, you're doing **secondary data analysis**. This is a particularly important part of criminal justice research because of the availability of so many important secondary data sets, such as the official criminal justice system statistics that describe the operation of police, courts, correctional facilities, juvenile justice organizations, and so on. In addition to these official statistics, criminal justice researchers and other social scientists have conducted hundreds of research studies. Many times, the data from these studies are contributed to a **data archive** maintained for use by others. The largest social science data archive is the Inter-university Consortium for Political and Social Research (**ICPSR**), located at the University of Michigan. It has a special collection of criminal justice studies (the National Archive of Criminal Justice Data) maintained at the request of the National Institute of Justice. With the skills you'll learn in this book and a tool like SPSS, you could use this archive of data sets. Not only are these secondary data sets available for the United States, but four different international surveys have now been conducted under the sponsorship of the United Nations. One of the most useful sources of secondary data for American research is the **General Social Survey (GSS)**, conducted with federal support by the National Opinion Research Center (NORC). You'll be using the GSS data throughout this book, so it's worth an introduction (see Section 2.2).

There's even a third kind of data analysis, called **meta-analysis**, in which the "data" are the results of other completed analyses, so that each "case" is a completed study. For example, several researchers (Ennett, Tobler, Ringwalt, & Flewelling, 1994) gathered all the published and unpublished studies of Project DARE, the largest drug prevention program for American children. Each "case" was a statistical summary of how large an effect (if any) the DARE program had on its participants. The researchers reported that when they summarize all that is known about the program, there was little evidence that it had any preventive effect.

2.2 Description of a Data Set: The General Social Survey

Several of the data sets on this book's CD come from the GSS. The data we provide for your use here are real. They come from the responses of more than 1,000 adult Americans selected as a representative sample of the nation in each year the survey has been conducted since it began in 1972. (These data are a major resource for professional social scientists and are the basis of many published books and articles.)

The GSS is conducted regularly by the NORC in Chicago, with financial support from the National Science Foundation and private sources. The purpose of the GSS program is to provide the nation's social scientists with accurate data for studying general social trends in American society. Because crime and justice are major social issues, the GSS is particularly rich in questions that criminal justice researchers will find useful. The brainchild of Jim Davis, one of the most visionary social scientists alive during your lifetime, the GSS began in 1972 and has continued more or less annually since then. (For more information about the GSS, see Davis & Smith, 1992. The Web page for this book explains how you can access through the Internet any of the data collected by the GSS since 1972.) In our discussions, we'll concentrate on the data collected by the 1990 GSS, but by using the Internet you will be able to compare the 1990 figures with those of any other year to check out whether there has been any change over time.

2.3   Sampling: How Representative Are Your Data?

The data provided by the GSS are representative of American adults. This means that anything we learn about the 1,500 people in our sample can be taken as a more or less accurate reflection (give or take some sampling error) of what all non-institutionalized, English-speaking American adults would have said if we could have interviewed them all. This is the case because of a technique known as **multistage probability sampling**.

The researchers began by selecting a random sample of cities and counties across the country, having grouped them in such a way as to ensure that those selected would reflect variations in cities and counties in the nation. At the second stage of sampling, the researchers selected a random sample of city blocks or equivalent units in rural areas within each of the selected cities and counties. This resulted in the selection of more than 500 blocks.

The researchers then visited each of the selected blocks and chose specific households at random on each. Finally, when interviewers visited each of the selected households, they determined the number of adults living in the household and selected one of them at random as the respondent.

This complex and sophisticated sampling process makes it possible for the responses of 1,000 to 2,000 individuals to provide an accurate reflection of the feelings of all adult Americans. Similar techniques are used by federal agencies for the purpose of government planning and by polling firms that predict voting behavior with relative accuracy. (Only the official U.S. census, taken every 10 years, actually tries to enumerate the entire population.)

The GSS data you have at hand, then, can be taken as an accurate reflection of the characteristics, attitudes, and behaviors of Americans aged 18 and older in a particular year. This statement needs to be qualified slightly, however. When you analyze the data and learn that 43% of the sample said they supported a woman's unrestricted right to have an abortion for any reason, you are safe in assuming that about 43% of the entire U.S. adult population feels that way. Because the data are based on a sample rather than on asking everyone, however, we need to anticipate some degree of sampling error. It would not be strange, for example, to discover that 42% or 44% of the total adult population (rather than exactly 43%) held the opinion in question. It is inconceivable, however, that as little as 10% or as much as 90% of the population supported unrestricted abortion.

As a rough rule of thumb, you can assume that the sampling error in this data set is plus or minus only a few percentage points. In Chapter 9, we'll see how to calculate the actual sampling error for specific pieces of data.

Even granting the possibility of sampling error, however, our best estimate of what's true among the total U.S. population is what we learned from the probability sample. Thus if you were to bet on the percentage of the total U.S. population who supported a woman's unrestricted right to an abortion, you should put your money on 43%. You would be better off, however, to bet that it was, say, between 38% and 48%.

Sampling is one of the most important topics in research methods, and we wish we could spend more time here discussing the many other sampling techniques in use by criminal justice researchers. Since we can't, we suggest that you consult either a general research methods text (such as Schutt, 2001) or a specialized introduction to sampling (Maisel & Persell, 1996).

2.4   Data Collection

The GSS data were collected in face-to-face household interviews. Once the sample households were selected, professional interviewers were dispatched to call on each. The interviewers asked each of the questions and wrote down the respondents' answers. Each interview took approximately an hour.

To maximize the amount of information that can be collected in this massive interviewing project, NORC asks some questions in only a random subsample of the households, and other questions in other households. Some questions are asked of all respondents. When we begin analyzing the GSS data, you will notice that some data items have a substantial number of respondents marked "missing data." For the most part, this refers to respondents who were not asked that particular question. Although only a subsample of respondents were asked some of the questions, you can still take their responses as representative of the U.S. adult population. The degree of sampling error, however, is larger.

This book introduces the use of SPSS by explaining one of its most accessible versions, SPSS for Windows Student Version. The Student Version is available at only a fraction of the cost of the full SPSS product and can handle data sets with no more than 50 variables and 1,500 cases. Fortunately, very elaborate, fully professional research can be done within those limits. The Web page for this book describes how to access the full range of variables and yearly samples through the Internet so that you can use your SPSS skills to study any part of this vast collection of data. (By the way, the data are available free of charge.)

2.5   General Social Survey Variables

The data set taken from the GSS has a rich collection of questions about American social and political attitudes and behaviors, including some fascinating variables about crime, justice, and social deviance. A list of variables drawn from the GSS is found on your CD in the file "GSS.SAV." We use this data set frequently in the remaining chapters, so you should become very familiar with this list of variables.

Two other data sets on your CD contain older GSS questions concerning crime and justice, "CJGSS1.SAV" and "CJGSS2.SAV." As the Web page for this book explains, with a bit of work and a willingness to venture onto the Internet, you can access any of the variables in the GSS from 1972 to the present. The Web page maintained for this text explains how to use the powerful software that can extract smaller data sets from any year or set of years of the GSS.

2.6   Harvard School of Public Health College Alcohol Study

The most sophisticated study of college student binge drinking—the College Alcohol Study (CAS)—was recently undertaken by researchers at the Harvard School of Public Health (HSPH). Full-time college students in a representative sample of 140 colleges in 40 states and the District of Columbia completed a

20-page questionnaire that had been mailed to them. The data you have on your CD is a random sample of 1,400 respondents drawn from the 17,592 respondents in the original CAS.

In this survey, shorter variable names that correspond to the original question numbers on the self-administered survey are used, followed by the questions asked in the survey.

The data from this study are found on your CD in the special SPSS file called "BINGE.SAV." Also on your disk is another file, "LOCAL.SAV," which will help you enter data if you decide to conduct your own "college alcohol study" using the questionnaire presented in Appendix B of this text.

In addition to the variables you can collect using the instrument in Appendix B, there are three variables at the end of the "BINGE.SAV" file you will want to use. One is called COLLBING, and it defines whether an individual student met the criteria for being a binge drinker. The criteria were reporting at least one episode of drinking five or more drinks in a row for a male or four or more drinks in a row for a female. This gender-specific definition of binge drinking was created because it makes the risk of an alcohol-related problem equal for men and women; gender-neutral definitions of binge drinking tend to undercount females who abuse alcohol.

Among the many variables in the "BINGE.SAV" data set are some rich indicators of crime perpetration and victimization on college campuses, variables with considerable application to criminal justice problems at colleges.

2.7   Criminal and Juvenile Justice in the American States

Many of the most important criminal justice issues concern how different jurisdictions—federal, state, and local—deal with some problem or concern. To take one extremely important issue, expenditures on criminal justice, the 50 American states vary substantially in how much they spend on their criminal justice systems. By contrast, other developed countries have less variation from place to place in such expenditures. So we've included an SPSS file (called "JUSTICE.SAV") that contains information about the 50 states and their criminal justice systems. In the next chapter, we will show you how you can add variables about issues you are concerned with—how you can explore your own criminal justice questions and test your own criminal justice hypotheses.

Another very important question in contemporary criminal justice deals with juvenile justice. For example, how many reports of child abuse and neglect are made across the 50 states? Why is there so much variation across the states? To find out, you might want to use the juvenile justice data found in the special SPSS file "JUVENILE.SAV."

SPSS for Windows allows you to add variables to an existing data set such as these easily, particularly if the cases are placed in the same order. The criminal justice and juvenile justice data sets have the 50 states and the District of Columbia in alphabetic order, so it should be very easy for you to find data about a topic you want to study and then add it to either data set. Just remember that if you are using the Student Version, you can have no more than 50 variables on a data set, so you may have to delete some variables to have room for the new ones.

2.8   World Crime Surveys

Is it true that there is a worldwide increase in serious crime? Have countries such as Australia, Canada, and the United Kingdom seen dramatic increases in crime? Or is the United States the only country that has experienced an increase? You'll be able to explore the answers using data from the World Crime Surveys (WORLD.SAV on the CD). The United Nations office that maintains these data can be reached through the Web page for this book.

2.9   Your Own Criminal Justice Survey

The next chapter also explains how you can use SPSS to analyze data you collect in your own survey. You might want to administer the questionnaire found in Appendix B at your own college to compare drug and alcohol use there with the national patterns found by the CAS. An alternative might be to develop your own questionnaire on whatever topic you choose to study. SPSS provides you with all the tools you'll need to complete the analysis.

2.10   Summary

In this chapter, we've introduced several data sets that will allow you to explore the world of criminal justice research. A biologist would reach for a microscope to begin testing hypotheses; we're going to reach for SPSS. The next chapter describes how to use this basic investigative tool on contemporary crime and justice problems.

Key Terms

data archive
General Social Survey (GSS)
ICPSR
meta-analysis

multistage probability sampling
primary data analysis
secondary data analysis

Chapter 3 Using SPSS

Like most data analysis programs, SPSS is capable of computing many different statistical procedures with different kinds of data. This makes SPSS a very powerful and useful tool, but because of its generality, we need to specify what we want SPSS to do for us.

In many ways, SPSS is a vehicle for discovering differences and relationships in data, the same way a car is a vehicle for discovering places we have not yet visited. The car does not know where we want to go or what we wish to see. We, rather than the car, plan the trip and set the direction. Similarly, when we use SPSS, we choose the data we wish to explore and select the statistical procedures we wish to use. Sitting at our computer keyboards, we are in SPSS's driver's seat.

We tell SPSS where to go and what to do in our criminal justice research adventure with SPSS commands. These commands instruct SPSS where to find our data, ways in which we want to modify the data, and the statistical procedures we want to use.

3.1 Using SPSS to Open Existing Data Sets

SPSS for Windows has probably already been installed for you by computer center personnel, lab assistants, or your instructor. You need to learn which of the machines available to you are equipped with the system.

Your instructor will no doubt help you get started, but we think you will find it pretty simple.

There will likely be only one SPSS icon on your screen. If there is more than one icon, your instructor will tell you which to choose. If you are using an older version of Windows (e.g., 3.1), your screen will look slightly different. Simply locate the SPSS icon and double-click on it to open SPSS. For those of you using Macintosh computers, consult your instructor for information on how to use SPSS for Macintosh.

With your cursor, all you need to do is double-click the SPSS icon. It will take SPSS a little while to respond, with the length of time depending on the kind of computer you are using. Another way to open SPSS is to click on the "Start" button and scroll up to "Program Files." Another menu will appear and you can search this list for SPSS and click on it. You will see a box asking you what you want to do.

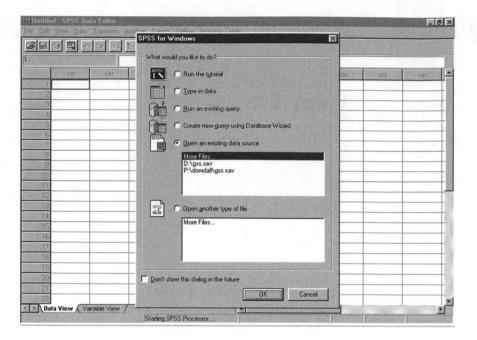

Click on "Type in data" and click "OK." Eventually you will be looking at a screen with a grid pattern. If it does not look like this, click on the Data View tab on the bottom left.

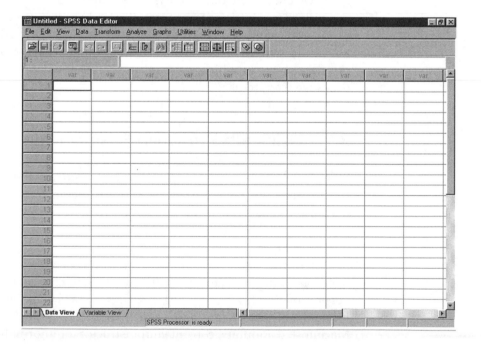

Right beneath the window's title is a set of menus called a **menubar**, running from File on the left to Help on the right. You are going to become very familiar with the menus on this menubar; they are the control system through which you will operate SPSS. The menubar is available in virtually identical form in all the versions of SPSS for Windows (and SPSS for Macintosh) and is therefore the key to being able to use any of them effectively.

Like other Windows programs, SPSS for Windows also provides other ways of using the program, such as a toolbar that makes a few functions from the menubar available even more quickly with just a single click on an icon. But for learning SPSS for Windows, nothing can beat the menubar for ease of use and access to any SPSS command regardless of which version of SPSS for Windows you are using. If you see a row of icons appear just beneath the menubar, you are looking at the toolbar. You can remove the toolbar from use by clicking on View in the menubar and then clicking on Toolbars and clicking off the checkmark that will appear next to the choice "Data Editor." ("Data Editor" is the name of the SPSS window that shows the raw data.)

As a preview, click on the word File on the menubar. Notice that a list of commands drops down below the title, with some of the commands in dark, black letters and some in faint gray. Whenever you see a list like this, you can execute the black commands (by clicking on them), but the gray ones are not currently available to you. Right now, for example, you could Open a data set, but you can't Save it because there's nothing to be saved just now.

Click on File again, and the list disappears. Do that to get rid of the File menu now; we'll come back to it shortly.

Now look in the upper right corner of the SPSS for Windows window and you'll find three squares, one with a dash (–), one with two overlapping windows, and one with an "X."

Click the first square with the dash (–) in it. Wow! The SPSS for Windows window has vanished. Looks like you're in big trouble now, but you're not. If you look along the bottom of the screen, you'll find a rectangle like the "Start" button but labeled "SPSS for Windows." This simply means that you have moved SPSS out of the way temporarily in case you want to work on something else for a while. To restore SPSS back to the screen you are working with, simply click on the SPSS rectangle.

Now click on the second square with the overlapping windows. Notice that the SPSS for Windows window has now shrunk in size. Notice also that the middle square in the upper right corner has now changed to a single window. Whenever you see this kind of square, it means that clicking it will return the window to its full screen size. Why don't you try that now? You may want to click it back and forth a few times to get comfortable with it.

Get back to the SPSS for Windows as a full screen. We will get to the third square with an "X" in it soon. For now, click on the Window menu from the menubar. Notice that there is a check next to "Untitled–SPSS Data Editor." This is the only window listed now. Later, after we've asked SPSS to produce some analysis for us, there will be another choice called an Output window. This is where SPSS will store the results of any commands we give it. You will become familiar with how to switch back and forth between viewing the Data Editor window and the Output window.

Right now, there is no Output window because we haven't given SPSS any commands that produced written results. Before long, however, you will begin seeing results here and will become very familiar with this window. Getting back to the Data Editor window, notice that it is titled "Untitled." This is the window that contains the data for SPSS to analyze, although right now it is empty. If you wanted, you could begin entering data for analysis. In fact, if you decide to conduct your own survey later on, this is how you would enter those data. As a quick preview of this feature, type "1" and press the "Enter" key on your keyboard.

You have now created the world's smallest data set, containing one piece of information about one person. The "1" at the left of the matrix represents "Person 1." If you entered another number, you would have brought "Person 2" into existence—with one piece of information. Do that now—enter a "2" for that person.

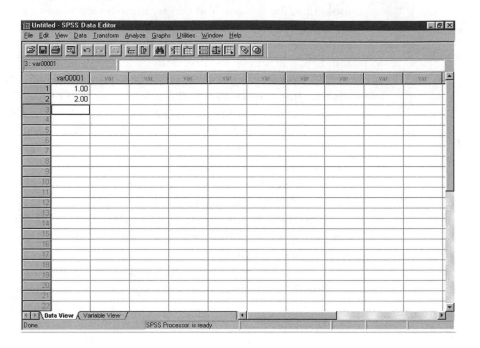

The "var00001" at the head of the column in the matrix represents the specific information we are storing about each person. It might represent gender, for example. Moreover, a value of 1.00 might mean "male" and a value of 2.00 might mean female. Therefore, we would have indicated that Person 1 is a man and Person 2 a woman.

This is the basic structure of the data sets analyzed by SPSS. The good news for you is that we've already prepared a large data set for your use, so you won't have to keep entering data in this way.

For our present purposes, we are going to load the GSS data provided with this book. This is easily done in SPSS for Windows. Click the word File again, and the file menu will open up below it. The second command in that menu is the one we want: Open. Click Open. A new menu list opens to the right giving you a choice of file types. We want Data.

Now you will find yourself with a new screen, listing files that might be loaded into SPSS. Unless your instructor has told you differently, locate the "GSS.SAV" file on the CD that accompanied this book. Make sure the "File type" is SPSS(*.SAV). With your cursor, click the file titled "GSS.SAV." Then click the "OK" button. As an alternative, you can double-click the file name rapidly.

Because we began to create a data set, SPSS will ask us if we want to "save the contents of data window Untitled." This is a protection to keep us from losing valuable data. In the present situation, however, we aren't interested in keeping our doodling, so just click "No."

Now you should be looking at the data in the GSS.SAV file, the data used for most of the exercises in this book. Now there are variable names across the top of the matrix and numbers in the cells. These are the GSS data. Again, if it does not look like this, click on the "Data View" tab on the bottom.

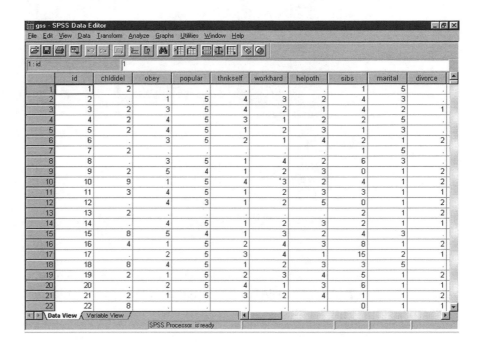

Notice that Case 15 (the case numbers run down the left side of the matrix) has an "8" in the column for CHLDIDEL. (Throughout the text, we put variable names in all capital letters.) This variable represents answers to the question of how many children is the ideal number of children to have. A score of 8 represents the opinion that as many children as one wants is the ideal number of children. Case 4, by contrast, believes two children are ideal. Respondents with a dot (".") in this column were not asked the question, and respondents with "9" in this column did not answer or answered "don't know."

If you want to look at other variables, you can accomplish this by clicking the two arrows at the bottom of the matrix. Why not experiment with this? The two arrows on the right side of the matrix will let you move up and down through the list of respondents. You could play with that, too. See if you can find the marital status of Respondent 10.

By clicking the arrows a bit, you should eventually arrive at the variable MARITAL. Respondent 10 has been coded "1" on that variable, but what does that mean? Here's an easy way to find out.

Click the Utilities menu. The first command in this menu is Variables. Click it. Now you will be looking at a new screen—one that tells you everything you might want to know about ABANY. In the left portion of the screen, however, you'll find a list of the variables. The two arrows will let you move up and down the list. Do that until you find MARITAL and click it. The variables may not be listed alphabetically. If not, go under the Edit menu to Options. With the general tab forward, click on Display names under variable lists and click on alphabetically.

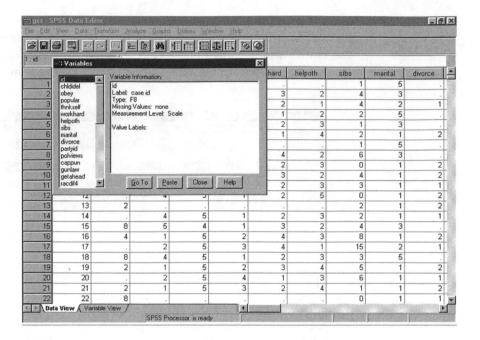

Now the information in the right portion of the window should tell you about MARITAL. Notice that a code of "1" stands for "married." Respondent 10 is married.

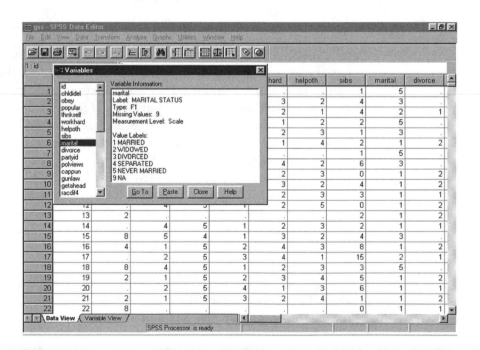

That's enough of a start. Spend a little time poking around the data set and examining the information about variables. When you finish with the Variables window, you can close it. Click the small box in the upper right corner of the window with an "X" in it. This will close the window.

When you've finished for this session, open the File menu by clicking it. Scroll down to the Save As command and click on it. The Save As box will ask you to locate where the file will be saved. At this point, you should make an extra working copy of the GSS.SAV file. If you are working from the CD with the book, simply save to your personal computer hard drive or some other drive.

Once you have saved your personal copy of GSS, you can now exit SPSS. You can do this in one of two ways. Click on the File menu and at the very bottom, you'll see the command Exit. Clicking this will instruct the computer to terminate the SPSS session and return you to the Windows desktop. The third square in the upper right corner with an "X" in it will do the same thing.

If you accidentally typed anything into the data file, it will ask if you want to save the changes. Because the data set has already been saved, we can safely click the "No" button now. If you had entered your own data, you definitely would have wanted to save the data—and the computer would have asked you to name the new data set.

Later in this book, we'll discuss how you can open the other data sets provided on the CD accompanying this book. But you probably already know how: It's as simple as making sure the name of the file you want appears inside the "File Name" field as part of the Open File window. It takes a little getting used to, but we think that you will find SPSS for Windows allows you to open and then use data files easily.

3.2   Learning More: The Windows Tutorial

If you've never used a Windows program before, you may find some of what you've just done confusing. You might find it helpful to learn a little more about Windows itself. This might be a good time to learn how to use one of the very popular Windows word processing programs, such as Word. You'll see many familiar things in any of those programs because all application programs developed for the Windows environment (such as SPSS or a word processor) have many common features. One important common feature is that there is usually a Help choice. When you're stuck, click Help and look around—you'll probably find a way to answer your question.

Another feature often found in Windows applications is a tutorial program. The one for SPSS is a bit involved, and we think you should follow our suggestions in this book before using it. But if you've used other Windows programs extensively or if you've used other non-Windows versions of SPSS, you might want to give it a try now. Choose Tutorial after clicking on Help. You may remember that running the tutorial was also a choice when you first opened SPSS.

3.3   Creating Your Own Data Set

For many criminal justice research questions, you will have to create your own data set—performing what we called primary data analysis. Most likely, the data will be collected through an original survey that you designed and executed, or else they will be official criminal justice system statistics that you assembled from original sources (e.g., a police department's data collection system, published FBI statistics, or data from the *Sourcebook of Criminal Justice Statistics* (Maguire & Pastore, 1995). In this chapter, we'll examine how to enter data of either type.

Getting data ready for analysis with SPSS is really a two-step process. The first step, often called data definition, involves establishing a computer file with names for variables, designated places for their storage, and supplying any variable or value labels and missing values that you may wish to associate with each variable. Normally, that would be done using the Variable View and Value Labels commands in SPSS for Windows. We have saved you the trouble of defining data you collect using the questionnaire in Appendix B. On the CD enclosed with this book is a file named "LOCAL.SAV" that contains a data definition. We'll show you how to use it a little later.

The second step in preparing for data analysis is editing and coding your data. People do not always follow instructions when filling out a questionnaire. Verbal or written responses have to be transformed into a number code for processing with SPSS. For ease of entry, questionnaires should be edited for proper completion and coding before you attempt to key them into a SPSS file.

3.4   Coding Your Data

To the extent we could, we have designed the questionnaire in Appendix B to be self-coding. Except for the three-digit identification number that begins the questionnaire, each question is closed-ended. The questions were taken from the 20-page Harvard School of Public Health College Alcohol Study self-administered questionnaire and are used here with permission of Dr. Henry Wechsler, the study's principal investigator.

Before the data for a single person can be entered into a file, the questionnaire needs to be edited. Each questionnaire should have a unique number in the ID field. We do this not because we want to identify individuals but because frequently in the coding process, errors are committed that show up later. For instance, we have coded GENDER with "1" for male and "2" for female, but in our analysis we might find a respondent with GENDER coded "7." What we will need to do is to find the record with the erroneous code "7," look up the ID number, go back to the original questionnaire, find out what code GENDER should have been, and fix it.

Next in the editing process, we have to code the open-ended questions, if there are any in the questionnaire. (The questionnaire in Appendix B doesn't have any.) All the persons coding questions should be following the same written instructions for coding. For example, social scientists who study occupations have put together codes for occupational prestige. You are much better off using such a coding scheme (see Babbie & Halley, 1995, Appendix A, for this code). Other coding schemes might not be as elaborate. For instance, in a medical study, patients might be asked about the illnesses that brought them to the hospital. Coding might be as simple as classifying the illnesses as acute or chronic, or it could use the very elaborate professional codes for physical disease (the International Classification of Diseases, Version 9, known as ICD-9) or for mental illnesses (the *American Psychiatric Association's Diagnostic and Statistical Manual,* fourth edition, known as *DSM-IV*). It's your job to decide whether you need very detailed or very general codes.

In criminal justice, you should pay particular attention to coding so that your study conforms with current professional practice. A good place to start is the *Sourcebook of Criminal Justice Statistics* (Maguire & Pastore, 1995), which presents a lot of the most important coding schemes in general use in studying crime and justice.

The coding for the College Alcohol Study has been designed to be very simple. If a person checks off the first box, that person receives a code "1"; if a person checks off the second box, that person receives a code "2"; and so on. How's that for simple?

Finally, the codes need to be written so that they are easy to read. We have designed our questionnaire to be edge-coded. If you look in the right margin, we have put a space for each variable's code.

Even with our simple coding scheme, you will need a copy of the codes used to define the "LOCAL.SAV" file. It's easy to get. Bring up SPSS for Windows, and place the CD that accompanied this book in a drive. Once the Data window is in the foreground, click the following sequence (we will use this type of notation from this point on to simplify the presentation of several separate steps, in this case clicking File and then clicking Open and then clicking Data):

File → Open → Data

At the open window, select the drive with the CD in it and locate "LOCAL.SAV" in the field under "File Name." Click on "LOCAL.SAV" and then on "OK." You will see a window of empty data cells. This is the empty, but defined, data file for your local data.

To have the codes printed out for your use in coding your data, click Utilities followed by File Info. The codes will print quickly on the screen. You should see the information for GENDER in the Output window. To have the codes printed, click on File and then Print. If there is a printer connected to your computer, you should have a hard copy of the codes printed in about a minute.

What happens if a person doesn't check off a response? That question then has a missing value.

Once you have edited and coded your questionnaires, you can move to the next step—entering data.

3.5   Entering Your Data

First, repeat the File → Open → Data sequence again. Click on "LOCAL.SAV" again to retrieve the empty data file. If necessary, click on the Data window to move it to the front. What you should be looking at is an empty data matrix with the names of the variable names across the top and record numbers down the left side. You will notice that the order of the variables across the record is the same as the order of the variables on the questionnaire. We placed them in that order to make data entry easier and less prone to error.

You can easily move from cell to cell in the data matrix. Pressing just the "Tab" key moves the active cell to the right, and pressing the "Shift" and "Tab" keys simultaneously moves the active cell to the left. You can tell the active cell by its thick black border. After you enter data, pressing the "Enter" key moves the active cell down to the next record. The directional arrows will also move the active cell, one cell at a time. The mouse can be used to make a cell active just by pointing and clicking. Long-distance moves can be made by pressing "Ctrl" and "Home" together to move to the leftmost cell in the first row and "Ctrl" and "End" to move to the rightmost cell in the last row.

When you key data in, they first appear on a line under the name of the file. When you move the active cell, the data jump to the cell. Data may be changed at any time just by moving to the cell and keying in new values.

If a particular row turns into a disaster, you can get rid of the entire row by clicking on the record number at the extreme left of a record and pressing the "Delete" key. After you are done entering data, or if you want to stop entering data and continue at a later time, click on File and Save Data. Your data will be

Table 1.8 State and Local Justice System per Capita Expenditures, by Type of Activity and State—Fiscal Year 1992[a]

State[b]	Estimated Population 1992[c] (in thousands)	Total Justice System	Police Protection	Judicial and Legal	Corrections
Total	254,493	$315.3	$136.1	$65.1	$114.2
Alabama	4,136	199.5	94.7	45.5	59.3
Alaska	587	572.6	217.1	130.4	225.2
Arizona	3,832	366.5	156.6	83.5	126.4
Arkansas	2,399	152.4	69.8	28.2	54.5
California	30,867	454.6	190.8	103.3	160.5
Colorado	3,470	302.8	133.1	57.9	111.8
Connecticut	3,281	332.4	142.0	62.1	128.3
Delaware	689	375.8	141.8	75.6	158.4
District of Columbia	607	1,184.6	449.3	210.8	524.4
Florida	13,488	382.0	169.9	72.5	139.7
Georgia	6,751	267.5	105.3	43.6	118.6
Hawaii	1,160	350.7	143.3	117.1	90.2
Idaho	1,067	219.4	105.1	47.3	67.1
Illinois	11,631	279.9	148.0	51.4	80.4
Indiana	5,662	181.2	75.8	34.8	70.5
Iowa	2,812	194.5	93.3	52.8	48.5
Kansas	3,523	171.3	76.4	35.8	59.2
Kentucky	3,755	195.3	81.8	42.2	71.3
Louisiana	4,287	256.3	127.0	47.5	81.9
Maine	1,235	199.1	80.4	35.6	83.2
Maryland	4,908	348.3	143.8	69.1	135.4
Massachusetts	5,998	296.9	131.2	57.7	108.0
Michigan	9,437	313.2	130.9	63.6	118.7
Minnesota	4,880	220.9	104.5	55.3	61.1
Mississippi	2,614	136.3	71.8	25.0	39.5
Missouri	5,193	192.3	102.0	36.1	54.2
Montana	824	209.5	89.4	65.1	55.0
Nebraska	1,606	193.6	88.3	38.9	66.5
Nevada	1,327	467.6	191.2	90.7	185.8
New Hampshire	1,111	224.7	114.7	46.1	63.9
New Jersey	7,789	370.7	170.1	81.9	118.7
New Mexico	1,581	293.1	134.8	53.2	105.1
New York	18,119	496.8	205.0	100.5	191.2
North Carolina	6,843	235.7	102.7	37.8	95.3
North Dakota	636	154.6	66.7	45.6	42.3
Ohio	11,016	261.9	120.9	59.3	81.7
Oklahoma	3,212	193.9	91.2	35.0	67.7
Oregon	2,977	286.6	120.9	64.0	101.8
Pennsylvania	12,009	245.1	102.6	55.8	86.8
Rhode Island	1,005	301.1	128.6	72.0	100.5
South Carolina	3,603	240.9	91.2	34.2	115.5
South Dakota	711	169.7	79.1	35.8	54.8

State[b]	Estimated Population 1992[c] (in thousands)	Total Justice System	Police Protection	Judicial and Legal	Corrections
Tennessee	5,024	226.0	93.5	41.7	90.8
Texas	17,656	300.2	115.1	63.0	122.1
Utah	1,813	218.6	96.4	47.7	74.5
Vermont	570	218.5	103.9	55.4	59.2
Virginia	6,377	266.3	115.1	45.9	105.3
Washington	5,136	327.0	122.1	62.6	142.3
West Virginia	1,812	117.3	51.3	33.8	32.2
Wisconsin	5,007	293.7	139.2	57.1	97.3
Wyoming	466	318.2	147.7	80.4	90.1

Note: See Note, Table 1.1. For survey methodology and definitions of terms, see Appendix 1.

[a]Detail may not add to total because of rounding.

[b]Local government portion of these data are estimates subject to sampling variation.

[c]Population figures are from the U.S. Bureau of the Census, Current Population Reports. Series P-25, No. 1045, July 1992.

Source: U.S. Department of Justice, Bureau of Justice Statistics, Justice Expenditure and Employment Extracts: 1992, NCJ-148821 (Washington, DC: U.S. Department of Justice, forthcoming). Table 8. Table adapted by *Sourcebook* staff.

saved under the name that was used at the beginning of the session. If you wish to save it under another name, click on File and Save As. Be careful of what disk drive you are saving on. If the computer is in a public place, you will want to save your work on a removable disk or CD so that you can take it with you.

If you save your data file at the end of a session, you can pick up where you left off by retrieving it in subsequent sessions. To retrieve a file and start adding data again, just click File → Open → Data.

Although a fair amount of work is involved in doing your own survey and entering your own data, you will experience a certain excitement about coming to understand the opinions and behaviors of a group of people with whom you have become directly familiar.

3.6   Using Published Criminal Justice Data

Unlike other areas of social science, criminal justice often uses a great deal of published data from official statistical sources. Because this is such an important task, we want to show you how to code and analyze data from official sources. We'll take as an example coding data from perhaps the most important single source of statistical data about the criminal justice system, the *Sourcebook of Criminal Justice Statistics* (Maguire & Pastore, 1995). Suppose that you want to code the per capita expenditures on the total justice system of each of the 50 states and the District of Columbia. (For many criminal justice statistics, the District of Columbia appears in data sets as if it were one of the states.) You find these data in Table 1.8 of the report, in a form just like the one you see reproduced on pages 34-35.

Following SPSS practice, you have to come up with an eight-character "variable name" for each piece of information, and each name must begin with an alphabetic character. So you decide to call the variable with each state's name STATE and the variable with the per capita expenditures on criminal justice PERCAPCJ.

(One caution: Be sure to check that all states are represented in the table.) First, give the 50 states and the District of Columbia a list of ID numbers from 1 to 51, making sure that they are all in alphabetic order. (You might want to pencil in each number next to the state or district name.)

When you first open SPSS, click on "Type in data" and click OK (as explained in Section 3.1). If you are in SPSS already, simply choose File → New → Data.

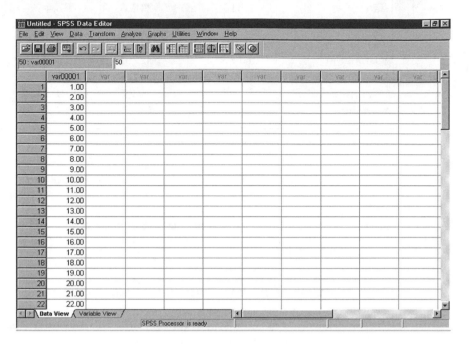

Let's first enter the state ID number and give it meaningful labels. Use the arrow to click on the first cell under "var00001" and then enter the first ID number, "1," in this cell; when you've done this, hit the "Enter" key, and the cell below will be highlighted and ready to enter "2," and so forth.

When you've entered all 51 numbers, use your mouse to click on the Variable View tab at the bottom of the screen.

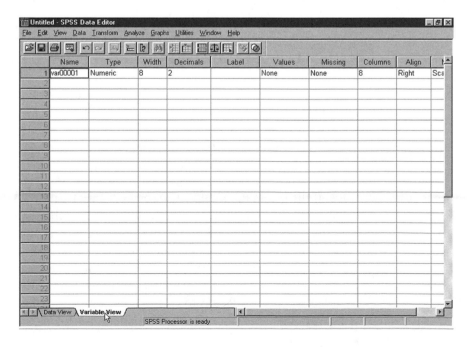

Highlight the first box in the first column. Change the variable name from "var00001" to "state."

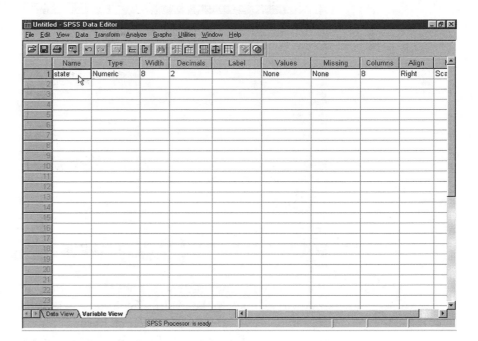

Under Type, the word "Numeric" appears. Leave that—that's fine.

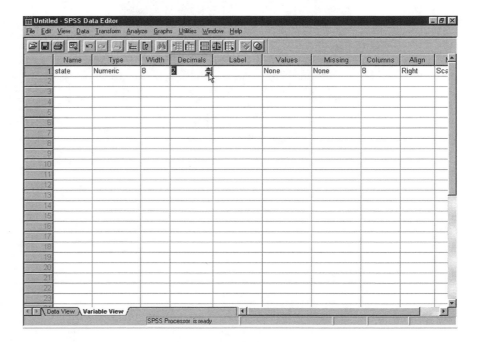

In the "Decimals" box will be a "2"—you should change that to a zero, "0." (This will make the print in later screens look more like what you will use to code the state data from this and other books.)

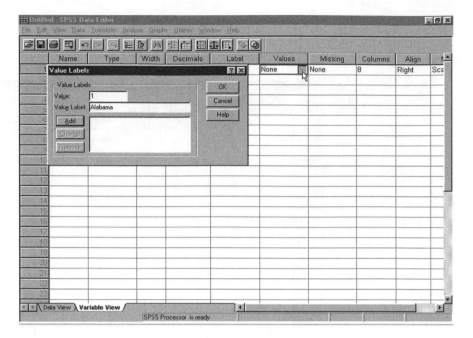

You now will enter each state code, followed by the name of each state as a separate value label. In the "Values" column, click on the box that says "None." A small gray box will appear, click on that. In the box that says "Value," enter a "1"; in the box below it marked "Value Label," enter the word "Alabama," then click on "Add." Your screen should look like this:

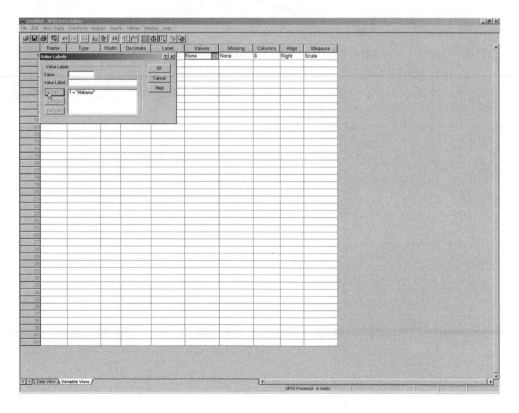

Referring to the text, enter each of the remaining values, followed by each of the state names and remember to click on "Add." When you are all done, click on "OK."

Before going any further, why not take this opportunity to save what you've done? (By now, you probably know what you need to do.) Use your mouse to move the arrow to File on the menubar, then choose File → Save As. Give your file any appropriate name—how about "CJSTATE"?—but make sure it has the extension .SAV and the correct drive (and path name, if appropriate). Just click "OK," and your work is saved!

Why not enter another variable into this data set? Try entering PERCAPCJ, the per capita expenditures on the total justice system. Other variables you can enter include the per capita expenditures on police protection, judicial and legal, or corrections. (The Web page for this book at www.sju.edu/~gdowdall explains how you can add variables about the criminal justice and juvenile justice systems of the 50 states that are included in other files on your CD.)

When you're done, print out the data file (assuming that it's the active file) by choosing File Print. You can use this printout to verify that you've coded the data correctly. Remember, from this point on, the famous expression GIGO is in operation: Garbage in, garbage out! If your coding is garbage, you can imagine what your results will be!

Here's an important piece of advice. Personal computers are usually very reliable, but occasionally a power failure or some computer problem might interrupt your session. If you haven't saved your data, you will lose your work.

One very final piece of advice. Even if you've saved your data onto a hard disk or a floppy, there is some risk that even that copy of the data set might be lost. Someone might take your floppy, or the hard disk your data are on might crash! You should always back up the working file of your data onto a second disk and then keep that disk in a safe place.

3.7   Summary

Believe it or not, you've just learned many of the important things to know about running SPSS for Windows. Nothing in the rest of this book will require you to do much more than the kinds of things you've learned in this chapter: how to move around among the several windows, how to use your cursor to make some choices, and how to save your data safely. If you follow our advice about backing up your data, there is nothing you can do that will harm them. So relax!

Key Terms

Data Editor   Variable View
menubar

Part II   Univariate Analysis

We begin our data analyses with some basic measurements of variables. First, we will examine three concepts: religiosity, political orientation, and attitudes toward abortion. We've chosen these on the basis of general interest and the possibilities they hold for taking a new look at some important questions of crime and justice.

In Part II, we will engage in univariate analysis, the analysis of one variable at a time. This is a basic act of measurement. In Chapter 4, for example, we will examine the different ways we might measure the religiosity of the respondents to the General Social Survey (GSS), distinguishing the religious from the nonreligious and noting variations in between. In Chapter 5, we take a first look at differences in political orientation. Depending on your interest in these topics, we think you may be surprised to learn how Americans in general feel about these issues. We will also begin to investigate college student binge drinking, a basic topic in studying deviant behavior and an issue that will help us understand crime victimization on campus.

Whereas the initial univariate analyses will focus on single questions asked in the interview questionnaire, we will see in Chapter 6 how social researchers often combine several such responses into more sophisticated measures of the concepts under study. You'll learn a couple of techniques for doing that.

In addition, the CD suggests a number of other topics you might be interested in exploring: binge drinking, attitudes about crime and justice, sexual behavior, poverty, and prejudice. We'll give you some guidance in approaching these topics, but our main purpose is to give you opportunities to strike out on your own and experience some of the open-endedness of research about crime and justice.

Chapter 4 **Describing a Variable**

Let's start analyzing some data now. You'll need to launch the SPSS program as described in Section 3.1. Double-click the SPSS icon or use the "Start" button to find SPSS to get things going. Once SPSS has been activated, click "OK" to open an existing data file with "more files" highlighted. You'll be given a list of files to choose from. You should have your saved GSS.SAV file on your computer now (from instructions given in Section 3.1 in the last chapter). If for some reason you don't have a file called GSS.SAV, be sure to open the GSS.SAV file from your CD and use the Save As command under the File menu to save the file as GSS.SAV onto your computer.

For our first illustration, we're going to look at some aspects of religious behavior. (Later in the book, we'll explore how a person's religious behavior might influence how the person feels about crime and justice issues.) We can get a list of the variables in our data set through the following steps:

1. Select the Analyze menu.

2. Choose Descriptive Statistics in that menu.

3. Choose Frequencies in the Descriptive Statistics menu.

From now on, we will use the notation introduced in Chapter 5 to simplify the description of such steps:

Analyze → Descriptive Statistics → Frequencies

Once you've completed these steps, you should be looking at the following screen.

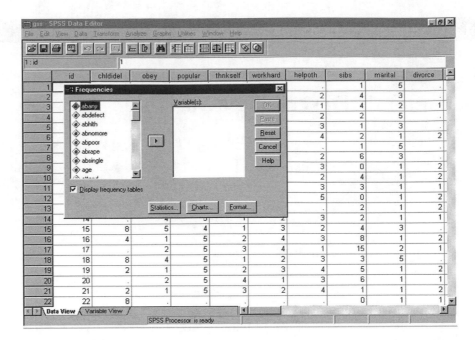

If the list of variables does not look like this and instead gives the whole variable label, rather than alphabetized variable name list, we can change the settings. To do this, click on the Edit menu from the menubar and click on Options at the bottom. In the "Options" box, make sure the tab marked General is forefront. On the right side are options for variable list. Click on "Display names," making sure "Alphabetical" is also selected. Then click "OK." A message will appear letting you know that the change will become the default and SPSS dialog boxes will close. You can click "OK" and then get back to the GSS data file and follow the steps Analyze → Descriptive Statistics → Frequencies.

Four of the variables in this data set have to do with religiosity:

RELIG   Respondent's religious preference

ATTEND   How often the respondent attends religious services

POSTLIFE   Belief in life after death

PRAY   How often the respondent prays

Variable names are limited to eight characters and are the key to identifying variables in SPSS commands. Sometimes it is possible to express the name of a variable clearly in eight or fewer characters (e.g., SEX, RACE), and sometimes the task requires some ingenuity (e.g., RINCOME for the respondent's annual income). Sometimes researchers prefer to use the name or number (e.g., A1) used in a questionnaire for the variable's name and then use a longer **variable label** to explain it more fully.

Let's start by looking at the distribution of religious preferences among the sample. This is easily accomplished as follows. First, move the scroll bar to the right of the list of variable names until RELIG is visible. Click that name so that it's highlighted. Then click the arrow to the right of the list. This will transfer the variable name to the field labeled "Variable(s)."

Once you've moved the name RELIG, click the "OK" button. This will set SPSS off on its assigned task. Depending on the kind of computer you are using, this operation may take a few seconds to complete. Eventually, however, a new window—the Output - SPSS Viewer—will be brought to the front of the screen, and you should see the following information.

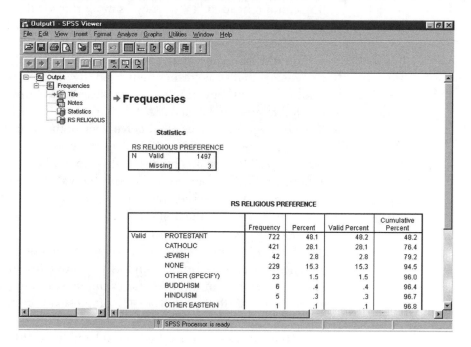

As a helpful hint, if you want to change the format of your Output window to see more of the output, you can place the cursor on the line dividing the outline on the left from the output on the right. When the cursor becomes arrows, hold down the mouse and drag the cursor to the left until the outline disappears. This will allow you to view more of the output in the window.

The small box titled "Statistics" tells us that of the 1,500 respondents in our subsample of the 2000 GSS, 1,497 gave valid answers to this question, whereas the remaining 3 have missing data. The box marked "RS RELIGIOUS PREFERENCE" contains the data we were really looking for. Scroll down using the window bar or arrows on the right side to view the frequency table.

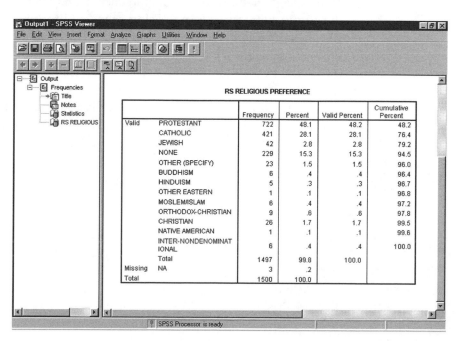

We'll go through this table piece by piece. The leftmost column in the table lists the **value labels** of the many categories constituting the variable.

The column headed "Frequency" simply records the **frequency** of occurrence of each label—how many of the 1,500 respondents said they identified with the various religious groups. We see, for example, that most—722—said they were Protestant, 421 said they were Catholic, and so forth. Note that in this context, "None" means that some respondents said they had no religious identification; it does not mean that they didn't answer. Near the bottom of the table, we see that three failed to answer, labeled NA.

The next column tells us what percentage of the whole sample each of the religious groups represents. Thus 48.1% are Protestants, for example, calculated by dividing the 722 Protestants by the total sample, 1,500.

Usually, you will want to work with the **valid percentage,** presented in the next column. As you can see, this percentage is based on the elimination of those who gave no answer, so the first number here means that 48.2% of those giving an answer said they were Protestant.

The final column presents the **cumulative percentage,** adding the individual percentages of the preceding column as you move down the list. Sometimes this will be useful to you. In this case, for example, you might note by combining the Protestants and Catholics that 76.4% of those giving an answer were either Protestant or Catholic.

Now that we've examined the method and logic of this procedure, let's use it more extensively. As you may have already figured out, SPSS doesn't limit us to one variable at a time. (If you tried that out on your own before we said you could, you get two points for being adventurous. Hey, this is supposed to be fun as well as useful.) From the Window menu on the top of the screen, choose "GSS – SPSS Data Editor" to get back to the Data window.

Return to the Frequencies window with

Analyze → Descriptive Statistics → Frequencies

If you are doing this all in one session, you may find that RELIG is still in the "Variable(s)" field. If so, you should click it, and once it's highlighted, notice that the arrow between the two fields changes direction. Clicking it now returns RELIG to its original location. Do that.

Now let's get the other religious variables. One at a time, click and transfer ATTEND, POSTLIFE, and PRAY. When all three are in the "Variables(s)" field, click the "OK" button.

After a few seconds of cogitation, SPSS will present you with the Output window again. Use the scroll bar to move down to the beginning of the newest data. Your screen should look like this:

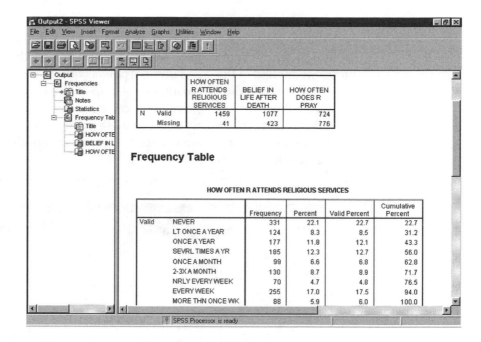

Take a few minutes to study the new table. The structure of the table is the same as the one we saw earlier for religious preference. This one presents the distribution of answers to the question concerning the frequency of attendance at religious services. Notice that the respondents were given several categories to choose from, ranging from "Never" to "More than once a week." The final category combines those who answered "Don't know" (DK) with those who gave no answer (NA).

Notice that church attendance is an *ordinal variable*. The different frequencies of church attendance can be arranged in order, but the "distances" between categories vary. Had the questionnaire asked, "How many times did you attend church last year?" the resulting data would have constituted a ratio variable. The problem with that measurement strategy, however, is one of reliability: We couldn't bank on all the respondents' recalling exactly how many times they had attended church.

The most common response in the distribution is "Never." Just over one-fifth of those giving an answer—22.7%—gave that answer. The most common answer is sometimes referred to as the ***mode***. If we combine the respondents who report never attending religious services with the category immediately below them— "Less than once a year"—we can say that 31.2% of our sample reports rarely or never attending religious services. If we added those who report attending once per year, we see that approximately 43.3% attend church once per year or less.

Combining adjacent values of a variable in this fashion is called collapsing categories. It is commonly done when the number of categories is large and/or some of the values have relatively few cases. In this instance, we might collapse categories further and round the percentages, for example:

About weekly	28%
1-3 times a month	16%
Seldom	33%
Never	23%
Total	100%

Compare this abbreviated table with the original, and be sure you understand how this one was created. Notice that we have rounded off the percentages here, dropping the decimal points. Typically, data such as these do not warrant the precision implied in the use of decimal points because the answers given are themselves approximations for many of the respondents. Later in this chapter, we'll show you how to tell SPSS to combine categories in this fashion. That will be especially important when we want to use those variables in more complex analyses.

Now let's look at the other three religious variables. Use the scroll bar of the Output window to move to POSTLIFE.

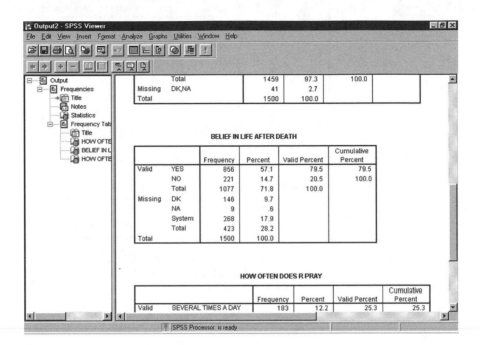

As you can see, significantly fewer attributes make up this variable: "Yes" and "No." Notice that 423 respondents are "Missing." This is the total number of respondents who responded "don't know" (DK) or gave no answer (NA) or were missing for other reasons (System), such as they were not asked the question.

To collect data on a large number of topics, the GSS asks only subsets of the sample some of the questions. Thus you might be asked whether you believed in an afterlife but not asked for your opinions on abortion. Someone else might be asked about abortion but not about the afterlife. Still other respondents would be asked about both.

Notice that more than half the American adult population believes in an afterlife. Is that higher or lower than you would have predicted? Part of the fun of analyses like these is the discovery of aspects of our society that you might not have known about. We'll have numerous opportunities for that throughout the remainder of the book.

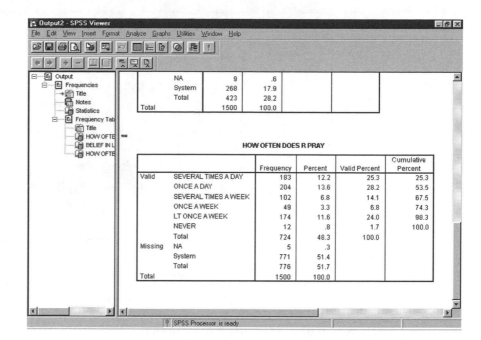

This completes our introduction to frequency distributions. Now that you understand the logic of variables and the values that constitute them and know how to examine them with SPSS, you should spend some time looking at other variables in the data set. You can see them by using the steps we've just gone through.

4.1   A Graphic View

Sometimes the information in a univariate analysis can be more quickly grasped if it is presented in graphic form rather than in a table of numbers. Take a moment to recall the distribution of religious affiliations examined earlier in this chapter. You may recall the most common affiliation (Protestant), but do you remember the relative sizes of the different groups? Was the Protestant group a little bigger than the others or a lot bigger? Sometimes a graphic presentation of such data sticks in your mind more than a table of numbers.

SPSS offers an easy method for obtaining a graphic display of a univariate analysis. In the Graphs menu, select Bar. This will give you the opportunity to select the kind of graph you would like. For now, let's choose the "Simple" type. Probably that's the one already selected, but you can click it again to be sure. Then click the "Define" button.

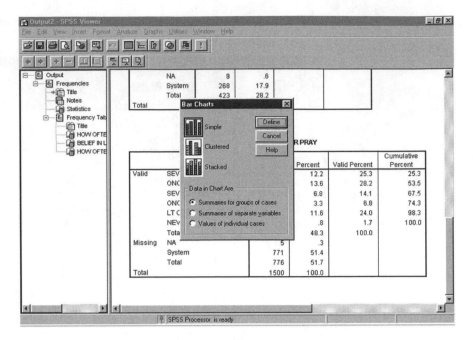

The next window allows you to specify further the kind of **bar chart** you would like, including a specification of the variable or variables to be graphed. As a start, let's just graph the religious affiliations. Find RELIG in the list, and click it. Then click the arrow beside the "Category Axis" box.

Near the top of the window, let's click "% of cases." We could accept the default, "N of cases," but we can as easily have SPSS calculate the percentage represented by each group. Next, click on "Options" in the lower right corner. Now you should have a screen that allows you to select how missing values will be treated. Since we are not interested in cases coded as missing, make sure that the check mark is turned off next to the line that says "Display groups defined by missing values." Then click "Continue" to go back to the "Define Simple Bar" screen. Click the "OK" button.

It may take SPSS a few seconds to construct the bar graph, but here's the result you should eventually get.

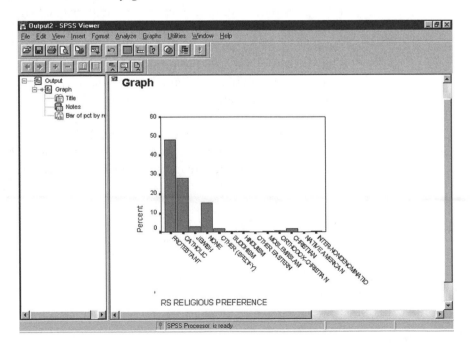

A graphic presentation like this can sometimes communicate the relative sizes of the different groups more powerfully than a table of numbers. Chances are you'll have a more vivid memory of the distribution of religious groups in the United States from having seen this graph.

When you are finished with the bar graph, click the small box in the upper right corner of the window (with the "X" in it). SPSS will now ask, "Save contents of output viewer?" This would be your opportunity to save the output—to paste later into your term paper, for example. For now, however, click "No" and let's move on.

Want to try a few more criminal justice variables? Why not examine CAPPUN ("Do you favor or oppose the death penalty for persons convicted of murder?")? You can find out how many respondents in the GSS took positions on this crucial question facing the criminal justice system by doing a univariate analysis, generating both a frequency distribution and a bar chart. Then turn your attention to GUNLAW ("Would you favor or oppose a law which would require a person to obtain a police permit before he or she could buy a gun?"). Again, you'll want to look at both the table and the bar graph.

4.2 Measuring Central Tendency and Dispersion

In the previous examples, frequency distributions have been appropriate because of the relatively few categories making up the variables we've examined. If you followed our suggestion that you run Frequencies for all variables, you will have turned up some oddities. You will have discovered, for example, that 0.5% of the sample is 18 years of age, 1.6% is 19, 1.2% is 20, and so forth. This display of AGE is not very useful for analysis.

Age is presented here as a **continuous variable,** measured at the ratio level of measurement. By contrast, other variables, such as belief in a life after death or whether a student is a binge drinker, are measured at the nominal or ordinal level and can be described as **discrete** or **categorical variables.** Sometimes **continuous variables** such as age (and also EDUC in this study) are more appropriately described in terms of their "average" values, such as the **mean.** As you may already know, the mean value in a set is calculated by adding all the individual values and dividing by the number of such values. Add up all the ages in a group and divide by the number of people in that group. This calculation is what people usually have in mind when they use the imprecise term *average.*

In SPSS, we can find the mean value for a variable rather simply, using the menu chain Analyze → Descriptive Statistics → Descriptives. SPSS once more offers you the opportunity to specify the variables you want to analyze.

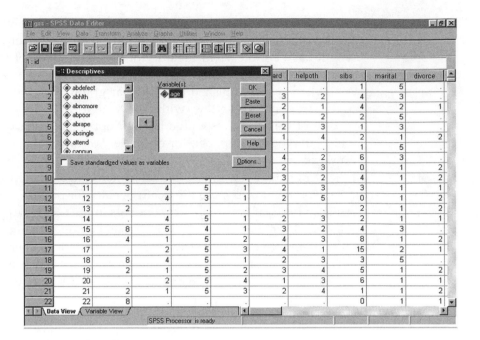

Since we're interested in measuring the central tendency, we should pick an appropriate variable. Let's choose AGE by clicking it. Then, to run Descriptives, click on "OK."

The mean age of respondents in this study is 45.32. This was calculated by adding the individual ages reported by the 1,495 valid respondents and dividing that total by 1,495.

We see that the minimum age reported was 18 and the maximum was 89. The distance between these two values—71 years—is known as the *range of* values.

As you may know, the **standard deviation** is a measure *of dispersion,* the extent to which the individual ages are clustered around the mean or spread out away from it. When a variable has a shape that approaches a normal or bell-shaped curve, the standard deviation helps us understand its dispersion around the mean.

You can check whether the variable you're working with is normally distributed by using another feature of SPSS. Click Analyze → Descriptive Statistics → Frequencies. When the Frequencies dialog box opens up, move AGE into the "Variable(s)" field, as you did before. But this time click on "Charts . . ." to open the Frequencies Charts dialog box, and select "Histogram(s)" and "With normal curve" and finally click on "Continue." Back in the Frequencies dialog box, click on "Statistics . . ." and select "Mean" and "Std. deviation" before clicking "Continue." You can turn off ("deselect") "Display frequency tables" and then go ahead and click "OK."

The result will be an interesting graph that will tell you whether your variable is normally distributed.

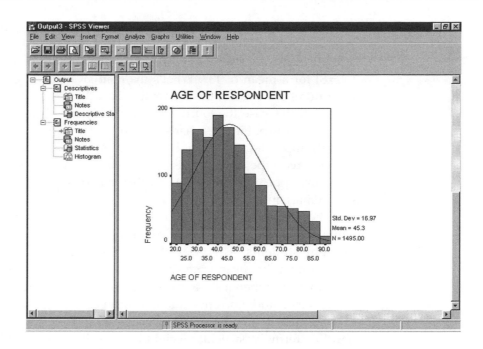

This chart shows that age doesn't fit a normal distribution too well. The distribution is "skewed" to the right.

Even though the fit to a normal curve isn't perfect, measures of dispersion such as the standard deviation can help us understand the distribution of a quantitative variable such as age. When a variable's distribution approaches a normal distribution, it is distributed according to the "68–95–99.7% rule." That means that about two-thirds of the cases (68%) are within one standard deviation of the mean, 95% of the cases are within two standard deviations on either side of the mean, and 99.7% of the cases are within three standard deviations of the mean.

The standard deviation tells us how far we would need to go above and below the mean to include approximately two-thirds of all the cases. In this instance, two-thirds of the 1,495 respondents have ages between 28.35 and 62.29: (45.32 − 16.97) and (45.32 + 16.97), respectively. Later, we'll discover other uses for the standard deviation.

How do you calculate the mean, median, mode, and standard deviation? Well, you've already done it using SPSS! But to help you appreciate how it's done, let's take a simple example using variables we all know quite well—a person's weight.

Let's look at the weight for the following eight people; we've arranged them from lowest to highest:

Person	Weight
Heather	92
Mary	111
Ruth	128
Marge	137
Eddy	144
Terry	153
Albert	165
Larry	166

Have a calculator handy? (If you're next to a PC using Windows, just click the Accessories icon and you'll find a calculator you can use!) What's the mean? Just add all the scores (for a sum of 1,096) and then divide by the number of cases ($N = 8$) for a mean of 137. What's the **median** or middle case? Since there is an even number of cases, the convention is to take the average of the two middle scores, in this case the fourth (Marge at 137) and fifth (Eddy at 144), yielding a median of 140.5. Finally, what's the **mode?** The mode is defined as the most frequently appearing score in a distribution. At a typical college, the most frequently encountered type of student is a freshman. But in the distribution of weights, no one score appears more frequently than any other, so the mode is not much help in summarizing these scores.

The following table presents the students and their weights in the first column of numbers. The next column presents the mean for the entire group of eight students. The "Deviation" column reports on what happens when you subtract the mean from each of the weights; the resulting number is a negative number when a student's weight is below the mean, zero when it is equal to the mean, and a positive number when it's above the mean. The next column is the square of the deviations; we square them to get a sense of how far off in absolute terms a particular weight is, regardless of whether it's above or below the mean.

	Weight	Mean	Deviation	Squared Deviation
Heather	92	137	−45	2,025
Mary	111	137	−26	676
Ruth	128	137	−9	81
Marge	137	137	0	0
Eddy	144	137	+7	49
Terry	153	137	+16	256
Albert	165	137	+28	784
Larry	166	137	+29	841
Sum	1,096		4,712	

To get a feeling for how typical the deviations about the mean are, we simply take the sum of the squared deviations around the mean (4,712) and divide it by the number of cases minus 1 ($8 - 1 = 7$). The resulting number (673.14) is called the **variance,** an important term in statistics but not very helpful to us mere mortals who want to describe our data. (The variance is based on squaring the deviations, so we lose all feel for our original units of measure, which were pounds of weight.) To get back to our original unit of measure, we take the square root of the variance to get the standard deviation—in this case, 25.94.

They may seem a bit strange, but note that the variance and the standard deviation are actually not complex to calculate if the number of cases is small and a calculator is handy. But what if we had to calculate them for all 1,500 cases in the GSS? No wonder SPSS is so popular with criminologists!

Now, to practice using the Descriptives command, why don't you examine the variable EDUC? See if you can complete the following sentence:

The mean education of the respondents is _____, and two-thirds of them have between ____ and _____ years of education.

Why not try to generate a histogram of EDUC and check out how close to a normal distribution it is?

Graphing your data is one of the very best ways to understand them better, and SPSS makes it easy to generate graphs that will impress your friends and probably get you better grades on your term papers.

4.3   Modifying Variables With Recode

You'll recall from earlier in this chapter that we found the variable ATTEND had so many categories that it was a bit difficult to handle. To simplify matters, we combined some adjacent answer categories.

Now we are going to see how SPSS can be instructed to do that, to **recode** old variable values into a new scheme, using the Recode command. In the Transform menu, select Recode. SPSS now asks if you want to replace the existing values of the variables with the new recoded ones. Select Into Different Variables, since we are going to assign a new name to the recoded variable. SPSS now presents you with the following screen in which to describe the recoding you want.

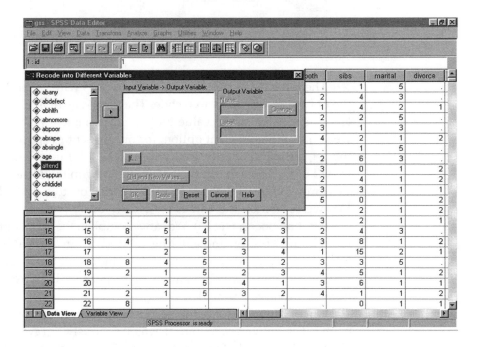

In the variable list at left, find and select ATTEND. Use the arrow to the right of the list to move the variable name to the "Numeric Variable → Output Variable" field in the middle of the window. Notice the question mark that indicates you need to tell SPSS what you would like to name the new recoded variable. You can accomplish this easily in the section of the window called "Output Variable." Let's name the recoded variable CHATT, for "church attendance." Type CHATT into the space provided for the "Output Variable" name. Click the "Change" button. As you can see in the middle field, SPSS will now modify the entry to read, "ATTEND → CHATT."

So far, we have created a new variable, but we haven't entered any data into it. We initiate this final step by clicking the "Old and New Values" button. Now SPSS presents you with the following window.

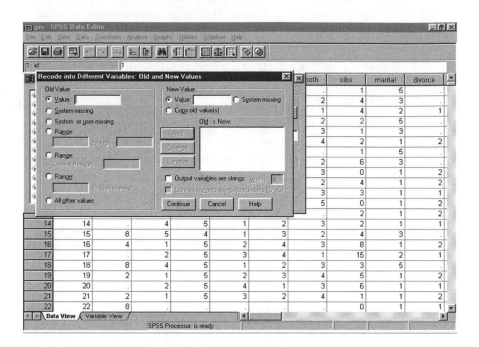

The left side of this window provides us with several options for specifying the old values we want to recode. The first, which SPSS has selected as a default, lets us specify a single value on the old variable—such as 8 ("More than once a week"). A more efficient option, for our present purposes, is found farther down the list, letting us specify a range of values. (To find the numerical codes assigned to ATTEND, you can return to Variable View in the Data Editor window.)

In our manual collapsing of categories on this variable earlier, you'll recall that we combined the values 6 ("Nearly every week"), 7 ("Every week"), and 8 ("More than once a week"). We can accomplish the same thing now by clicking the first "Range" button and entering "6" and "8" in the two boxes.

At the top of the right side of the window, notice a space for you to enter the new value for this combination of responses. Let's recode it "1." Enter that number in the box provided.

Once you've added the recode value, notice that the "Add" button just below it is activated. Where it was previously "grayed out," it is now a clear black and available for use. Click it. This action causes the expression "6 thru 8 – 1" to appear in the field. We've given SPSS part of its instructions. Now let's continue.

Click "Range" again, and now let's combine values 4 ("Once a month") and 5 ("Two to three times a month"). Give this new combined category the value of 2. Click "Add" to add it to the list of recodes.

Now combine categories 1 ("Less than once a year"), 2 ("Once a year"), and 3 ("Several times a year"). Rescore them as 3, and add it to the list.

Finally, let's recode 0 ("Never") as 4. On the left side of the window, use the "Value" button to accomplish this. Enter 0 there and enter 4 as the new value. Click "Add." Your Recode window should now look like this:

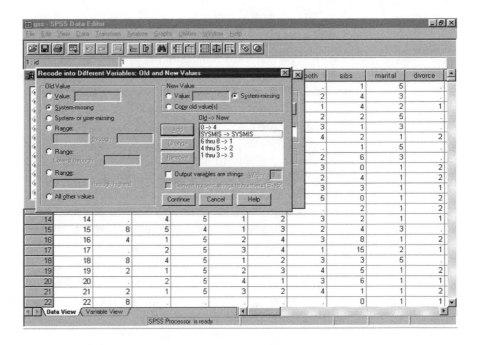

To tidy up our recoding, we could have SPSS maintain the "missing data" values of the original variable. We would accomplish this by clicking "System-missing" as an old value (on the left side) and as the new one (on the right side) and then clicking on "Add." Although it is a good practice to recode every category, in this case it is not necessary. Any cases that were not covered by the range of the old values would be undefined and treated as missing values.

As we wrap up, we should remind you that there are no hard-and-fast rules for choosing which categories to combine in a recoding process like this. There are, however, two rules of thumb to guide you—one logical, the other empirical.

First, there is sometimes a logical basis for choosing cutting points at which to divide the resulting categories. In recoding AGE, for example, it is often smart to make one break at 21 years (the traditional threshold of adulthood) and another at 65 (the traditional age of retirement). But in criminal justice research, you will want to decide how to categorize age on the basis of any legal definitions that might influence your research. In the case of church attendance, our first combined category observes the Christian norm of weekly church attendance.

The second guideline is based on the advantage of having sufficient numbers of cases in each of the combined categories, because a very small category will hamper subsequent analyses. Ideally, each of the combined categories would have roughly the same number of cases, so you might want to compute the median and then use it as a cutting point.

How do you suppose we'd continue the recoding process? Click "Continue," you say? Hey, you may be a natural at this. Do that.

This takes you back to the Recode into Different Variables window. Now that you've completed your specification of the recoding of this variable, all that remains is to click "OK" at the bottom of the window. SPSS may take a few seconds now to accomplish the recoding you've specified.

Go to the Data View of the Data Editor window again. To see your new variable, scroll across the columns of the window until you discover CHATT in the last column used thus far. Notice the values listed in the column. Person 1 has a value of 2.00 on the new variable.

Now find ATTEND. Notice that Person 1 has a 4 in ATTEND. That's correct, since everyone with a 4 or 5 in the original variable was recoded a 2 in the new one. You can check a few more people if you want to verify that the coding was accomplished as we instructed. This isn't a bad idea, by the way, to ensure that you haven't made a mistake. (Presumably, SPSS doesn't make mistakes.)

At this point, our recoding could be considered complete. You could now begin using the new variable in your analysis.

Let's take one more step in the interests of elegance. Click on the Variable View tab at the bottom of the Data Editor window. At the bottom you should see your newly created CHATT variable. The second column shows that it is numeric. That's fine; we can leave that. The third column shows the width as 8. We do not need this many spaces; we really only need 1 space, but there is no harm in leaving this. Column 4 shows the number of decimal places as 2, making the values appear as 1.00 or 2.00, and so on. We don't need those decimal places, so we will change the 2 to a 0. To do this, click on that box and when the arrows appear on the right, click the down arrow twice to make the number go to 0. Next, click on the box to the right. This is the variable "Label" column. We can label our variable simply "Church attendance recoded." Type that in the box now. You'll notice the box gets longer to accommodate your typing.

Finally, the "Values" column allows us to assign value labels to the recoded numeric scores on CHATT, so we don't have to remember what a 1 or a 2 represents on the recoded variable.

Click on the box in the "Values" column for our CHATT variable. It currently says "None"; but we'll change that now. Click on the small gray box that appears to the right. A "Value Labels" box will appear. SPSS is asking us to give names to the numeric values of the new variable. To start, enter 1 in the "Value" field. Recall that this value represents people who originally scored 6 ("Nearly every week"), 7 ("Every week"), and 8 ("More than once a week"). Let's call this new combined category "About weekly." Enter that description in the "Value Label" field, and click "Add."

Now enter the remaining value labels as indicated here.

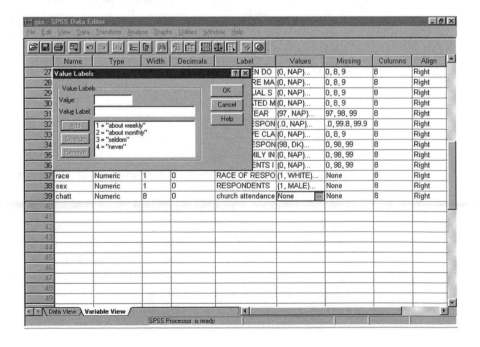

Once your screen looks like this, click "OK." Once you've been returned to the Variable View window, you can consider your work of creating a new variable almost complete at this time.

Let's review the results of our recoding process now. Go back to the Data View. We can check our recoded variable most easily through the use of the now familiar Frequencies command. Don't forget to check "Display frequencies table" (you no longer need the histogram). You'll see that CHATT is now included in the list of variables on the left. Remove AGE from the "Variables" box and put CHATT in there. You can also click on "Reset" to both take AGE out and recheck "Display frequencies table."

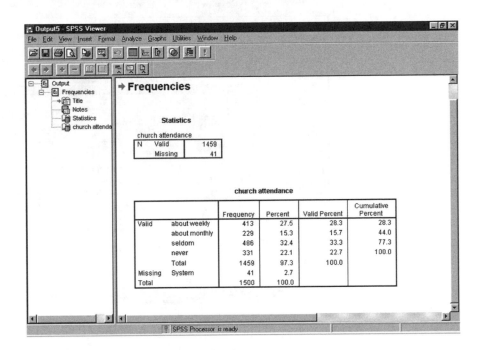

Notice how much more manageable the recoded variable is. Now we can use the recoded variable in our later analyses.

The value of recoding is especially evident in the case of continuous variables such as age and education. Because they have so many answer categories, they are totally unmanageable in some forms of analysis. Fortunately, we can recode continuous variables as easily as we just recoded ATTEND. In the case of AGE, for instance, we might establish categories "Under 21," "21 to 35," and so on. You can probably figure out how to do this, but we are going to take advantage of one additional feature in the recoding procedure.

Let's launch Transform Recode Into Different Variables again.

Notice that the Recode into Different Variables window still has our recoding of ATTEND. Clear the boards by clicking "Reset" at the bottom of the window. Then select AGE and move it to the "Input Variable" box.

Let's name the new variable AGECAT to represent "age categories." Notice there is a spot to put in the "Variable Label" here. You can do that now and save yourself the trouble of doing it later in the Variable View window. Once you've named the new variable, click "Change" to create the new name, and then click "Old and New Values."

In recoding AGE, we want to make use of the range option again, but for our first recode, check the second one: the one that specifies "Lowest through

_____." This will ensure that our youngest category will include the youngest respondents without our having to know what the youngest age is. Enter 20 in the box, specify the new value as 1, and click "Add."

Beware! Although the "lowest" and "highest" specifications are handy, they must be used with care. If you look at the frequency distribution for AGE, you will see that the five missing cases were coded "98" or "99." If we used "65 through highest," we would code five people we knew nothing about as being 65 or older.

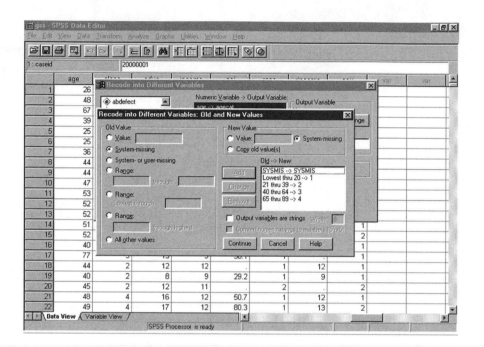

Do what you have to do to create the remaining recode instructions as indicated.

Click "Continue" to return to the main Recode window and then "OK" to make the recoding changes. Once again, you should be looking at the Data window, and you have a new variable in the rightmost column. Check it out.

To complete the process, let's tidy up the new variable. In the Variable View window, click on the "AGECAT decimals" column. Set the decimal places to 0. In the "Values" column, establish the labels for the new variable.

Once you've completed the recoding and labeling, check the results of your labors by running Frequencies on the new variable. Notice that CHATT is still in the list of variables to be analyzed. You can remove it by selecting it and then clicking the arrow that returns it to the main list of variables. If you fail to do this, SPSS will simply calculate and report the frequencies on CHATT again—not a really big crime.

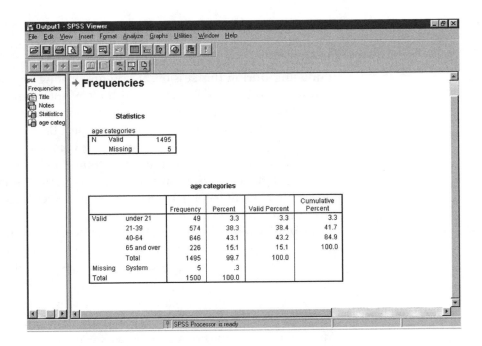

One last point to remember about recoding variables: When you take a continuous variable such as age and code it into categories (under 21 years old, 65 years old and over), the new variable may have a quite different level of measurement from the old one. It might have made sense to calculate a standard deviation and a mean for age, but it wouldn't make much sense to do so for the newly recoded age categories variable.

4.4   Practicing Recodes

To experiment further with this technique, why don't you try changing the age recodes into a somewhat more elaborate coding of age into teens, 20s, 30s, and so on? For even more practice, recode the variable EDUC. Later on, we are going to want to use it in a recoded form. See if you can create EDCAT with the following categories:

- Attended high school
- Graduated from high school
- Attended college
- Graduated from college
- Did graduate studies (beyond college)

If you have trouble, the proper commands and results are on the CD.

4.5   Saving Your Work

That's enough work for now. Before we stop, let's save the work we've done in this session so that we won't have to repeat it when we start again. The recoding you've done so far is being held only in the computer's volatile (temporary) memory. That means if you leave SPSS right now, all the recoding changes will disappear.

Because we will want to use the recoded variables AGECAT and EDCAT, there's a simple procedure that will save us time at our next session.

First, you may want to save a copy of the Output window that you've been accumulating during this session. If you are writing a term paper that will use these results, you can probably cut portions of the output and paste them into your word processing document. To save the Output window, first make sure it is the window frontmost on your screen, then select Save As from the File menu.

SPSS will present you with the following window. Note that the file type is called "Viewer files." Notice that the "File Name" field gives you "Output" and a number highlighted. SPSS wants you to name the file. You can name it anything you want (up to eight letters). We're going to use "OUT.613" to indicate that these were created on June 13.

Once you've entered a name, click "OK." Notice that the name of the Output window has been changed. After you leave SPSS, you should find the file and open it with SPSS to reassure yourself that you can get at the results whenever you wish.

Now let's save the data file with the recodes. Return to the Data window (labeled something like gss–SPSS Data Editor). Once the Data window is in front on your screen, go to the File menu. If you are already working from your backed-up version of the original data file, called GSS.SAV on your personal drive, simply select Save under the File menu. If you still have not saved the data file as GSS.SAV on your computer, select Save As under the File menu and do that now. Now your recodes have been saved. The next time you start an SPSS session and load the data set, it will have all the new recoded variables. (If you are using SPSS for Windows Student Version, bear in mind that you can't add variables forever, since you are limited to a maximum of 50. You may have to delete some variables if you want to add new variables.)

4.6   Summary

You've now completed your first interaction with data. Even though this is barely the tip of the iceberg, you should have begun to get some sense of the possibilities that exist in a data set such as this or the other data sets included on your disk. Many of the concepts criminologists and other social scientists deal with are the subjects of opinions in everyday conversations. A data set such as the one you have begun to use in this book is powerfully different from opinion.

From time to time, you probably hear people make statements like these: "Americans support capital punishment." "Most people don't want gun control." "Most people are opposed to abortion." Sometimes, opinions like these are an accurate reflection of the state of affairs; sometimes they are far from the truth. In ordinary conversation, the apparent validity of such assertions typically hinges on the force with which they are expressed or the purported wisdom of the speaker. Already in this book you have discovered a better way of evaluating such assertions, and you've learned how to establish the facts about such different issues as religion, gun control, and capital punishment in the United States today. The two chapters that follow will enable you to investigate crime and justice issues as well as the realms of politics and attitudes toward abortion.

Key Terms

bar chart

categorical variables

continuous variables

cumulative percentage

discrete variables

frequency

mean

median

mode

recode

standard deviation

valid percentage

value labels

variable label

variable names

variance

Chapter 5 **Working With Variables**

How Americans feel about crime and criminal justice is shaped powerfully by how they look at political issues more generally. In this chapter, we examine several items in the General Social Survey (GSS) data set about politics. Later we will study how these political questions are linked to criminal justice questions.

5.1   Political Views: Liberalism Versus Conservatism

We start our examination of political orientation with POLVIEWS. Let's see what that variable measures. Use the Frequencies command to find out.

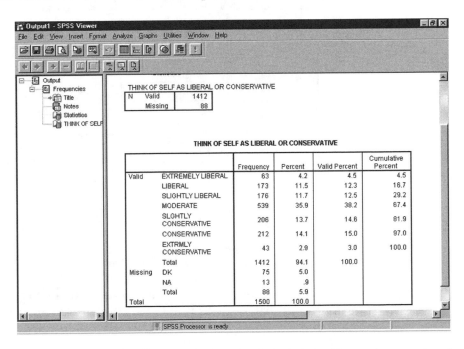

As you can see, POLVIEWS taps into basic political philosophy, ranging from extremely liberal to extremely conservative. As you might expect, most people are clustered near the center, with fewer numbers on either extreme.

As we continue to use this variable in our analyses, we will probably want to work with fewer categories. For now, let's recode the variable to just three categories: liberal, moderate, and conservative. Recall from Chapter 4 that there are two steps involved in recoding the categories of a variable. First, we combine categories; then we assign names to identify the new groupings.

First, let's create a new variable, POLREC, by recoding POLVIEWS as follows:

1 thru 3 → 1

4 → 2

5 thru 7 → 3

[MISSING] → SYSMIS

Then assign new labels to the values of POLREC:

1 "Liberal"

2 "Moderate"

3 "Conservative"

If you have any trouble accomplishing this, you can refer to the notes for this chapter on the CD.

To see the results of our recoding, we repeat the Frequencies command with the new variable:

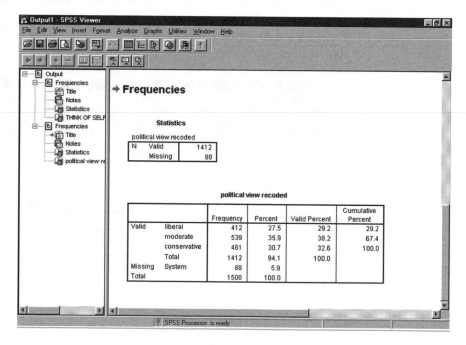

Now that we've recoded political orientation into a form we can use easily in our future analyses, let's turn to the other fundamental measure.

5.2   Political Party Affiliation

Another basic indicator of a person's political orientation is found in the party he or she tends to identify with. Let's turn now to the variable PARTYID. Get the Frequencies for that variable.

You should get the following result from SPSS.

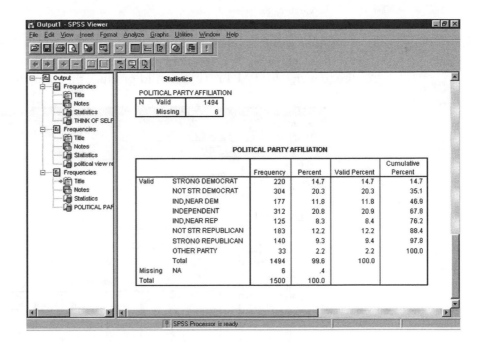

Once again, there are more answer categories here than we will be able to manage easily in our subsequent analyses, so let's consider recoding the variable. Let's call the recoded variable simply PARTY.

It makes sense to combine the first two categories, the "strong" and "not strong" Democrats. Similarly, we will want to combine the corresponding Republican categories (5 and 6). Two of the categories, however, need a little more discussion: the two Independent groups, who said, when pressed by interviewers, that they were "near" one of the two parties.

Should we combine those near the Democrats with that party, for example, or should we combine them with the other Independents? There are a number of methods for resolving this question. For now, however, we are going to choose the simplest method. As we continue our analyses, it will be useful if we have ample numbers of respondents in each category, so we will recode with an eye to creating roughly equal-sized groups. In this instance, that means combining the three Independent categories into one group. So let's recode as follows:

0 thru 1 → 1

2 thru 4 → 2

5 thru 6 → 3

7 → 4

[MISSING] → SYSMIS

Then label PARTY as follows:

1 "Democrat"

2 "Independent"

3 "Republican"

4 "Other"

Enter and execute these commands now. Once you've done so, we'll be ready to look again at the frequency distribution of the new variable. Let's run Frequencies for PARTY. That should produce the following result.

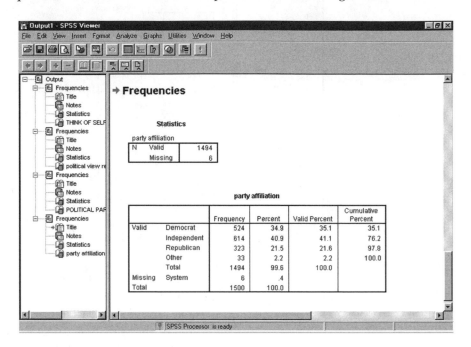

Now we have two basic measures of political orientation. There are other possibilities, however.

5.3   Gun Laws and Capital Punishment

The GSS data set contains other variables that also tap into people's political orientation. For instance, GUNLAW measures how people feel about the registration of firearms. This has been a controversial issue in the United States for a number of years, involving, on the one hand, Second Amendment guarantees of the right to bear arms and, on the other, high rates of violent crime, often involving firearms. CAPPUN measures whether respondents favor or oppose capital punishment, another topic associated with political attitudes.

As you can see, there is no lack of ways to explore people's political outlooks in the "GSS.SAV" data set. We're going to focus on some of these items in later sections of the book. You should take some time now to explore some of them on your own. Take capital punishment, for example. How do you think the American people feel about this issue? Do you think most Americans are in favor of it, or are most opposed? This is your chance to find out for yourself.

If you have any interest in political matters, you should enjoy this exercise. You may have your own personal opinion about extramarital sex or homosexuality, but do you have any idea how the general population feels about such things? You have the definitive answers to those questions at your fingertips right now, using the GSS data set and your developing mastery of SPSS.

5.4   Understanding Binge Drinking

Another data set on your CD has survey data about American college students. How many students are binge drinkers or abuse alcohol? How many use marijuana? What proportion of students run into problems with alcohol or drugs, such as being the victims of alcohol-related sexual assault or date rape? Or driving a car after heavy drinking? Or getting into trouble with the campus or community police?

To begin your exploration, follow the sequence File → Open → Data and choose "BINGE.SAV." Next, follow the now familiar sequence Analyze → Descriptive Statistics → Frequencies, and you will see on the left side of the "Frequencies" dialog box the variables from the Harvard School of Public Health College Alcohol Study. Begin your exploration of this important issue by selecting variables for inspection through frequency distributions and bar charts.

5.5   Other Survey Items About Crime and Justice

Other files on your CD contain GSS data from 1990 on a wide variety of topics dealing with crime and justice. All you have to do is follow the sequence File → Open → Data and choose either "CJGSSLSAV" or "CJGSS2.SAV." Next follow the now familiar sequence Analyze → Descriptive Statistics → Frequencies, and you will see on the left side of the "Frequencies" dialog box a long list of crime and justice variables waiting for your inspection. Explore them, using both frequency distributions and bar charts.

5.6   Crime and Justice Data for the American States

How do the 50 states vary in crime and crime control? Your CD contains up-to-the-minute information from official federal and state criminal justice agencies: Just look for the "JUSTICE.SAV" file. Another file, "JUVENILE.SAV," contains juvenile justice data for the 50 states.

5.7   Summary

This chapter has opened up a world of exploration for the criminal justice researcher. You can choose to explore crime, justice, and political attitudes through the GSS, college drug and alcohol use in the Harvard School of Public Health College Alcohol Survey, or justice data across the American states. Or you can create your own survey and explore what your respondents tell you about the issues. In any case, you'll find SPSS an indispensable tool in exploring these issues.

Chapter 6 Creating Composite Measures

Now that you've had a chance to get familiar with univariate analysis, we're going to add a little more sophistication to that process. As you're about to see, it is not necessary to limit your analysis to single measures of a variable. In this chapter, we're going to create **composite measures** made up of **multiple indicators** of a single concept.

Why would a criminal justice researcher want to do that? Many of the key concepts in criminal justice are complex and can't simply be indicated by the responses to a single variable or by a single piece of information. To take a very important example, how do we define crime among the most important concepts in criminal justice? If we were trying to measure how much crime takes place in a state, it would not be enough just to look at any one type of serious crime. The Uniform Crime Reporting Program uses seven crime categories to establish a "crime index" to measure the trend and distribution of crime in the United States: murder and nonnegligent manslaughter, forcible rape, robbery, aggravated assault, burglary, larceny and theft, and motor vehicle theft; the "total crime index" is the sum of these offenses.

Take another example: We have already suggested that you explore the kinds of harm binge drinking has on nonbingeing students. We called these "secondary binge effects." Suppose that you want to assess how many residential students experience any of these effects or you want to find out how many of the effects (ranging from none to all eight) any of the students on a campus experienced.

In this chapter, we will explore how SPSS can help you create composite measures such as the "crime index" or an index of secondary binge effects. For purposes of this discussion, let's look at attitudes toward abortion. Seven General Social Survey (GSS) items reflect people's attitudes. You can ask SPSS to generate frequency tables for all seven abortion variables from the GSS.SAV data set. (This exercise is also presented on the CD.) These tables on abortion suggest that attitudes toward abortion fall into three basic groups. A small minority of no more than 10% are opposed to abortion under any circumstance. We conclude this because 90% would support abortion if the woman's life was seriously endangered. Another group, a little under half of the sample population, would support a woman's free choice of abortion for any reason. The remainder of the sample population would support abortion in only a few circumstances involving medical danger and/or rape.

6.1   Using Crosstabs

To explore attitudes toward abortion in more depth, we need to use a new SPSS command: Crosstabs. This command provides us with a crossclassification or **crosstabulation** of people in terms of their answers to more than one question. The resulting table is sometimes called a **crosstab** or a **contingency table,** the latter term indicating that the values of one variable are examined for how contingent they are on the values of another variable. Later in this book, we'll explain how to use crosstabs to test hypotheses about two or more variables when each of the variables is measured on the nominal or ordinal scale. Here we'll use it to help us understand how to combine variables into a composite measure. Let's try a simple example.

The command pathway to this technique is Analyze → Descriptive Statistics → Crosstabs. Work your way through those menu selections, and you should reach a window that looks like the following.

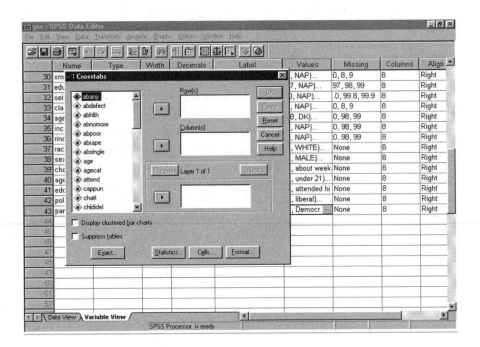

Because the logic of a crosstab will be clearer when we have an example to look at, we ask that you follow these steps on faith, and we'll justify your faith in a moment.

Let's analyze the relationship between the answers people gave to the question about whether a woman should be able to have an abortion if (1) her health was seriously endangered (ABHLTH) and (2) if she was too poor to have more children.

In the Crosstabs window, click ABHLTH and then click the arrow pointing toward the "Row(s)" field. Then click on ABPOOR and transfer it to the "Column(s)" field, producing the result shown next.

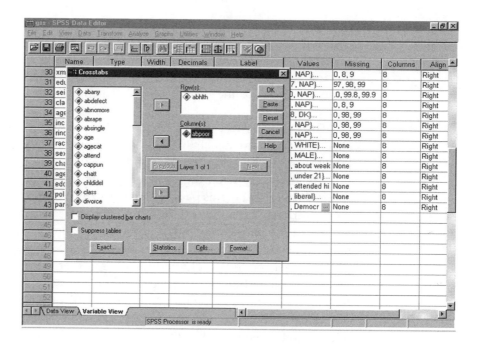

Once your window looks like this, click "OK." After a few seconds, you would be rewarded with the following data in your Output window.

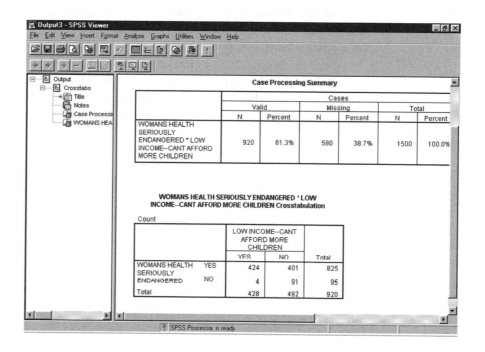

Notice that the table demonstrates the logic of the command we asked you to make. By specifying ABPOOR as the column variable, we have caused it to appear across the top of the table with its attributes, "Yes" and "No," representing the two columns of figures.

ABHLTH, as the row variable, appears to the left of the table, and its attributes constitute the rows of the table.

More important, this table illustrates a logic that operates within the system of attitudes people hold about abortion. First, we notice that 424 people say they would support a woman's right to choose abortion if her health was seriously endangered or if she was poor and felt she couldn't afford more children. At the opposite corner of the table, we find 91 people who would oppose abortion in both cases.

The table shows that 401 respondents said they would support the right to choose if the woman's health was seriously endangered but not on the basis of poverty. Notice that only four respondents would support abortion on the basis of poverty but deny it on the basis of threats to health. There are probably two elements involved in this pattern. Threats to the woman's life are probably seen as more "serious" than the suffering presented by another mouth to feed in a poor family. At the same time, few if any would blame a woman for ending a pregnancy that seriously threatened her health. Some people, however, do blame the poor for their poverty and would likely say that the woman in question should have avoided getting pregnant because she knew that it would be hard for her to feed another child. As a consequence, then, 401 of the respondents oppose abortion under some circumstances but are willing to make an exception in the case of a threat to the woman's health.

What are we to make of the four people who said they would approve an abortion for the poor but not for the woman whose life was threatened? Without ruling out the possibility of some complex point of view that demands such answers, it is most likely that these respondents misunderstood one or both of the questions. Fortunately, they are few enough in number that they will not seriously affect the analysis of this topic.

Additional information in the SPSS table will become more useful to us in later analyses. The rightmost column in the table, for example, tells us that a total of 825 respondents with an opinion said they would approve an abortion for a woman whose health was seriously endangered, and 95 would not. The bottom row of numbers in the table gives the breakdown regarding the other variable.

Let's try another example of the same phenomenon. The threat of a birth defect was considered a more compelling reason for abortion by the respondents than the fact that the woman was not married. Run that table now. Use Analyze → Descriptive Statistics → Crosstabs to get to the Crosstabs window; specify ABDEFECT as the row variable and ABSINGLE as the column variable. Notice that you can click the "Reset" button to remove the variables already in the fields or individually move the variables back to the list and put in the new ones. Click "OK." Next, use the scroll bar to give a complete view of the table. Here's what the output should look like.

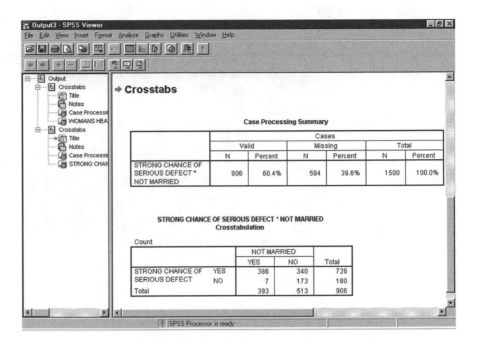

This table presents a strikingly similar picture. We see that 386 respondents support the woman's right to choose in both situations, and 173 oppose abortion in both instances. Of those who would approve abortion in only one of the two situations, almost all of them (340) make the exception for the threat of birth defects. Only 7 respondents would allow abortion for a single woman but deny it in the case of birth defects.

We could continue examining tables like these, but the conclusion forthcoming remains the same: There are three major positions regarding abortion. One group approves it on the basis of the woman's choice, another group opposes it under all circumstances, and the rest approve abortion only in the case of medical complications or rape.

To explore attitudes toward abortion further, it will be useful for us to have a measure of attitudes that is not limited to a single item. In particular, it might be nice to have a single variable that captures the three groups we have been discussing. We're going to create two such composite measures in this chapter.

6.2   Combining Two Items in an Index

To begin, let's create a simple index based on the two variables we just examined. Our aim is to create a new measure—we'll call it ABORT—made up of three scores: 2 for those who approve of abortion if birth defects are likely and approve abortion for a single woman, 1 for those who approve abortion in one circumstance (primarily birth defects) but not the other, and 0 for those who disapprove of abortion in both cases.

To do this, let's use the Transform → Compute command pathway. That will bring up the following window.

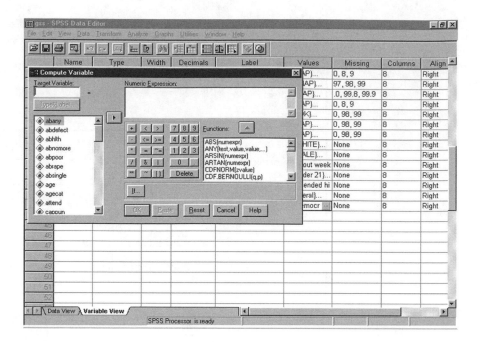

To initiate our index construction, we need to create the new variable so that SPSS will know where to put the results of our work. In the upper left corner of the Compute Variable window, click in the "Target Variable" field and type ABORT.

Notice that we've now begun a numeric expression that says "abort =," taking account of the equal sign already printed to the right of the "Target Variable" field. Our task from now on is to specify what ABORT equals by filling in the field titled "Numeric Expression." We'll do this in several steps.

Begin by entering 0 in that field. You can do this in one of two ways. You can simply type it in, or you can use the keypad in the center of the window. To use the latter, simply click the "0" key.

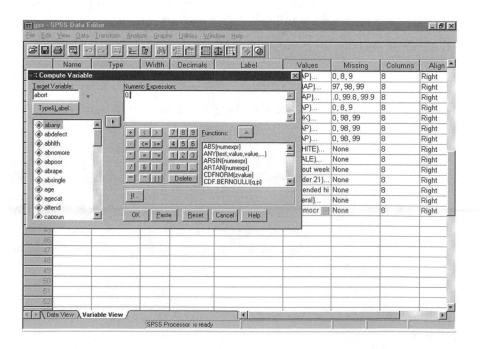

In either case, we've now instructed SPSS to create a new variable, named ABORT, and give everyone a score of 0 on it. Click the "OK" button at the bottom of the window to have SPSS execute the command.

Now let's start assigning index scores based on the answers people gave to the component items. First, if people agreed that a woman should be able to have an abortion in the case of a birth defect (scored 1 on ABDEFECT), we want to give them 1 point on our index. We do it as follows.

Select Transform Compute again. You'll see that the Compute Variable window still has your previous work in it. Click "Reset" at the bottom of the window to clear the boards.

Next, type ABORT into the "Target Variable" field. (As an alternative, you could have left ABORT on the screen and simply erased the earlier instruction in the "Numeric Expression" field instead of clicking "Reset.")

In the list of variables, click ABORT and transfer it to the "Numeric Expression" field by clicking the arrow. Then click "+" and "1" in the keypad, so the whole instruction to SPSS is "ABORT = ABORT + 1" at this point.

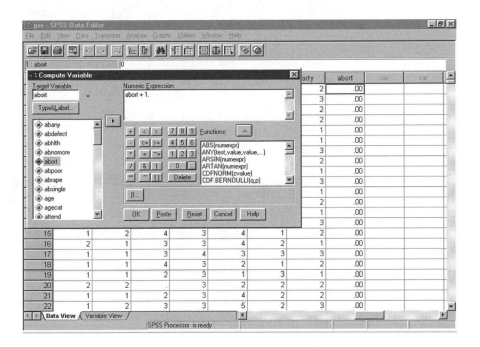

Now, we want SPSS to take this step only for respondents who agreed that a woman should be able to have an abortion in the case of a birth defect. To make this specification, click the "If" button near the bottom of the window. Now you should be looking at the following window:

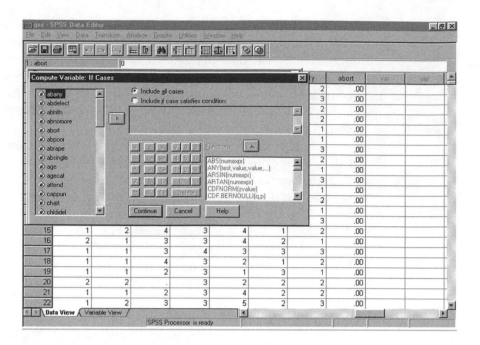

This new window will assist in specifying our instruction to SPSS. Begin by clicking the button "Include if case satisfies condition," which will engage the variable list.

Transfer ABDEFECT to the open field and then add "=1." using the keypad. Your screen should look like this:

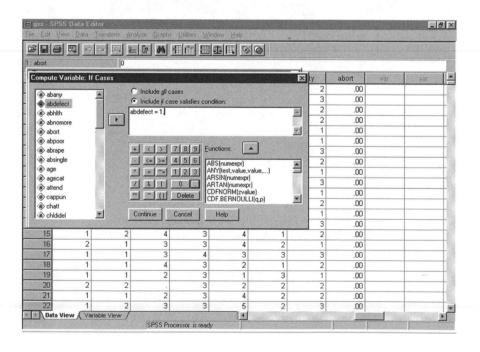

We have now told SPSS that we want it to execute the instruction to add a point to a person's ABORT index score only if the person's score on ABDEFECT is 1.

To continue, click the "Continue" button, and you will be returned to the Compute Variables window, where you will see the following:

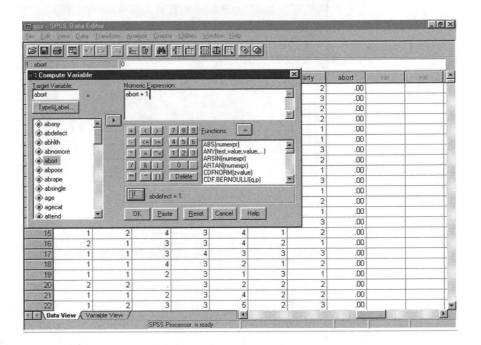

Take a minute to study the various elements of this window, and be sure you are clear on the logic of what we are asking SPSS to do. Once you are, click "OK." SPSS will ask, "Change the existing variable?" Say "OK."

Now you will be returned to your Data window, where you can watch the case counter at the bottom of the window indicate its progress through the data file, making the changes we've asked for. Eventually, you will see that the scores in the ABORT column now contain 0s and 1s.

Your next step is to repeat the same process using ABSINGLE in place of ABDEFECT. As you'll see, it's much easier the second time around. Select Transform → Compute. Notice that "ABORT = ABORT + 1" is still active, as is the conditional statement near the bottom of the window.

Click "If."

All we need to do now is change the name of the variable we want SPSS to check from ABDEFECT to ABSINGLE. The easiest way, perhaps, is to delete ABDEFECT from the field in the center of the window, click ABSINGLE in the list of variables, and move it with the arrow. Your window should look like this:

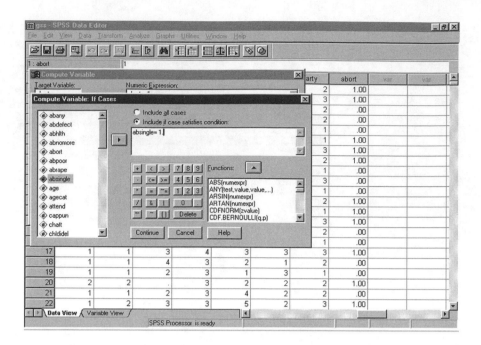

Click "Continue," then click "OK." When asked if you want to change the variable, click "OK."

Our index is nearly complete now. However, we must take account of the people who did not answer either or both of the questions included in the index, people scored as "missing data."

Recall that so far, we gave everyone a score of 0 to begin with, and then respondents who scored 1 on ABDEFECT or ABSINGLE were given additional points. Those who had missing data on the two items, however, are still scored 0 on our index. Thus they look as though they are strongly opposed to abortion, whereas they were actually never asked about it.

To complete our index, then, we must create a missing data code for ABORT and assign that code to the appropriate cases. Let's use –l, as that has no meaning on the index.

Return to Transform → Compute. Put –1 into the "Numeric Expression" field, and click "If" to tell SPSS when we want the –1 code assigned on ABORT.

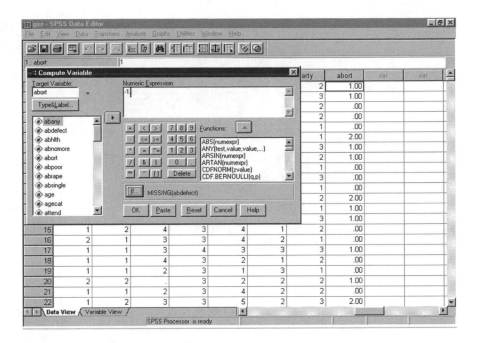

Instead of specifying a numeric value for ABDEFECT and ABSINGLE, we are going to use the list of functions found on the right side of the window. Scroll down the list until you find "MISSING(variable)." Select it and move it up to the open field using the up-pointing arrow.

Notice that the expression now has a highlighted question mark. Replace the highlighted question mark this time by selecting and transferring the variable name, ABDEFECT.

We have now created the following instruction for SPSS: If a person has a missing data code on ABDEFECT, we want that person scored as –1 on the index ABORT. Once you understand the logic of this instruction, click "Continue," then click "OK" to execute the instruction.

Now repeat the same procedure using ABSINGLE.

Our index is almost complete now, but we want to make two modifications to it.

In the Variable View of the Data Editor window, find and select the new variable, ABORT, at the bottom. Once you've done that, select the box in the "Missing" column for the new variable.

Notice that the index currently has "None" listed as missing. Click on the small gray box. Click "Discrete missing values" and type –1 into the first box underneath it. This tells SPSS that we have assigned that numeric score for all cases that got no index score on ABORT.

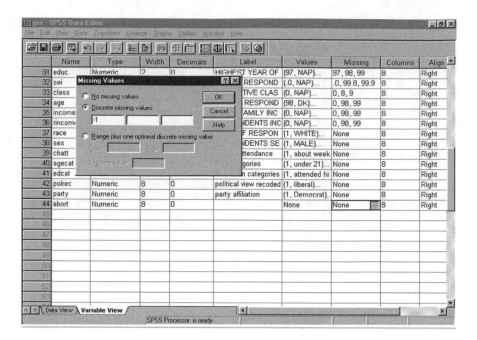

Once you are satisfied with the instruction, click "OK" to return to the Variable View window.

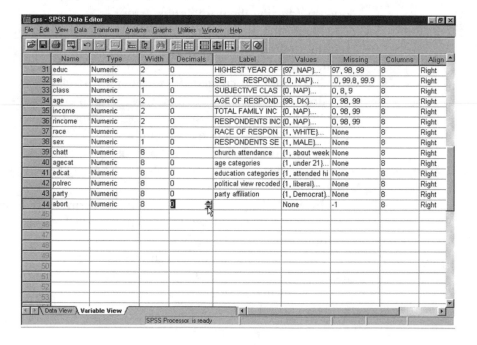

As we did the last time we were here, we want to set the number of decimal places to 0. Click on the box in the Decimals column and use the arrows to bring the 2 to a 0. We will not enter any labels at this point. Just go back to the Data View window, where you will see ABORT with its codes of −1, 0, 1, and 2.

Now let's see if all this really accomplished what we set out to do. Use the Frequencies command to find out. Run the frequency distribution of ABORT, and you should see this table on your screen now:

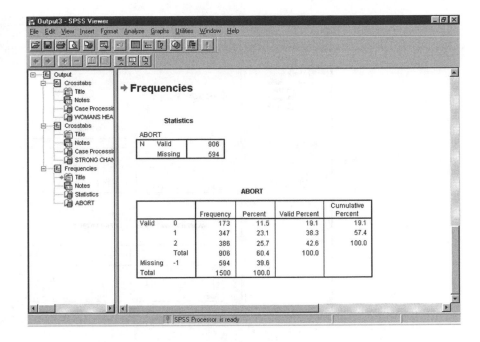

If you compare the index scores in this table with the crosstabs of the two component variables, you'll see a logical correspondence. In the earlier table, 173 people disapproved of abortion under both of the specified conditions; here we find that 173 people scored 0 on the index. And whereas we found that 340 people would approve abortion for birth defects but not for a single woman and 7 had the reverse view, the index shows 347 people (340 + 7) with a score of 1. Finally, the 386 people who approved of abortion in both cases are now scored 2 on the index. Notice also the 594 people who were excluded on the basis of missing data.

Congratulations! You've just created a composite index. We realize you may still be wondering why that's such good news. After all, it wasn't your idea to create the thing in the first place.

6.3   Checking to See How the Index Works

To get a clearer idea of the value of such a composite measure, let's move on to the next step in the process we've launched. Let's check whether the index works. Does it pull together and summarize all its components?

In creating the simple index, we've tried to put respondents in one of three groups: those strongly supportive of abortion, those strongly opposed, and those in the middle. If we've succeeded in that effort, the scores we've assigned people on the new index, ABORT, should help us predict how people answered other abortion items on the questionnaire. Let's begin with their answers to ABHLTH: approving abortion for a woman whose health is in danger.

To undertake this test of the index, we'll return to the Crosstabs command, introduced earlier in the chapter. As you'll see, it has some additional features that can be used to good effect. In this instance, we want to cross-classify people in terms of their scores on the index and on the variable ABHLTH.

Run the Crosstabs command with ABHLTH as the row variable and ABORT as the column variable. Here's the result you should get:

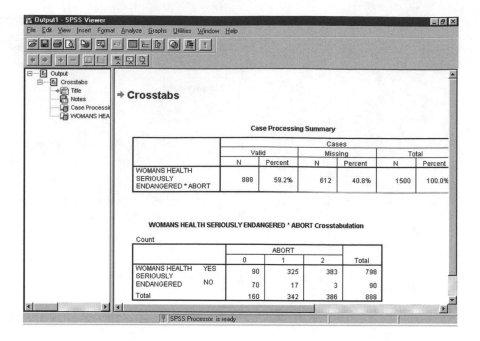

You may be able to look at this table and see the relationship between the index and ABHLTH, but the analysis will be much simpler if we convert the data in the table to percentages. Let's express the assumption of validity we are testing in terms of percentages. If respondents with a score of 2 on the index are the most supportive of abortion, we should expect to find a higher percentage of them approving abortion in the case of the woman's health being endangered than would be found among the other groups. Those scored 0 on the index, by contrast, should be the least likely—the smallest percentage—to approve abortion based on the woman's health.

Looking first at those with a score of 0, in the leftmost column of the table, we would calculate the percentage as follows. Of the 160 people scored 0, we see that 90 approved of abortion in the case of ABHLTH. Dividing 90 by 160 indicates that these 90 people are 56.25% of the total 160. Looking to those scored 2, in the right-most column, we find that the 383 who approve represent 99.22% of the 386 with that score. These two percentages support the assumption we are making about the index—it does seem to be working.

Happily, SPSS can be instructed to calculate these percentages for us. In fact, we are going to be looking at percentage tables for the most part in the rest of this book. Go back to the Crosstabs window. Your previous request should still be in the appropriate fields. Notice a button at the bottom of this window marked "Cells." Click it. This will take you to a new window as shown here:

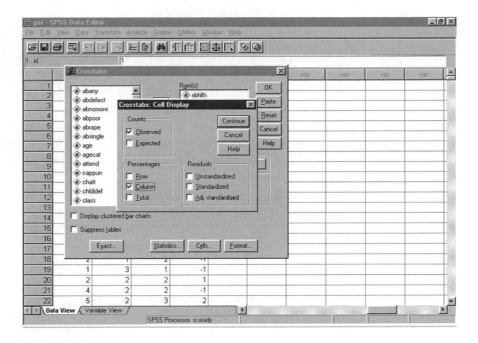

Notice that you can choose to have SPSS calculate percentages for you in one of three ways: either down the columns, across the rows, or total percentages. Click "Columns" and work your way back through the "OKs" to have SPSS run the table for you. Your reward should look like the following:

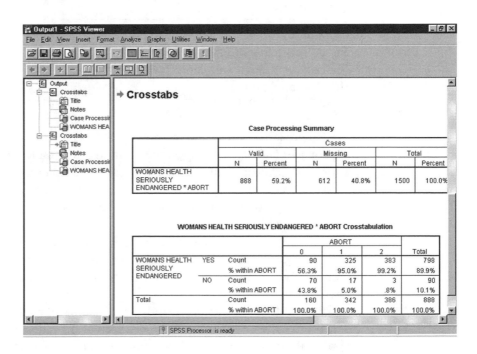

Take a moment to examine the logic of this table. For each score on the index, we have calculated the percentage of respondents saying they favor or oppose a woman's right to an abortion if her health is seriously endangered. It is as though we have limited our attention to one of the index-score groups (those scored 0, for example) and described them in terms of their attitudes on the abortion item; then we have repeated the process for each of the index-score groups. Once we've described each of the subgroups, we can compare them.

When you have created a table with the percentages totaling to 100 down each column, the proper way to read the table is across the rows. Rounding off the percentages to simplify matters, we would note, in this case, that 56% of those scored 0 on the index, 95% of those scored 1 on the index, and 99% of those scored 2 on the index said they would approve of abortion if the woman's health were seriously endangered. This table supports our assumption that the index measures levels of support for a woman's freedom to choose abortion.

Now let's check the index using the abortion variables not included in the index itself. Repeat the Crosstabs command, substituting the four other abortion items—ABNOMORE, ABRAPE, ABPOOR, and ABANY—for ABHLTH.

Run the Crosstabs command now and see what results you get. Look at each of the four tables and see what they say about the ability of the index to measure attitudes toward abortion. Here is an abbreviated table format that you might want to construct from the results of that command. SPSS doesn't create a table like this, but it's a useful format for presenting data in a research report.

Percentage of respondents who approve of abortion under various circumstances

Circumstance	Abortion Index		
	0	*1*	*2*
When the woman was raped	36	83	99
The couple can't afford more children	5	14	93
The couple doesn't want more children	4	12	92
The woman wants an abortion	5	13	90

Whereas the earlier table showed the percentages who approved and disapproved of abortion in specific situations, this table presents only those who approved. The first entry in the table, for example, indicates that 36% of those scored 0 on the index would approve of abortion for a woman who was raped. Of those scored 1 on the index, 83% approved of abortion for this reason, and 99% of those scored 2 approved.

As you can see, the index accurately predicts differences in responses to each of the other abortion items. In each case, those with higher scores on the index are more likely to support abortion under the specified circumstances than those with lower scores on the index.

By building this composite index, we've created a more sophisticated measure of attitudes toward abortion. Whereas each of the individual items allows only for approval or disapproval of abortion under various circumstances, this index reflects three positions on the issue: unconditional disapproval (0), conditional approval (1), and unconditional approval (2).

6.4 Creating a More Complex Index With Count

This first index was created from only two of the abortion items, but we could easily create a more elaborate index, using more items. To illustrate, let's use all the items except for ABANY (supporting a woman's unrestricted choice). Although we could create this new index following the same procedures as before, there is also a shortcut that can be used when we want to score several items the same way in creating the index. Suppose that we want to create a larger index by giving people one point for agreeing to an abortion in each of the six special circumstances. From the Transform menu, select Count. This will present you with the following window:

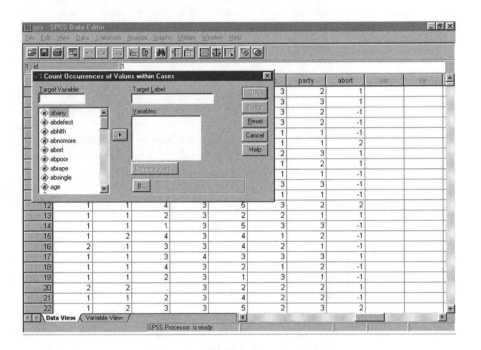

In creating our new index, we will once more need to deal with the problem of missing values. In using Count, we are going to handle that matter somewhat differently from before. Specifically, we are going to begin by creating a variable that tells us whether people had missing values on any of the six items we are examining. To do this, we'll create a variable called MISS. Type that name in the "Target Variable" field.

Next, we want to specify the items to be considered in creating MISS. Transfer the following variable names to the "Variable" field: ABDEFECT, ABHLTH, ABNOMORE, ABPOOR, ABRAPE, and ABSINGLE. You can do this by selecting a variable in the list on the left side of the window and clicking the arrow pointing to the "Variables" field, or you can simply double-click a variable name. (Where several variables are together in the list, you can click and drag your cursor down the several names, selecting them all, and then click the arrow.)

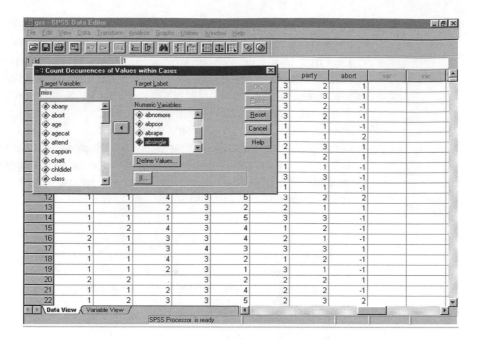

Having selected the variables to be counted, click "Define Values."

The left side of the window offers several options for counting, but we want to use the simplest: a single value. Click the button beside "System- or user-missing." Click the "Add" button to transfer the value to the "Values to Count" field. "MISSING" will now appear in that space. Click "Continue" to return to the Count Occurrences window.

Click "OK" to launch the procedure. Once SPSS has completed the procedure, you will find yourself looking at the Data window—with a new variable called MISS, with scores ranging from 0 to 6, indicating the number of missing values people had on the six items.

Now we are ready to create our new abortion index. Select Count from the Transform menu again. Notice that our earlier specifications are still there; these will be very useful to us.

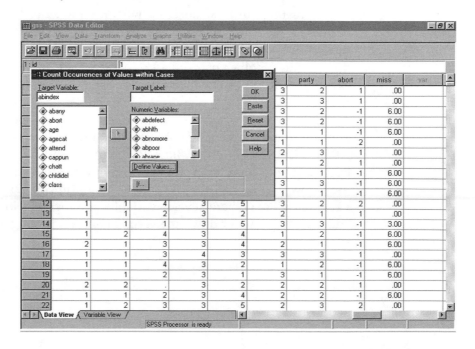

Replace MISS with ABINDEX in the "Target Variable" field. Click "Define Values." In the Values to Count window, you'll notice that MISSING is still showing in the specification field. Click it to select it. Then click "Remove." Now the field is empty.

Click the first option on the left, "Value," and type "1" in the field beside it. Click "Add" to transfer the value to the appropriate field.

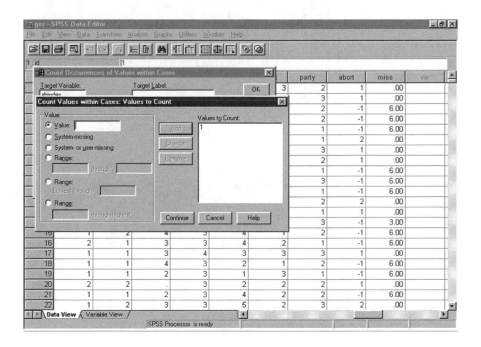

Then click "Continue." Since we left the six variable names in the "Numeric Values" field, we have now told SPSS to count the number of times a person had a score of 1 on any of those six items.

Before having SPSS do its counting, however, we can use the MISS index we created a moment ago.

Click "If." In the If Cases window, click "Include if case satisfies condition." Notice that the list of variables on the left is activated by that. You can either find MISS in that list and transfer it or simply type MISS in the field. Then add " = 0" after MISS. You can either type it in or use the keypad. We have now told SPSS that we want it to count pro-choice answers only for those who had no missing values on any of the six items.

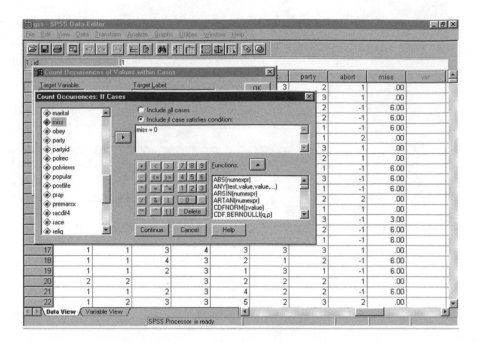

Click "Continue" and notice that the "If" field at the bottom of the window now contains our specification. Click "OK" to launch the counting.

Soon you should be looking at the Data window. Go to the rightmost column in the window and you will find ABINDEX. Some of the cells have scores between 0 and 6, and some have a simple period (indicating missing data).

Now we need to tidy up our new variable. Click on the Variable View tab. Go to ABINDEX in the last row. Click on the "Decimals" box and change the number of decimal places to 0.

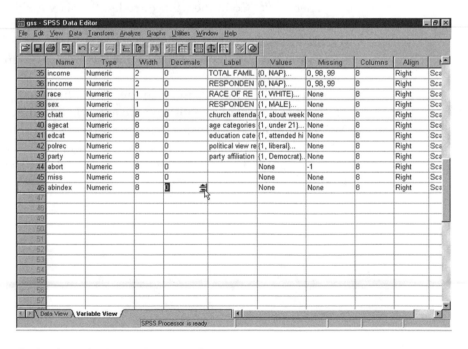

Go back to the Data View window.

Let's see what these instructions produced. Get the frequency distribution of ABINDEX. Here's what you should find:

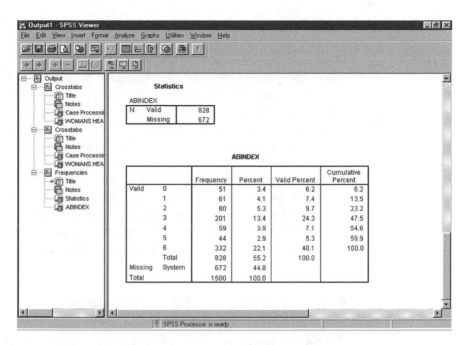

This table shows the distribution of scores on the new index, ABINDEX. (Use the scroll bar on the right hand side of the window to move the output text up and down so that you can see whatever output you want to look at.) As you can see, there are 332 people, about two-fifths of those with opinions, who support abortion in all the specified circumstances. A total of 51 disapprove of abortion in any of those circumstances. The rest are spread out according to the number of conditions they feel would warrant abortion.

For validation purposes this time, we have only one item not included in the index itself: ABANY. Let's see how well the index predicts respondents' approval of a woman's unrestricted choice of abortion.

Run the Crosstabs procedure, specifying ABANY as the row variable, ABINDEX as the column index, and cells to be percentaged by column.

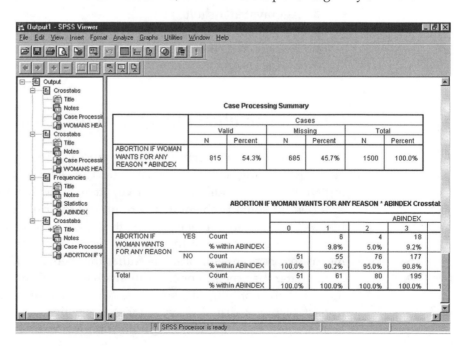

Looking at the SPSS output, using the scroll bars if necessary, we can see answers to ABANY are closely related to scores on ABINDEX. Of those with 0 on the index, no one said a woman had a right to an abortion for any reason. Only 6 of the persons who scored 1 on ABINDEX favored a woman's right to an abortion for any reason. For the scores 2 through 6, the percentage continues increasing across the index until we find that 95.1 percent of those scored 6 on the index say a woman has the unconditional right to an abortion. (You may have to scroll over to the right to see the entire table with all the columns.)

Once again, we find that the index works well. This means that if we wish to analyze peoples' attitudes toward abortion further (and we will), we have the choice of using a single item to represent those attitudes or using a composite measure. If we've constructed the index well, it should be superior to any one of its component parts, serving to provide much more information about a particular topic. We've seen, moreover, that we can create such an index in different ways.

6.5   Creating the FBI Crime Index

To take a very different example of creating a composite index, we will follow the simple steps necessary to create perhaps the most famous composite index in criminal justice. To do this, we'll use another file on your CD, so give SPSS the commands necessary to open the "JUSTICE.SAV" file. Once you've opened this file, follow this chapter's instructions to combine the crimes mentioned in the beginning of this chapter into an overall index. This index will be a simple addition of the component crimes into an overall sum of those crimes for each state. It is a simple index because none of the variables has any missing data.

So the index will include the following items:

- Murder and nonnegligent manslaughter
- Forcible rape
- Robbery
- Aggravated assault
- Burglary
- Larceny and theft
- Motor vehicle theft

6.6   "Secondhand Binge Effects": Creating an Index

How about a real challenge? A final example of index construction asks you to begin by opening the "BINGE.SAV" file. Concentrate your efforts on constructing an index that combines the survey items in which a student reports having experienced some problem as the result of the drinking of some other student. Just as "secondhand smoke" means that someone else's smoking causes a non-smoker to suffer some of the same ill effects as a smoker, "secondhand binge" means that nonbingeing students suffer those effects. This example is a bit more challenging than the last one. It will involve several steps. First, the index should include only nonbingeing students. Next, because you want to examine the impact of binge drinking on students who live on campus, make the index include only students who live in dormitories, fraternities, or sororities. Finally, include the following items from the College Alcohol Study, asking whether or not a student experienced each of these:

- Been insulted or humiliated
- Had a serious argument or quarrel
- Been pushed, hit, or assaulted
- Had your property damaged
- Had to "baby-sit" or take care of another student who drank too much
- Had your studying or sleep interrupted
- Experienced an unwanted sexual advance
- Been a victim of sexual assault or date rape

You can create an index that should count up the number of "secondary binge" effects that a student experienced. Since there are eight items, this index can vary from 0 to 8. Remember to construct this index variable taking missing values into account.

6.7   Summary

In this chapter, we've seen that it is often possible to measure criminal justice and other social scientific concepts in a number of ways. Sometimes the data set contains a single item that does the job nicely. Measuring gender by asking people for their gender is a good example.

In other cases, the mental images that constitute our concepts (e.g., attitudes about abortion, serious crime in a state, or the experience of secondary binge effects) are varied and ambiguous. Typically, no single item in a data set provides a complete representation of what we have in mind. Often we can resolve this problem by combining two or more indicators of the concept into a composite index. As we've seen, SPSS offers the tools necessary for such data transformations.

If you continue your studies in criminal justice research, you will discover many more sophisticated techniques for creating composite measures. However, the simple indexing techniques you have learned in this chapter will serve you well in the analyses that lie ahead.

Key Terms

composite measures
contingency table
crosstab

crosstabulation
multiple indicators

Part III Bivariate Analysis

This set of chapters adds a new dimension to your analyses of crime and the criminal justice system. By moving from the analysis of one variable, univariate analysis, to the analysis of two variables at a time, bivariate analysis, we open the possibility of exploring why variables take on the values they do. Chapter 7 poses the question "Why do some college students use (or abuse) drugs and alcohol, while others do not?" This is the sort of question that leads investigators toward matters of cause and effect. Also in Chapter 7, we'll begin to discover what makes some people liberal and others conservative, as well as what makes some Democrats, others Republicans, and still others Independents. In addition, we'll begin to explore some of the consequences of a person's political orientation. What difference does political orientation make in terms of other attitudes about criminal justice issues, such as gun control and capital punishment?

In Chapter 7, we will limit our analyses to percentage tables, a basic format for such investigations in criminal justice research. There are many other methods for measuring the extent to which variables are related to one another, however, and we'll examine some of these in Chapter 8: lambda, gamma, Pearson's *r* product-moment correlation coefficient, and linear regression. You'll learn the logic that lies behind them, and you'll see how to use them through SPSS.

Chapter 9 adds another set of techniques for your use in assessing the associations you discover among variables. Whenever samples have been chosen from a larger population, as is the case with the General Social Survey or the Harvard School of Public Health College Alcohol Study data, there is always some danger that the associations we discover among variables in our sample are merely results of sampling error and do not represent a genuine pattern in the larger population. Chapter 9 will demonstrate several techniques used by criminal justice researchers to guard against being misled in that fashion.

Chapter 7 **Investigating the Correlates of Binge Drinking and Attitudes Toward Gun Control and Capital Punishment: Independent Versus Dependent Variables**

So far, we have limited our analyses to single variables. Although we have examined a number of variables, we have looked at them one at a time. This process is appropriate to description, but we are going to shift our attention now to the beginnings of explanation.

7.1 Moving Beyond Description: Comparing Two Variables

Although it is important in criminal justice to be able to describe variables clearly, it is often more important to investigate what accounts for them. That usually means testing causal hypotheses, statements that one variable is the cause of another. Scientists—including social scientists such as criminologists—assume that there are **three criteria for testing causal hypotheses.** To say that one thing causes another, three basic questions have to be answered. First, the presumed cause must precede the effect in time, so scientists have to establish the **time order** between variables. Second, the presumed cause has to occur or change along with a change or occurrence of the effect, meaning that scientists have to establish **covariation.** Finally, other possible reasons that might explain the occurrence or change in the presumed effect have to be eliminated, so scientists have to rule out **rival causal factors.**

Data analysis in criminal justice research allows the researcher to answer whether there is covariation between variables that indicates causes and effects. Moreover, data analysis allows the researcher to take into account the impact of alternative causal variables, controlling for their impact statistically. Finally, logic and careful measurement help the researcher sort out which variables precede others in time.

Of these several issues, the most critical one we will examine in the remaining pages is the issue of covariation. How can we establish whether two variables covary (change together)? Fortunately, a statistical package such as SPSS for Windows can provide us with some powerful answers.

We've discussed earlier that surveys on crime and justice provide us with variables about the many issues we're concerned with. In any one research project, one or more of those variables are the center of attention, for it is their variation from case to case that is the subject or topic of the research. For example, the College Alcohol Study conducted by the Harvard School of Public Health wanted to understand how college students use (and often abuse) alcohol. Not surprisingly, binge drinking is the subject or topic of that research, and binge drinking is considered its major **dependent variable.** To understand why some students binge drink and others do not, a whole bunch of other variables will be examined, such as gender and religiosity, and those other variables are considered **independent variables** in this study. (Think of it this way: Whether any one student binge drinks is thought to depend on those other variables. Those other variables are largely independent of the research investigation, with the researcher not attempting to understand why a particular student is a male or a female, just whether binge drinking is higher for males or females.)

The research purposes define what are considered independent and dependent variables. In most of the College Alcohol Study, binge drinking was the dependent variable and gender and religiosity were independent variables. But in other parts of the study, binge drinking was considered the independent variable while some other event—whether a college student was the victim of date rape due to alcohol abuse or whether a student drove after drinking—was considered the dependent variable. So whether a variable is considered dependent or independent is largely a matter of what the researcher intends to study. In much criminal justice research, the dependent variables involve crime perpetration or victimization or attitudes and values about crime and justice, while the independent variables are the characteristics of individuals, groups, or situations.

These ideas probably sound pretty abstract. We can make them much more concrete by examining several real criminal justice research questions using our data sets. It is very important that we distinguish between our dependent and independent variables.

We also want to begin watching our language! As researchers, we can say with some certainty what the independent and dependent variables are in our study. But often it is premature to begin talking about cause and effect, at least without much more investigation, since we usually don't know very much about the time order of the variables or the status of other plausible explanations, and our data are often collected at a single point in time (so-called cross-sectional data).

7.2   Comparing Binge Drinking and Gender

In this new venture, we will also make use of a different data set than the General Social Survey (GSS) that we've been using so far. So now turn your attention to the "BINGE.SAV" data set. We mentioned in introducing this data set in Chapter 2 that one of its most important variables is called COLLBING, whether a student was a binge drinker. You'll recall that binge drinking was defined as a male student's having five or more drinks in a row or a female student's having four or more drinks in a row. (You'll remember that this definition makes the overall risks of alcohol-related problems equal between men and women.) Univariate analysis of this binge drinking variable assesses how many of the students in the College Alcohol Study turn out to be binge drinkers, or bingers. But where univariate analysis looks at the extent of binge drinking, for example, we are now going to turn our attention to why: What are the reasons some people abuse alcohol more than others?

This analysis requires us to advance our analytic procedures to what social researchers call **bivariate analysis,** involving two variables: an independent variable and a dependent variable. (In situations where our theory makes us think the independent variable causes the dependent variable, we might call these variables the causal variable, or cause, and the effect variable, or effect. But most of the time in criminal justice research, we simply refer to them as independent and dependent variables.)

Let's tackle one of the most interesting and challenging questions about college binge drinking: Have men and women achieved equality in terms of binge drinking? Or to put it another way, do men and women have the same likelihood of being binge drinkers, meaning that gender does not affect the likelihood of bingeing? (Later we'll explore whether gender makes a difference in whether one is the victim of alcohol-related violence, but for now let's look at gender and bingeing.)

The best way to start is with a clearly stated hypothesis: Gender is associated with binge drinking (men are more likely to binge than women).

Which is the independent variable, and which is the dependent variable? Since gender is a constant through one's life and since the kinds of childhood, adolescent, or young adult experiences that might shape binge drinking happen well before the period of binge drinking measured by this survey, let's assume that gender is the independent variable and binge drinking (we assume) is the dependent variable.

Once your hypothesis specifies which variables to look at and you are able to clarify which variable you consider dependent and which you consider independent, the next steps are straightforward.

To test this hypothesis, we need measures of both variables. We turn to one of the data files on your CD: "BINGE.SAV." Gender is easy: The variable GENDER handles that nicely.

As you begin this analysis, you might want to review how to get univariate frequency distributions (in the early part of Chapter 4). Next, run the univariate frequency distributions for each of the variables (COLLBING and GENDER). You might want to look again at the bar charts for each variable—you can never be too familiar with the individual variables in your study, details such as how they are coded, how the variables are distributed, and how many cases are valid and how many are missing.

We will now use one of SPSS's most helpful commands to construct a table in which the values of one variable are cross-tabulated with the values of the other variable. (As explained in Chapter 6, this table is called *a crosstabulation,* or *crosstab* for short; it is also known as a contingency table because one variable is contingent—depends on—the other.) Instead of just learning how many men and women were in the sample or how many binge drinkers or nonbinge drinkers there were (just a description of gender and bingeing separately), we're going to learn how many men were or were not bingers and how many women were or were not bingers. This evidence will be used to test our hypothesis.

Now we can request the Crosstab, specifying COLLBING (the dependent variable) as the row variable, GENDER (the independent variable) as the column variable. Also request the cells to be percentaged by columns. Once you specify which variable is independent and which is dependent, setting up a crosstabulation in this way will always give you tables that are correctly percentaged and ready for you to interpret.

Execute this command, and you should get the following result:

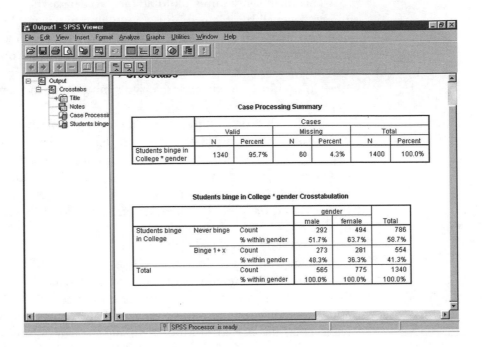

Epsilon is a simple statistic often used to summarize percentage differences such as these. In comparing men and women in terms of binge drinking, we look across the bottom set of cells, noting that 48.3% of males but only 36.3% of females are binge drinkers. Epsilon is simply the remainder when the smaller of these percentages is subtracted from the larger: 48.3% − 36.3% = 12%. So the percentage difference between men and women is 12%, a simple and clear demonstration that men and women have different rates of binge drinking.

Before moving on, let's emphasize the value of looking closely at simple percentage differences. Many of the statistics used in criminal justice are more "high-powered" than the lowly epsilon, but few are as helpful in making sense of your data.

We can request more tables. In the Crosstab window, replace COLLBING with CIGARETT, the variable about cigarette use, in the "Row Variable" field. Again, remember that the row variable is the dependent variable; the column variable, in this case GENDER, is the independent variable, and you should percentage the table down its columns.

Before you execute the Crosstabs command, try to hypothesize what you expect to see. Based on the binge drinking results, do you expect also to see a large difference in cigarette use between men and women? Now go ahead and run the table. The result should be the following output:

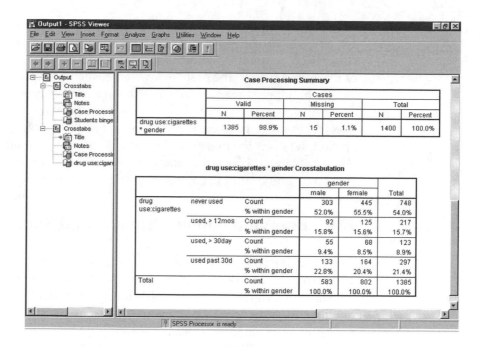

What is the epsilon, the percentage difference, between men and women in terms of cigarette use during the past 30 days? The percentage difference is very small, only a little more than 2%—noticeably different from the results for binge drinking.

Now you have evidence that college men and women use the two most commonly abused substances, alcohol and tobacco, in quite different ways. What would you hypothesize might be the case for marijuana use?

To test your hypothesis, keep GENDER as the independent variable, but substitute USEGRASS as the dependent variable. Run the table again and you should get output like the following:

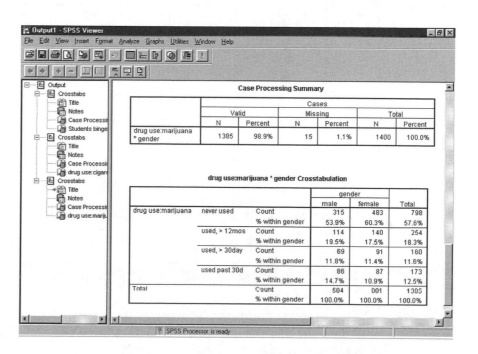

Again, compare the percentages across the rows. The top row shows that there is a noteworthy difference between men and women in the percentages who have never used marijuana. By contrast, the bottom row shows a clear difference in use of marijuana during the past 30 days, an epsilon of almost 5%.

Each of these bivariate analyses, therefore, has supported our thesis that men and women would differ in their use of these substances, but we learned that the differences range from almost insignificant to quite large. Judging by the value of epsilon, which is the biggest difference? Which is the smallest?

What is your conclusion about the equality of men and women in the area of substance use, confining your examination to college men and women?

7.3 Examining Binge Drinking and Race

One of the most striking social differences on American college campuses today concerns race. For better or for worse, students of different racial backgrounds often live in different social worlds. Would you expect to see any sharp differences in binge drinking by race, or do you expect that this is one area of behavior where the different racial groups behave similarly? Again, the best way to proceed is to state precisely, in the form of a testable hypothesis, what you expect to find.

Once again, the binge drinking variable will be considered the dependent variable, so it should be entered as the row variable. RACE will be considered the independent variable, so it is the column variable. Percentaging by column yields the following:

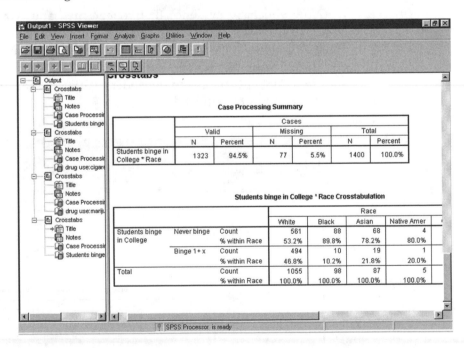

If you hypothesized sharp differences, these data support your ideas. The percentage difference between the two largest racial groups is particularly large, and it is clear that every minority group has substantially lower rates of binge drinking than whites.

Are you curious about whether the same patterns hold up between race and the two other substance use variables, CIGARETT and USEGRASS? Why not run the appropriate crosstabulation now?

7.4   Continuing the Analysis: Binge Drinking and Religiosity

This completes our initial foray into the world of bivariate analysis. We hope you've gotten a good sense of the potential for detective work in criminal justice research. To continue the present line of analysis, why don't you test the notion, from Wechsler and his colleagues (Wechsler, Dowdall, Davenport, & Castillo, 1995), that binge drinking is related to a person's religiosity? This means that college students who say that religion is an important or very important activity to participate in at college will tend to be less likely to be binge drinkers than those who say it is only somewhat important or not important at all. (Many people think that the changing importance of religion has been one of the most important changes in American life.) You find out. Does binge drinking covary with religiosity? More precisely, does the variable COLLBING covary with RELIGION? Use your skills at constructing a crosstabulation, and see what conclusions you reach.

7.5   The Impact of the Minimum Purchase Law: Bingeing and Age

In part because of rising fear about drinking and underage driving, all 50 states raised the age for legal purchase of alcoholic beverages to 21. Despite this legal barrier, it is widely known that many younger Americans drink before they are 21. In fact, most full-time college students are under 21. What's the impact of this law on binge drinking? Would you hypothesize that students who are 21 and over would engage in more binge drinking than younger students (thereby indicating the impact of the law on everyday behavior)? Or would you hypothesize that students under 21 will binge more (perhaps indicating the allure of "forbidden fruit" and the impulse by younger students to try out enjoined behavior)?

Let's check out this relationship by using a crosstabulation table. Request a Crosstab using COLLBING as the row variable, AGE as the column variable, and cells to be percentaged by column. Run the data, and then assess which of the two competing hypotheses appears to be supported by these data. Wouldn't it be easier to reach a conclusion if the data for age were regrouped into two categories, students who are under 21 and students who are 21 and over? Try recoding AGE into a new variable (AGECAT2, for example) with your recoded categories of under 21 and 21 and over. Then run the crosstab table again and compare the two age groups with regard to binge drinking.

7.6   Political Orientation, Guns, and Capital Punishment: Independent Versus Dependent Variables

In criminal justice research, it's usually best to begin an investigation with a coherent body of theory, such as routine activity theory. Where possible, that's usually the preferable approach to data analysis. Sometimes, however, it's appropriate to take a less structured route. As we turn our attention to politics, gun control, and capital punishment in this chapter, we're going to be more inductive than deductive so that you can become familiar with this approach. We'll return to using the GSS data in "GSS.SAV," so you'll again use your SPSS skills to open that file.

In Chapter 5, we examined two GSS variables, POLVIEWS and PARTYID. In the analyses to follow, we'll begin by looking at the statistical relationship between these two variables. You can do that now that you understand the Crosstabs command. Next, we'll explore some of the variables associated with differences in political philosophies and party identification. Finally, we'll look at POLVIEWS and PARTYID as *independent variables*: We'll see what impact they have on other variables, especially the crucial criminal justice questions of attitudes about gun control (GUNLAW) and capital punishment (CAPPUN).

In this chapter, then, we'll be looking at the same variables, but in two different ways. First, we'll explore how the two political orientation variables are associated. Later, we'll treat them both as *dependent variables*—trying to examine the extent to which a person's political views or party identification is dependent on other variables. Finally, these two variables will be treated themselves as independent variables, and we'll try to figure out how a person's attitudes about gun control or capital punishment depend on these independent variables.

In criminal justice research as a whole, most research concerns variables about crime or punishment of some type. In some investigations, these variables are treated as independent variables; in others, they are treated as dependent variables. The category depends on the researcher's approach to the topics of the research. As we discussed earlier, treating one variable as the cause and the other variable as the effect requires meeting criteria regarding time order and covariation and then eliminating rival causal factors. With this topic, we can't really establish time order among the variables or eliminate other plausible causal factors, so we are content to treat one variable as dependent and assess its covariation with another considered as independent.

7.7   The Relationship Between POLVIEWS and PARTYID

Let's begin with our two key variables, POLVIEWS and PARTYID, recoded as in Chapter 5. As we indicated earlier, there is a consensus that in contemporary U.S. politics, Democrats are more liberal than Republicans and Republicans are more conservative than Democrats, although everyone recognizes the existence of liberal Republicans and conservative Democrats.

The GSS data allow us to see what the relationship between these two variables actually is. Since neither is logically prior to the other, we could treat either as the independent variable. For present purposes, it is probably useful to explore both possibilities: that political philosophy depends on party identification and that party identification depends on political philosophy.

To begin, then, let's see if Democrats are more liberal or more conservative than Republicans. To check this, we'll use the two recoded political variables. You will want to make POLREC the row variable (because we consider it the dependent variable) and PARTY the column variable (because we consider it the independent variable). Remember that you want to arrange the table so that the percentages add up to 100 down the column—in SPSS, you want "column percents."

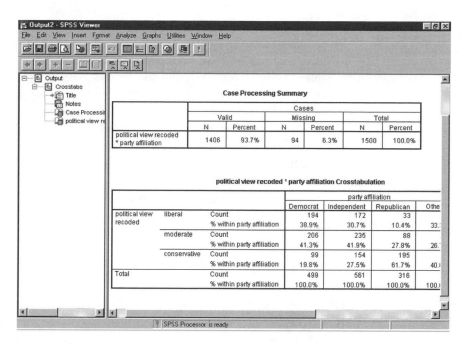

The data in this table confirm the general expectation. Of the Democrats in the GSS sample, 39% describe themselves as liberals, in contrast to 10% of the Republicans. The Independents fall between the two parties, with 31% saying they are liberals. The relationship can also be seen by reading across the bottom row of percentages: 20% of the Democrats call themselves conservatives, versus 62% of the Republicans.

We can also turn the table around logically and ask whether liberals or conservatives are more likely to identify with the Democratic or Republican Party.

By the way, before we move on, which do you now consider the independent variable? (If you said PARTY, you're correct! If you didn't get this right, review the difference between independent and dependent variables—it's important!) You can get this table by simply reversing the location of the two variable names in the earlier command. Make PARTY the row variable and POLREC the column variable and rerun Crosstabs. Here's what you'll get:

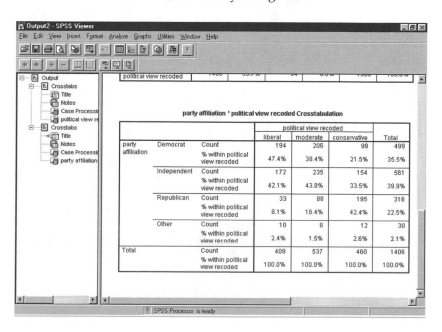

Again, the relationship between the two variables is evident. Liberals are more likely (47%) to say they are Democrats than moderates (38% are Democrats) or conservatives (only 22% are Democrats) are.

Now why don't you state the relationship between these two variables in terms of the likelihood that the respondents will support the Republican Party? Either way of stating the relationship is appropriate.

In summary, then, there is an affinity between liberalism and the Democrats and between conservatism and the Republicans. At the same time, it is not a perfect relationship, and you can find plenty of liberal Republicans and conservative Democrats in the tables.

Now let's switch gears and see if we can discover some of the reasons people are liberal or conservative, Democrats or Republicans.

7.8   Age and Politics

Often the search for useful independent variables involves the examination of **demographic** or **background variables** (such as age, sex, and race) that define important social or economic identities for an individual. Such variables often have a powerful impact on attitudes and behaviors about crime and the justice system. Let's begin with age.

There is a common belief that young people are more liberal than old people, that people get more conservative as they get older. As you can imagine, liberals tend to see this as a trend toward stodginess, whereas conservatives tend to explain it as a matter of increased wisdom. Regardless of the explanation you might prefer, let's see if it's true that old people are more conservative than young people.

To find out, run Crosstabs using POLREC as the row variable and AGECAT as the column variable. Here's what you should get:

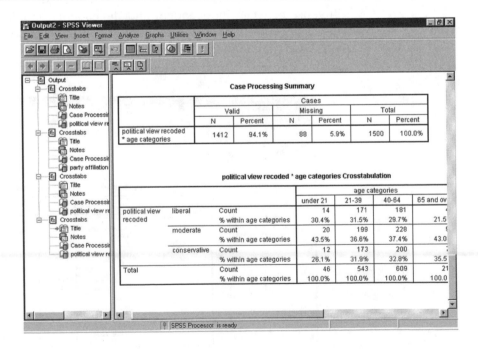

Which of the following statements is a more accurate interpretation of the table?

People appear to become more conservative as they grow older.

People appear to become more liberal as they grow older.

If you chose the first answer, you have just won the right to continue with the analysis. (Oh, never mind—you can continue even if you got it wrong.)

What would you expect to find in terms of political party identification? If that relationship corresponds to the one we've just examined, we'd expect to find growing strength for Republicans as people grow older. Young people should be more likely to identify themselves as Democrats. Here's an opportunity to test "common sense." Why don't you try it out and see what you get? How would you interpret the table?

7.9   Religion and Politics

In the United States, the relationship between religion and politics is somewhat complex, especially regarding Roman Catholics. Let's begin with political philosophies. Now would be a good time for you to ask SPSS for the crosstab connecting RELIG with POLREC. If you do, you should soon be looking at this table:

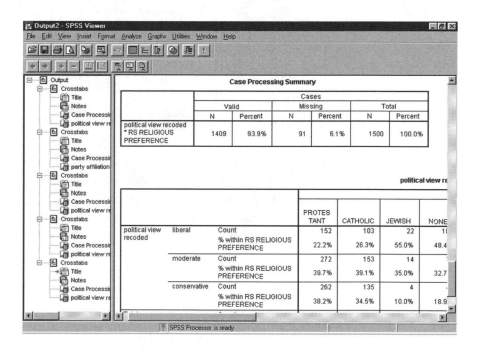

To begin, you should recognize that the many "other" religion categories make this table difficult to read and somewhat meaningless. If you were to work extensively with RELIG, you might want to recode it to put many of the religions with few respondents in with the "other" category.

"None" is a very meaningful category made up of agnostics and atheists. Notice that the people in this category are pretty liberal; but Jewish respondents are the most politically liberal. Protestants are the most conservative, followed by Catholics. Jews are apparently the least conservative of the groups.

If you were to make a gross generalization about the relationship between religious affiliation and political philosophy, it would place Protestants and Catholics on the right end of the political spectrum and Jews and "Nones" on the left.

Political party identification, however, is a somewhat different matter. Like the Jews, Roman Catholics have been an ethnic minority through much of U.S. history, and the Democratic Party, in the 20th century at least, has focused more on minority rights than the Republican Party has. That would explain the relationship between religion and political party. Why don't you run that table now? Make PARTY the row variable and RELIG the column variable.

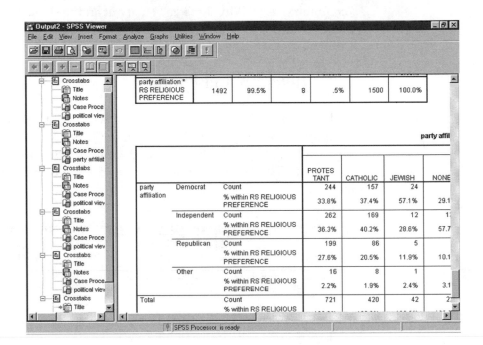

As we see in the table, Jews are indeed the most likely to identify with the Democratic Party. Although Catholics are the next most likely, they do not differ much from the Protestants in this regard.

If you are interested in these two variables, you might want to explore the relationship between politics and other religious variables such as POSTLIFE and PRAY.

You could also look for other consequences of RELIG. What else do you suppose might be affected by differences of religious affiliation?

7.10   Gender and Politics

Gender is a demographic variable associated with a great many attitudes and behaviors and turns out to be a particularly important variable in understanding crime and justice as well as politics. Take a minute to think about the reasons women might be more liberal or more conservative than men. Once you've formed an expectation in this regard, why don't you look for the actual relationship by using SPSS?

7.11   Race, Class, and Politics

In light of the comments made about politics and minority groups, what relationship do you expect to find between politics and race? The variable available to you for analysis codes only "white," "black," and "other," so it's not possible to examine this relationship in great depth, but you should be able to make some educated guesses about how Caucasians and African Americans might differ politically.

After you've thought about the likely relationship between race and politics, why don't you run the tables and test your ability to predict such matters?

The Democratic Party has also traditionally been strong among the working class, whereas the well-to-do have seemed more comfortable as Republicans. Why don't you check to see if this relationship still holds true in the 1990s? You can use the variable CLASS, which is a measure of subjective social class, asking respondents how they view themselves in this regard.

7.12   Education and Politics

Education, a common component of social class, is likely to be of interest to you, especially if you are currently a college student. From your own experience, what would you expect to be the relationship between education and political philosophy? Run Crosstabs for EDCAT (column variable) and POLREC (row variable), and you can find out the facts of the matter. Recall that we recoded EDUC into EDCAT in Chapter 4.

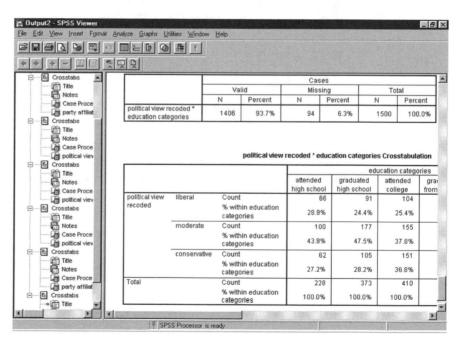

As you can see, there is almost a consistent pattern of increasing liberalism with higher levels of education. This does not mean that conservatism declines with increasing education, however. Instead, the rise in liberalism is accounted for by a decline in the number of moderates as education increases. But how about political party? You decide how to structure your Crosstabs instruction to obtain the following table:

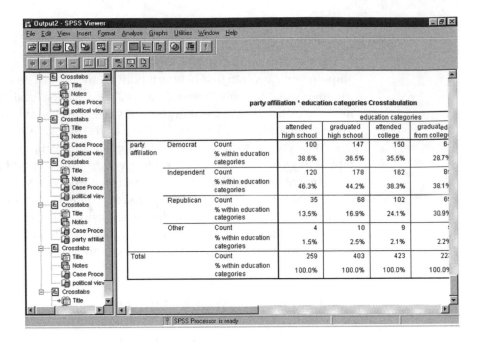

The relationship here is fairly consistent, but it is possibly in the opposite direction from what you expected. We've seen throughout these analyses that the association of liberalism with the Democratic Party is hardly a perfect one, and these latest two tables point that out very clearly.

Whereas liberalism increases with rising educational levels, Democratic Party identification mostly decreases. Why do you suppose that would be the case? Think about this, and we'll return to this issue in Chapter 11, when you have the ability to analyze multivariate tables.

7.13   Marital Status and Politics

Sometimes the inductive method of analysis produces some surprises. As an example, you might take a look at the relationship between MARITAL and our political variables. It wouldn't seem as though marital status would relate to political orientation, but your analysis is likely to present you with some odd results.

Once you've run the tables, try to think of some good reasons for the observed differences. Here's a clue: Try to think of other variables that might account for the patterns you've observed. Then, in Chapter 11, when we engage in multivariate analysis, you'll have a chance to check out some of your explanations.

7.14   Gun Laws and Capital Punishment

Let's shift gears now and consider politics as an independent variable while examining a set of crucial criminal justice issues. What impact do you suppose political philosophy or political party might have in shaping people's attitudes on some of the criminal justice issues we looked at earlier?

Ask yourself where liberals and conservatives would stand on the registration of firearms (our GUNLAW variable) and capital punishment (CAPPUN). Then run the tables to find out if your hunches are correct. (Remember, when POLREC is the independent variable, you need to alter its location in the Crosstabs command by making it the column variable.)

Once you've examined the relationship between political philosophies and these crime and justice issues, consider the impact of political party. In forming your expectations in this latter regard, you might want to review recent political platforms of the two major parties or the speeches of political candidates from the two parties. Then see if the political party identifications of the American public fall along those same lines.

7.15   Summary

In this chapter, we made a critical logical advance in the analysis of social scientific data. Up to now, we have focused our attention on description. With this examination of binge drinking, drug use, and political attitudes, we've crossed over into explanation. We've moved from asking *what* to asking *why*. We've begun by assessing whether two variables covary so that we see differences in the values of the dependent variable given different values of the independent variable.

We hope that this chapter has given you a taste of the excitement inherent in the detective work called criminal justice research. We're willing to bet that some of the results you've uncovered in this chapter pretty much squared with your understanding of American politics and criminal justice, whereas other findings came as a surprise. The skills you are learning in this book, along with your access to SPSS and important data about crime and justice issues, make it possible for you to conduct your own investigations into the nature of American criminal justice and other issues that may interest you.

Key Terms

background variables
bivariate analysis
covariation
demographic variables
dependent variable
epsilon

independent variable
rival causal factors
three criteria for testing causal
   hypotheses
time order

Chapter 8 **Measures of Association**

In the preceding analyses, we've depended on percentage tables as our format for examining the relationships between variables. In this chapter, we are going to explore some other formats for that examination. By and large, these techniques summarize relationships, in contrast to the way percentage tables lay the details out before you.

8.1 Lambda

To introduce the logic of statistical association, we would like you to take a minute for a "thought experiment." Imagine there is a group of 100 people in a lecture hall and you are standing in the hallway outside the room. The people will come out of the room one at a time, and your task will be to guess the gender of each before he or she comes into view. Take a moment to consider your best strategy for making these guesses.

If you know nothing about the people in the room, there really is no useful strategy for guessing, no way to make "educated guesses." But now suppose you know that 60 of the people in the room are women. This would make educated guesses possible: You should guess "woman" every time. By doing this, you would be right 60 times and wrong 40 times.

Now suppose that every time a person prepares to emerge from the room, his or her first name is announced. This would probably improve your guessing substantially. You'd guess "woman" for every Nancy or Joanne and "man" for every Joseph and Wendell. Even so, you probably wouldn't be totally accurate, given the ambiguity of names such as Pat, Jan, and Leslie.

It is useful to notice that we could actually calculate how much knowing first names improved your guessing. Let's say you would have made 40 errors out of 100 guesses without knowing names and only 10 errors when you knew the names. You would have made 30 fewer mistakes. Out of an original 40 mistakes, that's a 75% improvement. Statisticians refer to this as a **proportionate reduction of error,** which they abbreviate **PRE.**

Lambda is a measure of association appropriate for use with nominal variables, and it operates on the PRE logic. Essentially, **association** means that the two variables are related to the extent that knowing a person's attribute on one will help you guess his or her attribute on the other.

Here's a very simple example of lambda. Suppose that we have data on the employment status of 1,000 people. Half are employed; half are unemployed. If we were to begin presenting you with person after person, asking you to guess whether each was employed or not, you'd get about half wrong and half right by guessing blindly. So the logic of lambda begins with the assumption that you'd make 500 errors, in this case. Let's call these your "uneducated errors."

Now take a look at the table below, which gives you additional information: the ages of the subjects.

Status	Young	Old	Total
Employed	0	500	500
Unemployed	500	0	500
Total	500	500	1,000

Suppose now that we were to repeat the guessing exercise. This time, however, you would know whether each person is young or old. What would be your strategy for guessing employment status?

Clearly, you should make an educated guess of "unemployed" for every young person and "employed" for every old person. Do that and you'll make no errors. You will have reduced your errors by 500 in comparison with the first attempt. Given that you will have eliminated all your former errors, we could also say that you have reduced your errors by 100%.

Here's the simple equation for lambda that allows you to calculate the reduction of errors:

$$\frac{\text{Uneducated errors} - \text{educated errors}}{\text{Uneducated errors}} = \frac{500 - 0}{500} = 1.000$$

Notice that the calculation results in 1.00, which we treat as 100% in the context of lambda.

To be sure the logic of lambda is clear to you, let's consider another hypothetical example, similar to the previous example:

Status	Young	Old	Total
Employed	250	250	500
Unemployed	250	250	500
Total	500	500	1,000

In this new example, we still have half young and half old, and we have half employed and half unemployed. But the relationship between the two variables is very different. Just by inspection, you should be able to see that they are independent of each other. In this case, age has no impact on employment status. The lack of a relationship between age and employment status here is reflected in the educated guesses you would make about employment status if you knew a person's age. It wouldn't help you at all, and you would get half the young people wrong and half the old people wrong. You would have made 500 errors in uneducated guesses, and you wouldn't have improved your score by knowing their ages.

Lambda reflects this new situation:

$$\frac{\text{Uneducated errors} - \text{educated errors}}{\text{Uneducated errors}} = \frac{500 - 500}{500} = 0.000$$

Knowing age would have reduced your errors by 0%.

The real relationships between variables are seldom this simple, of course, so let's look at a real example using SPSS and the General Social Survey (GSS) data. You'll be pleased to discover that you won't have to calculate the errors or the proportion of reduction, because SPSS does this for you.

Let's look at the relationship between religion and attitude toward abortion. First we need to recode the RELIG variable into RELIGCAT in order to collapse all the religions with few respondents into one "other" category. In your Recode into Different Variable window, set it up this way:

RELIG → RELIGCAT

1 → 1

2 → 2

3 → 3

4 → 4

5-13 → 5

MISSING → SYSMIS

Then remember to label your new RELIGCAT values as 1 "Protestant," 2 "Catholic," 3 "Jewish," 4 "none," and 5 "Other."

Now back to lambda. Set up a Crosstabs request using ABANY as the row variable and RELIGCAT as the column variable. This time, it will be useful to request no percentaging of the cells in the table. Click "Cells" and turn off "Column" if that's still selected. Return to the Crosstabs window. Before executing the Crosstabs command, however, click the "Statistics" button. Here's what you should see:

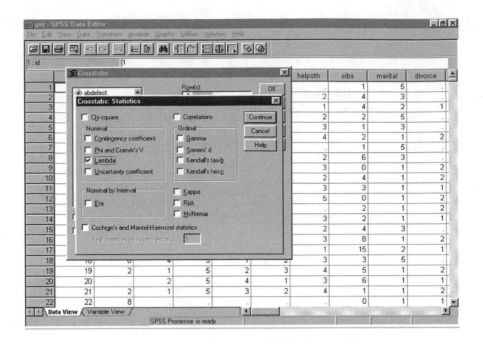

Click the button for "Lambda." Leave the Statistics window, and execute the Crosstabs command. Here's the result that should show up in your Output window:

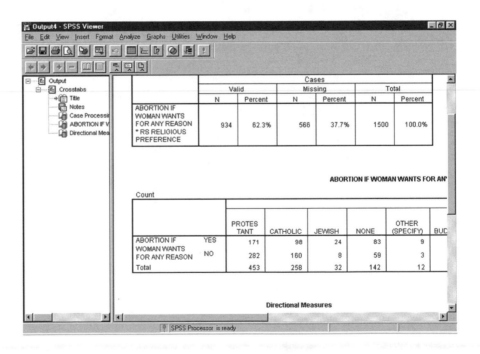

We've omitted the request for percentages in this table because it will be useful to see the actual number of cases in each cell of the table. At the far right of the table, notice that 404 people supported the idea of a woman's being able to have an abortion just because she wanted one; 530 were opposed. If we were to make uneducated guesses about people's opinion on this issue, we'd do best always to guess "no." By doing that, however, we would make 404 errors.

If we knew each person's religion, however, we would improve our record somewhat. Here's what would happen:

Religion	Guess	Errors
Protestant	Oppose	171
Catholic	Oppose	98
Jewish	Favor	8
None	Favor	59
Other	Favor	21
Total		357

To calculate lambda, then,

$$\frac{\text{Uneducated errors} - \text{educated errors}}{\text{Uneducated errors}} = \frac{404 - 357}{404} = 0.11634$$

This indicates that we have improved our guessing of abortion attitudes by almost 12% as a result of knowing religious affiliation. Here's how SPSS reports this result:

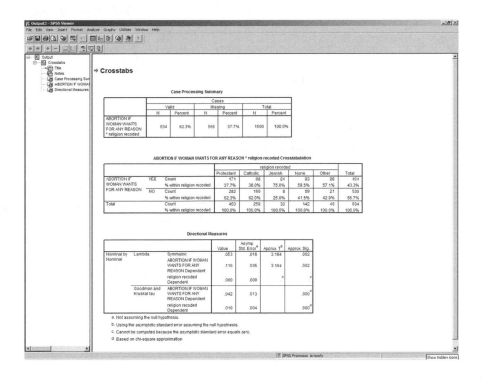

SPSS reports more information than we need right now, so let's focus our attention on the second row of numbers. Because we have been testing whether we could predict abortion attitudes (ABANY) by knowing religion, that makes ABANY the dependent variable. As you can see, the value of lambda in that instance is 0.116, the value we got by calculating it for ourselves.

Knowing a person's religious affiliation, then allows us to predict their attitude on abortion 12% more accurately. The implicit assumption in this analysis is that religious affiliation causes, to some degree, attitudes toward abortion. We use the value of lambda as an indication of how strong the causal link is.

However, it is important that you bear in mind that association alone does not prove causation. When we observe a statistical relationship between two variables, that strengthens the probability that one causes the other, but it is not sufficient proof. To be satisfied that a causal relationship exists, social scientists also want the link to make sense logically (in this case, the role of churches and clergy in the abortion debate offer that reasoning). And finally, we want to be sure that the observed relationship is not an artifact produced by the effects of a third variable. This latter possibility will be examined in Part IV on multivariate analysis.

For curiosity's sake, notice the next line, which treats RELIGCAT as the dependent variable. This deals with the possibility that we might be able to guess people's religions by knowing where they stand on abortion. Take a moment to look again at the crosstabulation of ABANY and RELIGCAT.

If we were to make uneducated guesses about people's religions, we'd always guess Protestant, because Protestants are by far the largest group. Knowing attitudes toward abortion wouldn't help, however. In either case, we'd still guess Protestant, even among those who were in favor of abortion rights.

So if RELIGCAT were the dependent variable, knowing ABANY would improve our guessing by 0%, which is the calculation presented by SPSS.

Now why don't you experiment with lambda on some other nominal variables?

8.2   Gamma

Whereas lambda is appropriate to nominal variables, **gamma** is a measure of association based on the logic of PRE appropriate to ordinal variables. What is a **statistical relationship?** We judge two variables to be related to each other to the extent that knowing what a person is like in terms of one variable helps us guess what he or she is like in terms of the other. Whereas the application of this logic in the case of lambda lets us make predictions for individuals (e.g., if a person is Protestant, we guess that he or she is also Republican), the logic is applied to pairs of people in the case of gamma.

To see the logic of gamma, let's consider the following nine people, placed in a matrix that indicates their social class standing and their level of prejudice—two ordinal variables.

Prejudice	Lower Class	Middle Class	Upper Class
Low	Jim	Tim	Kim
Medium	Mary	Harry	Carrie
High	Nan	Jan	Fran

Our purpose in this analysis is to determine which of the following best describes the relationship between social class and prejudice:

1. The higher your social class, the more prejudiced you are.

2. The higher your social class, the less prejudiced you are.

3. Your social class has no effect on your level of prejudice.

To begin our analysis, we should note that the only pairs who are appropriate to our question are those who differ in both social class and prejudice. Jim and Harry are an example; they differ in both social class and level of prejudice. Here are the 18 pairs that qualify for analysis:

Jim-Harry	Kim-Mary	Harry-Nan
Jim-Carrie	Kim-Harry	Harry-Fran
Jim-Jan	Kim-Nan	
Jim-Fran	Kim-Jan	
Tim-Mary	Mary-Jan	Carrie-Nan
Tim-Nan	Mary-Fran	Carrie-Jan
Tim-Carrie		
Tim-Fran		

Take a minute to assure yourself that no other pairs of people meet the criterion that they differ in both social class and prejudice.

If you study the table, you should be able to identify pairs of people who would support conclusion 1. We'll come back to 3 a little later.

Suppose now that you have been given the list of pairs, but you've never seen the original table. Your task is to guess which member of each pair is the more prejudiced. Given that you will simply be guessing blind, chances are that you'll get about half right and half wrong: nine correct answers and nine errors. Gamma helps us determine whether knowing how two people differ on social class would reduce the number of errors we'd make in guessing how they differ on prejudice.

Let's consider Jim-Harry for a moment. If they were the only two people you could study, and you had to reach a conclusion about the relationship between social class and prejudice, what would you conclude? Notice that Harry is higher in social class than Jim (middle class versus lower class), and Harry is also higher in prejudice (medium versus low). If you were to generalize from this single pair of observations, there is only one conclusion you could reach: "The higher your social class, the more prejudiced you are."

In the language of social research, we would refer to this as a **positive association:** The higher on one variable, the higher on the other. In the more specific language of gamma, we'll refer to this as a "same" pair: The direction of the difference between Jim and Harry on one variable is the same as the direction of difference on the other. Harry is higher than Jim on both.

Suppose that you had to base your conclusion on the Jim-Jan pair. What would you conclude? Look at the table and you'll see that Jan, like Harry, is higher than Jim on both social class and prejudice. This pair would also lead you to conclude that "the higher your social class, the more prejudiced you are." Jim-Jan, then, is another "same" pair, in the language of gamma.

Suppose, by contrast, that we observed only Tim and Mary. They would lead us to a very different conclusion. Mary is lower than Tim on social class, but she is higher on prejudice. If this were the only pair you could observe, you'd have to conclude that "the higher your social class, the lower your prejudice." In the language of gamma, Tim-Mary is an "opposite" pair: The direction of their difference on one variable is the opposite of their difference on the other.

Now we hope you've been feeling uncomfortable about the idea of generalizing from only one pair of observations, although that's what many people do in everyday life. In social research, however, we would never do that.

Moving a little bit in the direction of normal social research, let's assume that you have observed all nine of the individuals in the table. What conclusion would you draw about the association between social class and prejudice? Gamma helps you answer this question.

Let's see how well each of the alternative conclusions might assist you in guessing people's prejudice based on knowing about their social class. If you operated on the basis of the conclusion that prejudice increases with social class, for example, and I told you Fran is of a higher social class than Harry, you would correctly guess that Fran is more prejudiced. If, conversely, I told you that Harry is higher in social class than Nan, you would incorrectly guess that he is more prejudiced.

Take a minute to go through the list of pairs above and make notations of which ones are same pairs and which ones are opposite. Once you've done that, count the numbers of same and opposite pairs.

You should get nine of each type. This means that if you assume that prejudice increases with social class, you will get the nine opposite pairs wrong; if you assume that prejudice decreases with social class, you will get the nine same pairs wrong. In other words, neither strategy for guessing levels of prejudice based on knowing social class will do you any good in this case. In either case, we make as many errors as we would have made if we didn't know the social class differences in the pairs. Gamma gives us a method for calculating that result.

The formula for gamma is as follows:

$$\frac{\text{Same} - \text{opposite}}{\text{Same} + \text{opposite}}$$

To calculate gamma, you must first count the number of same pairs and the number of opposite pairs. Once you've done that, the mathematics is pretty simple.

Once you have that, you can complete the formula as follows:

$$\frac{9-9}{9+9} = \frac{0}{18} = 0$$

In gamma, this result is interpreted as 0%, meaning that knowing how two people differ on social class would improve your guesses as to how they differ on prejudice by 0%—not at all.

Consider the following modified table, however. Suppose for the moment that there are only three people to be studied:

Prejudice	Lower Class	Middle Class	Upper Class
Low	Jim		
Medium		Harry	
High			Fran

Just by inspection, you can see how perfectly these three people fit the pattern of a positive association between social class and prejudice. Each of the three pairs—Jim-Harry, Harry-Fran, Jim-Fran—is a same pair. There are no opposite pairs. If we were to give you each of these pairs, telling you who was higher in social class, the assumption of a positive association between the two variables would let you guess who was higher in social class with perfect accuracy.

Let's see how this situation would look in terms of gamma.

$$\frac{\text{Same} - \text{opposite}}{\text{Same} + \text{opposite}} = \frac{3 - 0}{3} = 1.00$$

In this case, we would say that gamma equals 1.00, meaning that you have reduced the number of errors by 100%. To understand this meaning of gamma, we need to go back to the idea of guessing prejudice differences without knowing social class.

Recall that if you were guessing blind, you'd be right about half the time and wrong about half the time. In this hypothetical case, you'd be wrong 1.5 times (that would be your average if you repeated the exercise hundreds of times). As we've seen, however, knowing social class in this instance lets us reduce the number of errors by 1.5—down to zero. It is in this sense that we say we have reduced our errors by 100%.

Now let's consider a slightly different table.

Prejudice	Lower Class	Middle Class	Upper Class
Low	Nan		
Medium		Harry	
High			Kim

Notice that in this case we could also have a perfect record, if we use the assumption of a **negative association** between social class and prejudice: The higher your social class, the lower your prejudice. The negative association shows up in gamma as follows:

$$\frac{\text{Same} - \text{opposite}}{\text{Same} + \text{opposite}} = \frac{0 - 3}{3} = -1.00$$

Once again, gamma indicates that we have reduced our errors by 100%. The minus sign in this result simply signals that the relationship is negative.

Now we are finally ready for a more realistic example. Just as you would not want to base a generalization on as few cases as we've been considering so far, neither would it make sense to calculate gamma in such situations. Notice how gamma helps you assess the relationship between two variables when the results are not as obvious to the nonstatistical eye.

Prejudice	Lower Class	Middle Class	Upper Class
Low	200	400	700
Medium	500	900	400
High	800	300	100

In this table, the names of individuals have been replaced with the numbers of people having a particular social class and level of prejudice. There are 200 lower-class people in the table, for example, who are low on prejudice. By contrast, there are 100 upper-class people who are high on prejudice.

Perhaps you can get a sense of the relationship in this table by simple observation. The largest cells are those lying along the diagonal running from lower left to upper right. This would suggest a negative association between the two variables. Gamma lets us determine with more confidence whether that's the case and gives us a yardstick for measuring how strong the relationship is.

In the simpler examples, every pair of cells represented one pair because there was only one person in each cell. Now it's a little more complex. Imagine for a moment just one of the people in the upper left cell (lower class, low prejudice). If we match that person up with the 900 people in the center cell (middle class, medium prejudice), we'd have 900 pairs. The same would result from matching each of the people in the first cell with all those in the second. We can calculate the total number of pairs produced by the two cells by simple multiplication: 200 × 900 gives us 180,000 pairs. Notice, by the way, that these are same pairs.

As a further simplification, notice that there are 900 + 400 + 300 + 100 people who will match with the upper left cell to form same pairs. That makes a total of 1,700 × 200 = 340,000. Here's an overview of all the same pairs in the table:

$$
\begin{aligned}
200 \times (900 + 300 + 400 + 100) &= 340,000 \\
500 \times (300 + 100) &= 200,000 \\
400 \times (400 + 100) &= 200,000 \\
900 \times 100 &= 90,000 \\
\text{Total same pairs} &= 830,000
\end{aligned}
$$

Following the same procedure, here are all the opposite pairs:

$$
\begin{aligned}
700 \times (500 + 800 + 900 + 300) &= 1,750,000 \\
400 \times (800 + 300) &= 440,000 \\
400 \times (500 + 800) &= 520,000 \\
900 \times 800 &= 720,000 \\
\text{Total opposite pairs} &= 3,430,000
\end{aligned}
$$

Even though this procedure produces quite a few more pairs than we've been dealing with, the formula for gamma still works the same way:

$$
\frac{\text{Same} - \text{opposite}}{\text{Same} + \text{opposite}} = \frac{830,000 - 3,430,000}{830,000 + 3,430,000} = \frac{-2,600,000}{4,260,000} = -.61
$$

The minus sign in this result confirms that the relationship between the two variables is a negative one. The numeric result indicates that knowing the social class ranking in each pair reduces our errors in predicting their ranking in terms of prejudice by 61%.

Suppose for the moment that you had tried to predict differences in prejudice blind for each of the 4,260,000 pairs. You would have been wrong about 2,130,000 times. By assuming that the person with higher social class is less prejudiced, you would have made only 830,000 errors, or 2,130,000 − 830,000 = 1,300,000 fewer errors. Dividing the 1,300,000 improvement by the 2,130,000 baseline gives .61, indicating that you have reduced your errors by 61%.

Now here's the good news. Although it's important for you to understand the logic of gamma, it is no longer necessary for you to do the calculations by hand. Whenever you run Crosstabs in SPSS, you can request that gamma be calculated by making that request when you set up the table.

Go to Crosstabs. Make CHATT the row variable and AGECAT the column variable. Then click "Statistics."

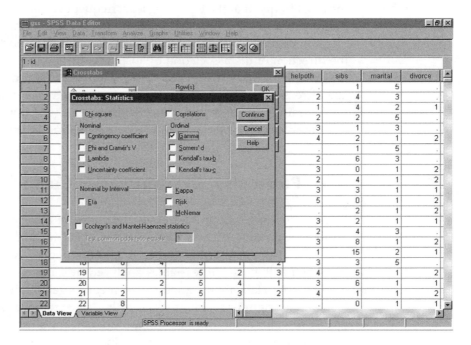

Notice that gamma is a choice for ordinal data. Click it and unclick lambda. Return to the main window and click "OK." You should get the following table and report on gamma:

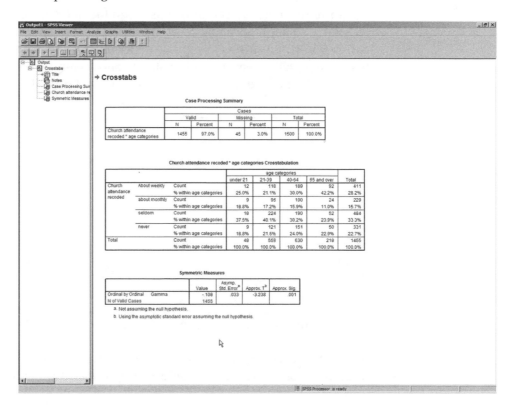

Notice that gamma is reported as –0.108. This means that knowing a person's age would improve our estimate of his or her church attendance by almost 11%. The minus sign in this case needs extra explanation.

Although you might reasonably think that this indicates a negative relationship between age and church attendance, that would be incorrect. In this case, the minus sign results from our choosing to arrange attendance categories from the most frequent at the top to the least frequent at the bottom. If we had arranged the categories in the opposite direction, gamma would have been positive.

Whenever you ask SPSS to calculate gamma, it is important that you determine the direction of the association by inspection of the table. Look at the first row in the table displayed on the screen. For the most part, church attendance increases as age increases; hence the relationship between the two variables is positive.

To gain some more experience with gamma, why don't you select some ordinal variables that interest you and examine their relationships by using gamma?

8.3   Pearson's *r*, the Correlation Coefficient

Finally, we are going to work with a measure of association appropriate to continuous, ratio data such as age, education, and income. Although this measure also reflects the PRE logic, its meaning in that regard is not quite so straightforward as for the discrete variables analyzed by lambda and gamma. Although it made sense to talk about "guessing" someone's gender or employment status and being either right or wrong, there is little chance that we would ever guess someone's annual income in exact dollars or someone's exact age in days. Our best strategy would be to guess the mean income, and we'd be wrong almost every time. **Pearson's *r*** lets us determine whether knowing one variable would help us "come closer" in our guesses of the other variable and calculates how much closer we would come.

To understand *r*, also known as a product-moment **correlation coefficient,** let's take a simple example of eight young people and see whether there is a correlation between their heights (in inches) and their weights (in pounds). To begin, then, let's meet the eight subjects once again—we first met them back in Section 4.2 when we were discussing measures of central tendency.

Person	Height	Weight
Eddy	68	144
Mary	58	111
Marge	67	137
Terry	66	153
Albert	61	165
Larry	74	166
Heather	67	92
Ruth	61	128

Take a minute to study the heights and weights. Begin with Eddy and Mary, at the top of the list. Eddy is both taller and heavier than Mary. If we were forced to reach a conclusion about the association between height and weight based only on these two observations, we would conclude that there is a positive correlation:

The taller you are, the heavier you are. We might even go a step further and note that every additional inch of height corresponds to about 3 pounds of weight.

Conversely, if you needed to base a conclusion on observations of Eddy and Terry, see what that conclusion would be. Terry is 2 inches shorter but 9 pounds heavier. Our observations of Eddy and Terry would lead us to just the opposite conclusion: The taller you are, the lighter you are.

Sometimes it's useful to look at a **scattergram,** which graphs the cases at hand in terms of the two variables. The diagram shown next presents the eight cases in this fashion. Notice that there seems to be a general pattern of increasing height being associated with increasing weight, although there are a couple of cases that don't fit that pattern.

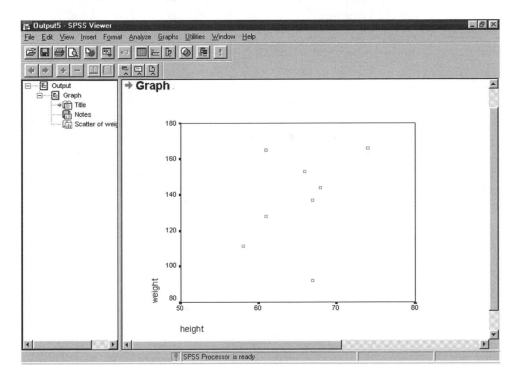

Pearson's r allows for the fact that the relationship between height and weight may not be completely consistent but nonetheless lets us discover any prevailing tendency in that regard. In the gamma logic presented earlier, we might consider a strategy of guessing who is heavier or lighter on the basis of who is taller or shorter, assuming either a positive (taller means heavier) or negative (taller means lighter) relationship between the two variables. With r, however, we'll take account of *how much* taller or heavier.

To calculate r, we will need to know the *mean* value of each variable. As you recall, this is calculated by adding all the values on a variable and dividing by the number of cases. If you do these calculations in the case of height, you'll discover that the eight people, laid end to end, would stretch 522 inches, for a mean height of 65.25 inches. Do the same calculation for their weights, and you'll discover that the eight people weigh a total of 1,096 pounds, for a mean of 137 pounds.

From now on, we are going to focus less on the actual heights and weights of our eight people and deal more with the extent to which they differ from the means. The next table shows how much each person differs from the means for height and weight. Notice that plus and minus signs have been used to indicate whether a person is above or below the mean. (If you want to check your calculations in this situation, you should add all the deviations from height and notice that they total 0; the same is true for deviations from mean weight.)

Person	Height	Weight	Height Deviation	Weight Deviation
Eddy	68	144	+2.75	+7
Mary	58	111	−7.25	−26
Marge	67	137	+1.75	0
Terry	66	153	+0.75	+16
Albert	61	165	−4.25	+28
Larry	74	166	+8.75	+29
Heather	67	92	+1.75	−45
Ruth	61	128	−4.25	−9
Means	65.25	137		

As our next step, we want to determine the extent to which heights and weights vary from their means overall. Although we have shown the plus and minus signs, it is important to note that both +2.00 and −2.00 represent deviations of 2 inches from the mean height. For reasons that will become apparent shortly, we are going to capture both positive and negative variations by squaring each of the deviations from the means. The squares of both +2.00 and −2.00 are the same: 4.00. The next table shows the squared deviations for each person on each variable. We've also totaled the squared deviations and calculated their means.

Person	Height	Weight	Height Deviation	Weight Deviation	Height Deviation Squared	Weight Deviation Squared
Eddy	68	144	+2.75	+7	7.5625	49
Mary	58	111	−7.25	−26	52.5625	676
Marge	67	137	+1.75	0	3.0625	0
Terry	66	153	+0.75	+16	0.5625	256
Albert	61	165	−4.25	+28	18.0625	784
Larry	74	166	+8.75	+29	76.5625	841
Heather	67	92	+1.75	−45	3.0625	2,025
Ruth	61	128	−4.25	−9	18,0625	81
Means	65.25	137	Totals		179.5000	4,712

Now we're going to present a couple of steps that would require more complicated explanations than we want to subject you to in this book. So if you can simply hear what we say without asking why, that's sufficient at this point. (If you are interested in learning the logic of the intervening steps, that's great. Check discussions of variance and standard deviations in statistics textbooks or refer to Section 4.2 for a brief explanation.)

Dividing the sum of the squared deviations by one less than the number of cases ($N - 1$) yields a quantity that statisticians call the **variance.** With a large number of cases, this quantity is close to the mean of the sum of squared deviations.

The variances in this case are 25.643 for height and 673.143 for weight. The square root of the variance is called the **standard deviation.** Thus the standard deviation for height is 5.063891; for weight, it is 25.94499.

Now we are ready to put all these calculations to work for us. We are now going to express all the individual deviations from mean height and mean weight in units equal to the standard deviations. For example, Eddy was 2.75 inches taller than the average. Eddy's new deviation from the mean height becomes +0.54 (+2.75/5.064). His deviation from the mean weight becomes +0.27 (+7/25.945).

Our purpose in these somewhat complex calculations is to standardize deviations from the means of the two variables because the values on those variables are of very different scales. Whereas Eddy was 2.75 inches taller than the mean and 7 pounds heavier than the mean, we didn't have a way of knowing whether his height deviation was greater or lesser than his weight deviation. By dividing each deviation by the standard deviation for that variable, we can now see that Eddy's deviation on height is actually greater than his deviation in terms of weight. These new measures of deviation are called *z* **scores.** The table presents each person's *z* score for both height and weight.

	Height	Weight	z Height	z Weight	z Cross
Eddy	68	144	0.54	0.27	0.15
Mary	58	111	−1.43	−1.00	1.43
Marge	67	137	0.35	0.00	0.00
Terry	66	153	0.15	0.62	0.09
Albert	61	165	−0.84	1.08	−0.91
Larry	74	166	1.73	1.12	1.93
Heather	67	92	0.35	−1.73	−0.60
Ruth	61	128	−0.84	−0.35	0.29
Total					2.38

You'll notice that there is a final column of the table called "z Cross." This is the result of multiplying each person's *z* score on height by the *z* score on weight. You'll also notice that we've begun rounding off the numbers to two decimal places. That level of precision is sufficient for our present purposes.

Thanks to your perseverance, we are finally ready to calculate Pearson's *r* product-moment correlation. By now, it's pretty simple.

$$r = \frac{\text{sum of (z scores for height} \times z \text{ scores for weight)}}{N - 1}$$

In our example, this amounts to

$$r = \frac{2.38}{8 - 1} = \frac{2.38}{7} = 0.34$$

There is no easy, commonsense way to represent the meaning of *r*. Technically, it has to do with the extent to which variations in one variable can explain variations in the other. In fact, if you square *r*, 0.12 in this case, it can be interpreted as meaning that 12% of the variance in one variable can be accounted for by the variance in the other. Recall that the variance of a variable reflects the extent to which individual cases deviate from the mean value. Reverting to the logic of PRE, this means that knowing a person's height reduces by 12% the extent of our errors in guessing how far he or she is from the mean weight.

In large part, r's value comes with use. When you calculate correlations among several pairs of variables, the resulting values of r will tell which pairs are more highly associated with each other than is true of other pairs.

Now here's the really good news. Your reward for pressing through all these calculations to gain some understanding of what r represents is that you'll never have to do it again. SPSS will do it for you.

Let's consider the possible relationship between two of the continuous variables in the data set: AGE and RINCOME. If you think about it, you would expect that people tend to earn more money as they grow older. So let's check the correlation between age and respondents' incomes. (Note: RINCOME is personal income; INCOME is family income.)

You might be reluctant to calculate the deviations, squared deviations, and so on for the 1,500 respondents in your data set (if not, you need a hobby), but computers thrive on such tasks.

Before we tell SPSS to take on the task of computing correlations for us, we need to do a little housekeeping. If you run a frequency distribution on RINCOME, you will see this:

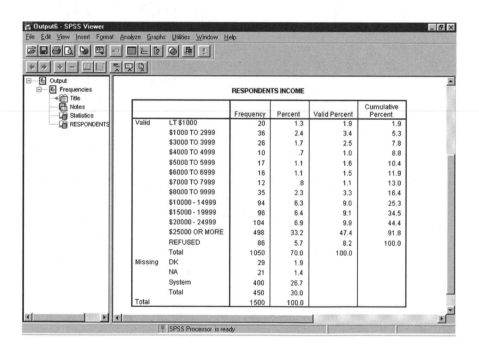

There is a problem in using the codes for RINCOME. The code categories are not equal in width. Code category 8 includes respondents whose incomes were only between $8,000 and $9,999, while code category 9 includes incomes between $10,000 and $14,999.

We can use Recode to improve on the coding scheme used for recording incomes. If we simply substitute the midpoints of the interval widths for the codes used in RINCOME, we can rid ourselves of the problems created by the interval widths' not being equal. Code 23, $25,000 or more, has no upper limit; we just took a guess that the midpoint would be about $35,000. As SPSS commands, the recoding looks like this:

Transform → Recode → Into Different Variables

Old Variable → New Variable
RINCOME → RINCOME2

Old and New Values

1	→	500
2	→	2000
3	→	4000
4	→	4500
5	→	5500
6	→	6500
7	→	7500
8	→	9000
9	→	12500
10	→	17500
11	→	22500
12	→	35000

Notice that we did not specify new values for code 0 (not applicable), 98 (don't know), and 99 (no answer). Also, we didn't recode 13 (refused). This was mistakenly not listed as a missing value in the original RELIG variable, but it should be. SPSS assigns "SYSMIS," the system missing value, to any of the cases not specifically identified with an old value in the "Old and New Values" list. By ignoring RINCOME's codes 0, 98, 99, and 13, the corresponding cases in RINCOME2 are set to SYSMIS.

Here's what the recoded variable looks like (the authors greatly appreciate the suggestion of this analysis by Prof. Gilbert Klajman, Montclair State College):

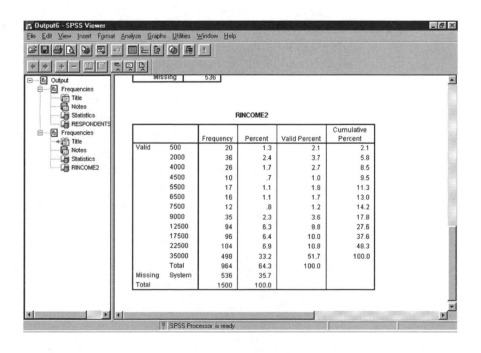

With the housekeeping out of the way, you need only move through this menu path to launch SPSS on the job of computing *r*:

Analyze → Correlate → Bivariate

This will bring you to the following window:

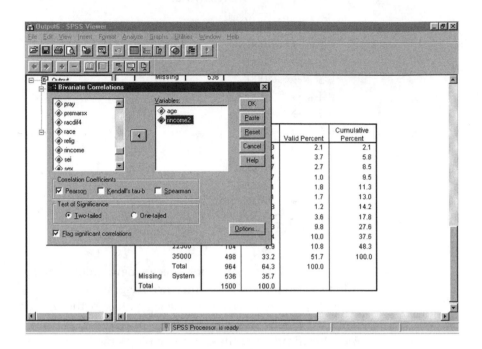

Transfer AGE and RINCOME2 to the "Variables" list. (Be sure to use AGE and not AGECAT, since we want the original ratio variable.)

Below the "Variables" list, you'll see that we can choose from among three correlation coefficients. We have described Pearson's *r*, and this should be the default. If not, click on "Pearson."

Did you ever think about what we would do if we had an AGE for someone, but we did not know the person's RINCOME2? Since we have only one score, we would have to throw that person out of our analysis. But suppose we had three variables and we were missing a score on a case. Would we throw out just the pair that had a missing value, or would we throw out the whole case?

SPSS lets us do it either way. Click on "Options," and you will see we can choose to exclude cases "pairwise" or "listwise. " If we exclude pairwise, we discard a pair only when either score is missing. But with listwise deletion, we discard the entire case if only one pair is missing.

We will use listwise exclusion. With a sample as large as ours, it does not hurt to lose a few cases. However, if our sample were small, we would probably want to use pairwise deletion.

Now click on "OK" until you are rewarded with the following in your Output window:

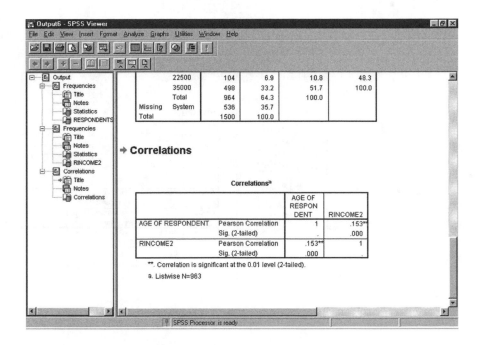

The Pearson's *r* product-moment correlation between AGE and RINCOME2 is 0.153. Notice that the correlation between AGE and itself is perfect (1.0000), which makes sense if you think about it.

You now know that the 0.153 is a measure of the extent to which deviations from the mean income can be accounted for by deviations from the mean of age. By squaring *r*, we learn that about 2.3% of the variance in income can be accounted for by how old people are.

What else do you suppose might account for differences in income? If you think about it, you might decide that education is a possibility. Presumably, the more education you get, the more money you'll make. Your understanding of *r* through SPSS will let you check it out.

The Correlations command allows you to request several correlation coefficients at once. Go back to the Bivariate Correlations window and add EDUC to the list of variables being analyzed. Execute the command.

Here's what you should get in your Output window:

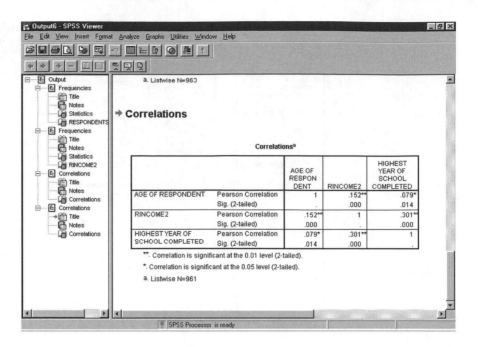

This new correlation matrix is a little more complex than the previous one. The fact that each variable correlates perfectly with itself should offer assurance that we are doing something right.

The new matrix also tells us that there is a stronger correlation between EDUC and RINCOME2: 0.301. Squaring the *r* tells us that about 9.1% of the variance in income can be accounted for by how much education people have.

We'll be using the Correlations command and related statistics as the book continues. In closing this discussion, we'd like you to recall that Pearson's *r* is appropriate only for continuous variables. It would not be appropriate in the analysis of nominal variables such as RELIG and ABANY, for example. But what do you suppose would happen if we asked SPSS to correlate *r* for those two variables? Look first at the crosstabulation of these two variables.

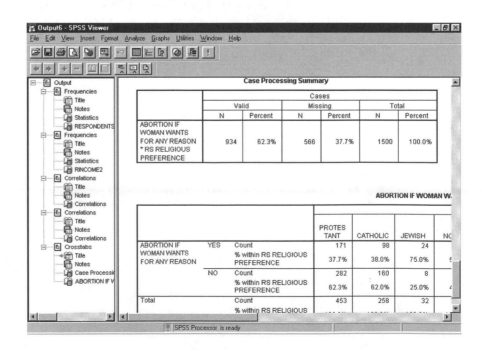

If we ask SPSS to correlate these two variables, SPSS has no way of knowing that we've asked it to do a stupid thing. It will stupidly comply. It tells us that there is a significant relationship between a person's attitude about abortion and the religion he or she belongs to, when in truth the correlation calculated here has no real meaning.

SPSS has been able to do the requested calculation because it stores "yes" (for favor abortion) as 1 and "no" (for oppose abortion) as 2 and stores "Protestant" as 1, "Catholic" as 2, and so on, but these numbers have no numeric meaning in this instance. Catholics are not "twice" Protestants, and people who oppose abortion are not "twice" people who favor it.

Here's a thought experiment we hope will guard against this mistake: (1) Write down the telephone numbers of your five best friends; (2) add them up and calculate the "mean" telephone number; (3) call that number and see if an "average" friend answers. Or go to a Chinese restaurant with a group of friends and have everyone in your party select one dish by its number on the menu. Add all those numbers and calculate the mean. When the waiter comes, get several orders of the "average" dish and see if you have any friends left.

Pearson's r is designed for the analysis of relationships between continuous, ratio variables. We have just entrusted you with a powerful weapon for understanding. Use it wisely. Remember, statistics don't mislead; people who calculate statistics stupidly mislead.

8.4   Regression

The discussion of Pearson's r correlation coefficient opens the door for discussion of a related statistical technique known as **regression.** When we looked at the scattergram of weight and height in the hypothetical example that introduced the discussion of correlation, you will recall that we tried to "see" a general pattern in the distribution of cases. Regression makes that attempt more concrete.

To begin, let's imagine an extremely simple hypothetical example, which relates the number of hours spent studying for an examination and the grades students got on the exam. Here are the data in a table:

Student	Hours	Grade
Fred	0	0
George	2	25
Kim	4	50
Bernie	6	75
Earl	8	100

Can you see a pattern in the data presented? The more you study, the better the grade you get.

Now let's look at these data in the form of a graph. (This is something you can do by hand, using graph paper.)

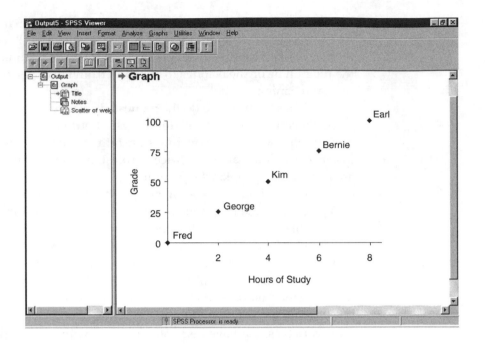

As you can see, the five people in this example fall along a straight line across the graph. This line is called the *regression line*. As you may recall from plane geometry, it is possible to represent a straight line on a graph in the form of an equation. In this case, the equation would be as follows:

$$Grade = 12.5 \times hours$$

To put this **regression equation** in more general form, let's say that grade is the Y variable and that its value is predicted by the multiplication of the value of the X variable by the **slope** b (the rate of change in Y, given a change of a single unit in X). Another part of the equation concerns the value of Y when the value of the X variable is zero: This value is called a in the equation, and is known as the **y-intercept** or simply the **intercept.** The general form of the regression equation is:

$$Y = a + bX$$

To determine a person's grade, using this equation, you need only multiply the number of hours studied by 12.5. Multiply Earl's 8 hours of study by 12.5 and you get his grade of 100. Multiply Bernie's 6 hours by 12.5 and you get 75. Multiply Fred's 0 hours by 12.5 and, well, you know Fred.

Whereas correlation considers the symmetrical association between two variables, regression adds the notion of asymmetry or direction. One of the variables is considered the *dependent variable*—grade, in this example—and the other is considered the *independent variable*—hours of study. Thus the equation we just created is designed to predict a person's grade based on how many hours the person studied. Thus if we were to tell you someone not included in these data studied 5 hours for the exam, you could predict that this person got a 62.5 on the exam (5 × 12.5).

If all social science analyses produced results as clear as these, you probably wouldn't need SPSS or a book like this one. In practice, however, the facts are usually a bit more complex. Luckily, SPSS is up to the challenge.

Given a set of data with an imperfect relationship between two variables, SPSS can discover the line that *comes closest* to passing through all the points on the graph. To understand the meaning of the notion of coming close, we need to recall the squared deviations used in our calculation of Pearson's *r*.

Suppose that Kim had gotten 70 on the exam, for example. How would she look on the graph we just drew?

Notice that the improved Kim would not fall on the original regression line: Her grade represents a deviation of 20 points. With a real set of data, most people fall to one side or the other of any line we might draw through the data. SPSS, however, is able to determine the line that would produce the smallest deviations overall—measured by squaring all the individual deviations and adding them up. This calculated regression line is sometimes called the **least-squares regression line.**

Requesting such an analysis from SPSS is fairly simple. To use this technique to real advantage, you will need more instruction than is appropriate for this book. However, we wanted to introduce you to regression because it is a popular technique among social scientists and is now probably the single most important statistical approach in contemporary criminology.

To experiment with this technique, let's make use of a new variable: SEI. This variable is a socioeconomic index of respondents' occupations on a scale from a low of 0 to a high of 100, based on other studies that have asked a sample from the general population to rate different occupations.

Here's how we would ask SPSS to find the equation that best represents the influence of EDUC on SEI. You should realize that there are a number of ways to request this information, but we'd suggest that you do it as follows.

From the Analyze menu, select Regression and then Linear. Here's what you get:

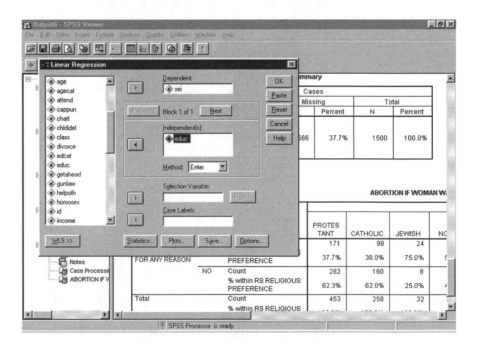

Click "OK," and SPSS is off and running. Here's the output you should get in response to this instruction:

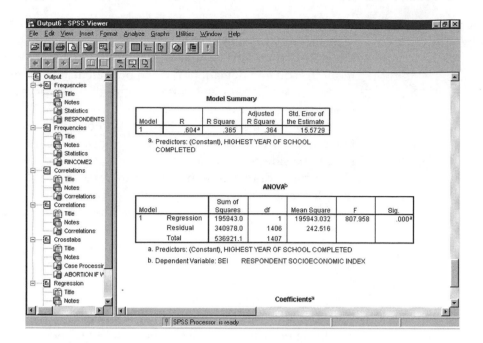

The key information we are looking for is contained in the final table of information called "Coefficients."

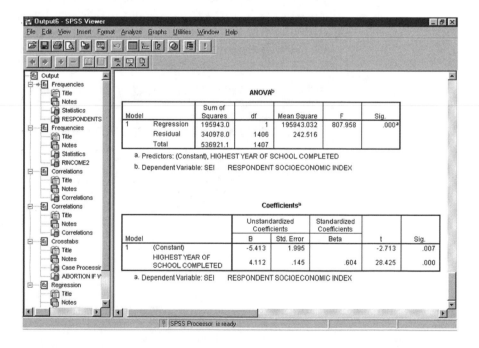

We want to focus on the **constant** and the slope. The constant is –5.413 and the slope (**unstandardized coefficient B** for EDUC) is 4.112. These are the data we need to complete our regression equation. Use them as follows:

$$SEI = -5.413 + (EDUC \times 4.112)$$

The constant or the intercept is the value of prestige when a person has 0 years of education—when the regression line intercepts the y-axis. The unstandardized coefficient or slope means how much prestige changes for each unit change in education. This means that we would predict the occupation prestige ranking of a high school graduate (12 years of schooling) as follows:

$$SEI = -5.413 + (12 \times 4.112) = 43.931$$

We would predict the occupational prestige of a college graduate (16 years of schooling), as

$$SEI = -5.413 + (16 \times 4.112) = 60.379$$

That's enough for now. We'll return to regression later, when we discuss multivariate analysis in Chapter 10.

8.5   Summary

In this chapter, we've explored a number of statistical techniques that can be used to summarize the degree of relationship or association between two variables. We've seen that the appropriate technique depends on the level of measurement represented by the variables involved. Lambda is appropriate for nominal variables, gamma for ordinal variables, and Pearson's *r* product-moment correlation coefficient and regression for ratio variables.

You may not always have known what to make of the results of these calculations. How do you decide, for example, if a gamma of 0.25 is high or low? Should you get excited about it or yawn and continue looking? The following chapter, about the existence, strength, and direction of an association, offers one basis for making such decisions.

Key Terms

association	regression
constant	regression equation
correlation coefficient	scattergram
gamma	slope
intercept	standard deviation
lambda	statistical relationship
least-squares regression line	unstandardized coefficient B
negative association	variance
Pearson's *r*	y-intercept
positive association	z scores
proportionate reduction of error (PRE)	

Chapter 9 **The Existence, Strength, and Direction of an Association**

So far, in Chapters 7 and 8 we've been looking at the relationships between pairs of variables. There are three big questions you should ask about a statistical relationship. First, is there evidence for its *existence*? If so, then there is a second question: What is its *strength*? Third, in a relationship involving variables measured at the ordinal, interval, or ratio level, what is its *direction*? In this chapter, we'll look at ways of understanding the existence, strength, and direction of relationships between variables.

In our previous discussions, you may have been frustrated over the ambiguity as to what constitutes a "strong" or a "weak" relationship. Ultimately, there is no absolute answer to this question. The strength or significance of a relationship between two variables depends on many things, but we'll try to pin down the basic answers.

If you are trying to account for differences between people on some variable, such as their attitudes about the death penalty, the explanatory power of one variable, such as education, needs to be contrasted with the explanatory power of other variables. So you might be interested in knowing whether education, political affiliation, or region of upbringing has the greatest impact on a person's attitudes about the death penalty.

Sometimes the importance of a relationship is based on practical policy implications. Thus the impact of some variable in explaining (and potentially reducing) auto theft rates, for example, might be converted to a matter of dollars. Does the very popular antidrug abuse program Project D.A.R.E. actually bring about any measurable decline in drug or alcohol abuse among young people? Other relationships might be expressed in terms of lives saved, students graduating from college, and so forth.

In this chapter, we address another standard for judging the significance of relationships between variables, one commonly used by social scientists. Whenever analyses are based on samples selected from a population rather than on data collected from everyone in that population, there is always the possibility that what we learn from the samples may not truly reflect the whole population. Thus we might discover that women are more religious than men in a sample, but that could simply be an artifact of our sample: We happened to pick too many religious women and/or too few religious men.

Social scientists often test the **statistical significance** of relationships discovered between variables. Although this does not constitute a direct measure of the *strength* of a relationship, it tells us the likelihood that the observed relationship could have resulted from the vagaries of probability sampling, which we call **sampling error.** These tests relate to the strength of relationships in that the stronger an observed relationship, the less likely it is that it could be the result of sampling error. Likewise, it is more probable that the observed relationship represents something that exists in the population as a whole.

9.1   Chi-Square

To learn the logic of statistical significance, let's begin with a measure, **chi-square,** that is based on the kinds of crosstabulations we've been examining in previous chapters. For a concrete example, we'll return to one of the tables that examines the relationship between religion and abortion attitudes.

Let's reexamine the relationship between religious affiliation and unconditional support for abortion.

Do a Crosstab of ABANY (row variable) and RELIGCAT (column variable), with cells percentaged by column.

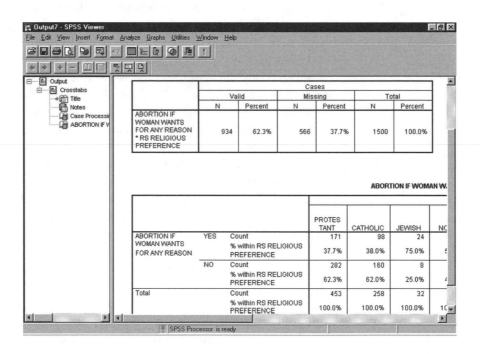

The question this table is designed to answer is whether a person's religious affiliation affects his or her attitude toward abortion. You'll recall that we concluded it does: Catholics and Protestants are the most opposed to abortion, and people with no religion or "other" religion are the most supportive. The question we now confront is whether the observed differences point to some genuine pattern in the U.S. population at large or if they result from a quirk of sampling.

To assess the observed relationship, we are going to begin by asking what we should have expected to find if there were no relationship between religious affiliation and abortion attitudes. An important part of the answer lies in the rightmost column in the table. It indicates that 43.3% of the whole sample supported a woman's unconditional right to an abortion and 56.7% did not.

If there were no relationship between religious affiliation and abortion attitudes, we should expect to find 43.3% of the Protestants approving, 43.3% of the Catholics approving, 43.3% of the Jews approving, and so forth. But recall that the earlier results did not match this perfect model of no relationship. So the question is whether the disparity between the model and our observations would fall within the normal degree of sampling error.

To measure the extent of the disparity between the model and what's been observed, we need to calculate the number of cases we'd expect in each cell of the table if there were no relationship. The following table shows how to calculate the expected cell frequencies.

ABANY	Protestant	Catholic	Jewish	None	Other
Approve	453	258	32	142	49
	×0.433	×0.433	×0.433	×0.433	×0.433
Disapprove	453	258	32	142	49
	×0.567	×0.567	×0.567	×0.567	×0.567

If there were no relationship between religious affiliation and abortion attitudes, we would expect that 43.3% of the 453 Protestants ($453 \times 0.433 = 196$) would approve and 56.7% of the 453 Protestants ($453 \times 0.567 = 257$) would disapprove. If you continue this series of calculations, you should arrive at the following set of expected cell frequencies.

ABANY	Protestant	Catholic	Jewish	None	Other
Approve	196	112	14	61	21
Disapprove	257	146	18	81	28

The next step in calculating chi-square is to calculate the difference between expected and observed values in each cell of the table. For example, if religion had no effect on abortion, we would have expected to find 196 Protestants approving; in fact, we observed only 171. Thus the discrepancy in that cell is –25. The discrepancy for Catholics approving is –14 (observed – expected = 98 – 112). The following table shows the discrepancies for each cell.

ABANY	Protestant	Catholic	Jewish	None	Other
Approve	−25	−14	10	22	7
Disapprove	25	14	−10	−22	−7

Finally, for each cell, we square the discrepancy and divide it by the expected cell frequency. For the Protestants approving of abortion, then, the squared discrepancy is 625 (-25×-25). Dividing it by the expected frequency of 196 yields 3.19 (rounded off a bit). When we repeat this for each cell, we get the following results.

ABANY	Protestant	Catholic	Jewish	None	Other
Approve	3.19	1.75	7.14	7.93	2.33
Disapprove	2.43	1.34	5.56	5.98	1.75

Chi-square is the sum of all these latest cell figures: 39.4. We have calculated a summary measure of the discrepancy between what we would have expected to observe if religion did not affect abortion and what we actually observed. Now the only remaining question is whether that resulting number should be regarded as large or small. Statisticians often speak of "goodness of fit" in this context: How well do the observed data fit a model of two variables' being unrelated to each other? The answer to this question takes the form of a probability: the probability that a chi-square this large could occur as a result of sampling error. A probability of .05 in this context would mean that it should happen five times in 100 samples. A probability of .001 would mean that it should happen only once in 1,000 samples.

To evaluate our chi-square of 39.4, we would need to look it up in a table of chi-square values, which you'll find at the back of any statistics textbook. Such tables have several columns marked by different probabilities (e.g., .30, .20, .10, .05, .01, .001). The tables also have several rows representing different **degrees of freedom** (*df*).

If you think about it, you'll probably see that the larger and more complex a table is, the greater the likelihood that there will be discrepancies from the perfect model of expected frequencies. We take account of this by one final calculation.

Degrees of freedom are calculated from the data table as (rows − 1) × (columns − 1). In our table, there are five columns and two rows, giving us $4 \times 1 = 4$ degrees of freedom. Thus we would look across the fourth row in the table of chi-square values, which would look, in part, like this:

df	.05	.01	.001
4	9.488	13.277	18.465

These numbers tell us that a chi-square as high as 9.488 from a table like ours would occur only five times in 100 samples if there were no relationship between religious affiliation and abortion attitudes among the whole U.S. population. A chi-square as high as 13.277 would happen only once in 100 samples, and a chi-square as high as 18.465 would happen only once in 1,000.

Thus we conclude that our chi-square of 39.4 could result from sampling error less than once in 1,000 samples. This is often abbreviated as "$p < .001$": The probability is less than 1 in 1,000.

They have no magical meaning, but the .05 and .001 levels of significance are often used by social scientists as a convention for concluding that an observed relationship reflects a similar relationship in the population rather than arising from sampling error. Obviously, if a relationship is significant at the .001 level, we are more confident of our conclusion than if it is significant only at the .05 level.

There you have it—all the basics you need to know about chi-square. By sticking it out and coming to grasp the logical meaning of this statistical calculation, you've earned a reward.

Rather than going through all the preceding calculations, we could have simply modified our Crosstabs request slightly. In the Crosstabs window, click "Statistics" and select "chi-square" in the upper left corner of the window. Then run the Crosstabs request.

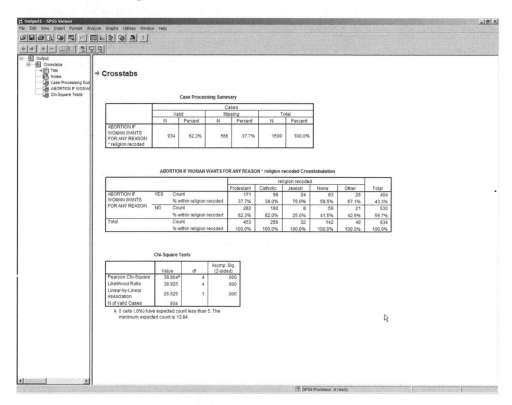

We are interested primarily in the first row of figures in this report. Notice that the 38.864 value of chi-square is slightly different from our hand calculation. This is due to our rounding off in our cell calculations and shouldn't worry you. Notice that we're told there are 4 degrees of freedom. Finally, SPSS has calculated the probability of getting a chi-square this high with 4 degrees of freedom and has run out of space after five zeros to the right of the decimal point. Thus the probability is far less than .001, as we determined by checking a table of chi-square values.

The reference to a "minimum expected frequency" of 13.84 is worth noting. Because the calculation of chi-square involves divisions by expected cell frequencies, it can be greatly inflated if any of them are very small. By convention, adjustments to chi-square should be made if more than 20% of the expected cell frequencies are below 5. You should check a statistics text if you want to know more about this.

While it is fresh in your mind, why don't you have SPSS calculate some more chi-squares for you? For example, why don't you see what the chi-square is for the relationship between SEX and ABANY?

To experiment more with chi-square, you might rerun some of the other tables relating various demographic variables to abortion attitudes. Notice that chi-square offers a basis for comparing the relative importance of different variables in determining attitudes on this controversial topic.

It bears repeating here that tests of significance are different from measures of association, although they are related. The stronger an association between two variables, the more likely it is that the association will be judged statistically significant—that is, not a simple product of sampling error. Other factors also affect statistical significance, however. As we've already mentioned, the number of degrees of freedom in a table is relevant. So is the size of the sample: The larger the sample, the more likely the association will be judged significant.

Researchers often distinguish between *statistical* significance (examined in this section) and *substantive* significance. The latter refers to the importance of an association, and it can't be determined by empirical analysis alone. As we suggested at the outset of this chapter, **substantive significance** depends on practical and theoretical factors. All this notwithstanding, social researchers often find statistical significance a useful device in gauging associations.

Whereas chi-square operates on the logic of the contingency table, which you've grown accustomed to through the Crosstabs procedure, we're going to turn next to a test of significance based on means.

9.2   *t*-Tests

Who do you suppose lives longer, men or women? Whichever group lives longer should, as a result, have a higher average age at any given time. Regardless of whether you know the answer to this question for the U.S. population as a whole, let's see if our General Social Survey (GSS) data can shed some light on the issue.

We could find the average ages of men and women in our GSS sample with the simple command path

Analyze → Compare Means → Means

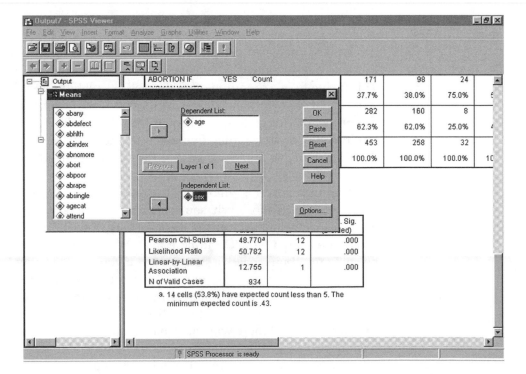

Since age is the characteristic we want to compare men and women on, AGE is the dependent variable and SEX the independent. Transfer those variables to the appropriate fields in the window. Then click "OK."

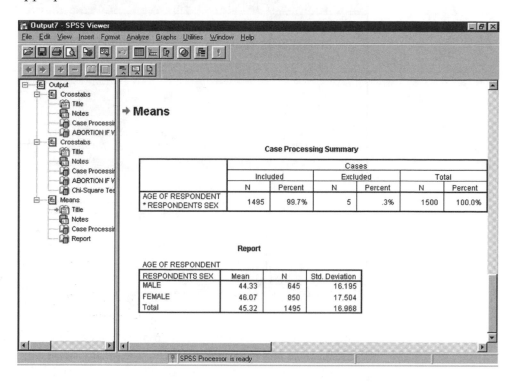

As you can see, our sample reflects the general population in that women have a mean age of 46.07, compared with 44.33 for men. The task facing us now parallels the one pursued in the discussion of chi-square. Does the observed difference reflect a pattern that exists in the whole population, or is it simply a result of a sampling procedure that happened to get too many old women and/or too many young men this time? Would another sample indicate that men are older than women or that there is no difference?

Given that we've moved very deliberately through the logic and calculations of chi-square, we are going to avoid such details in the present discussion. The *t*-test examines the distribution of values on one variable (age) among different groups (men and women) and calculates the probability that the observed difference in means results from sampling error alone.

To request a *t* test from SPSS to examine the relationship between AGE and SEX, you enter the following command path:

Analyze → Compare Means → Independent-Samples T-Test

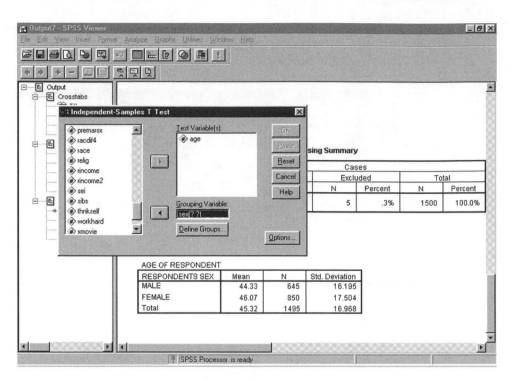

In this window, we want to enter AGE as the "Test Variable" and SEX as the "Grouping Variable." This means that SPSS will group respondents by sex and then examine and compare the mean ages of the two groups.

Notice that when you enter the "Grouping Variable," SPSS puts "SEX[??]" in that field. While the comparison groups are obvious in the case of SEX, it might not be so obvious with other variables, so SPSS wants some guidance. Click "Define Groups."

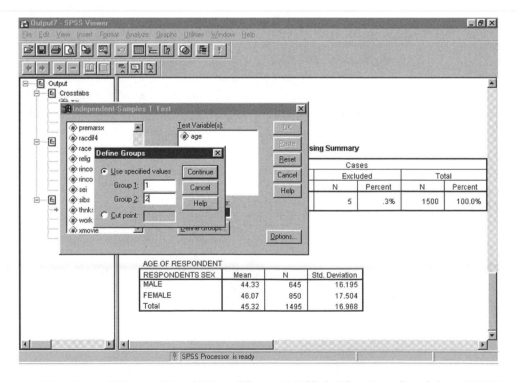

Type 1 into "Group 1" and 2 into "Group 2." Click "Continue" and then "OK."

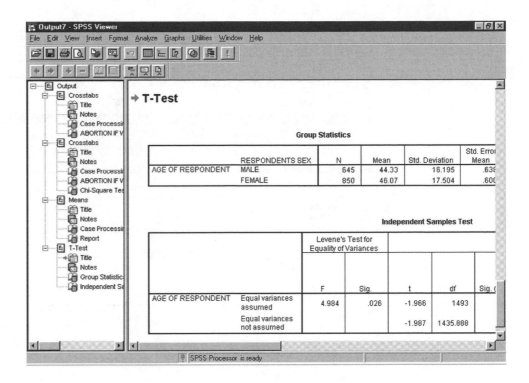

The program gives you much more information than you need for present purposes, so let's identify the key elements. Some of the information is a repeat of what we got earlier from the **Means** command: means, standard deviations, and standard errors for men and women.

The additional value we want from this table is the .049 under the heading "Sig. (2-tailed)" and in the row designated "Equal variances assumed." For our purposes, this is the result that we will use from the table. If you are interested in learning more about statistics, you will want to make use of some of the other information in this table.

As you have anticipated, .049 in this context indicates a probability of 49 in 1,000. The "two-tail" notation requires just a little more explanation.

In our sample, the average age for women is 1.74 years higher than for men. SPSS has calculated that 49 times in 1,000 samples, sampling error might produce a difference this great in either direction. That is, if the average age of men and the average age of women in the population were exactly the same and we were to select 1,000 samples like this one, we could expect 49 of those samples to show women at least 1.74 years older than men or men as much as 1.74 years older than women.

When you don't have theoretical reasons to anticipate a particular relationship, it is appropriate for you to use the "two-tail" probability in evaluating differences in means like these. In some cases—when you have deduced specific expectations from a theory, for example—you might come to the data analysis with a hypothesis that "women are older than men." In such a case, it might be more appropriate to note there is a probability of 26 in 1,000 ($p = .026$) that sampling error would have resulted in women being as much as 1.74 years older than men. For our purposes in this book, however, we'll stick with the two-tail test.

Some of the variables in your GSS data set allow you to explore this issue further. For example, it would be reasonable for better-educated workers to earn more than poorly educated workers. So if the men in our sample have more education than the women, that might explain the difference in pay. Let's see.

Return to the T-Test window and substitute EDUC for AGE as the "Test Variable." Leave "SEX[1 2]" as the "Grouping Variable." Run the new T-Test.

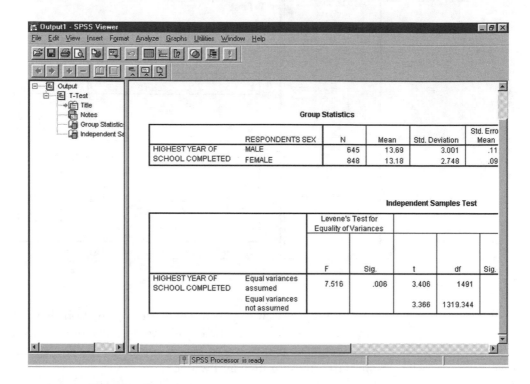

What conclusion do you draw from these latest results? Notice first that the men and women in our sample have a slightly different mean number of years of education. This fact is confirmed by the probability reported: Even though the difference is small, such a difference could be expected by chance alone in about 1 sample in 1,000 ($p = .001$).

In concluding from this that men do not have more education than women, we rule out that "legitimate reason" for women's earning less than men. That's not to say that there aren't other legitimate reasons that may account for the difference in pay. For instance, it is often argued that women tend to concentrate in less prestigious jobs than men: nurses rather than doctors, secretaries rather than executives, teachers rather than principals. Leaving aside the reasons for such occupational differences, that might account for the differences in pay. As you may recall, your GSS data contain a measure of socioeconomic status (SEI). We used that variable in our experimentation with Correlations. Let's see if the women in our sample have less prestigious jobs, on the average, than the men.

Go back to the T-Test window and replace EDUC with SEI. Run the procedure, and you should get the following result.

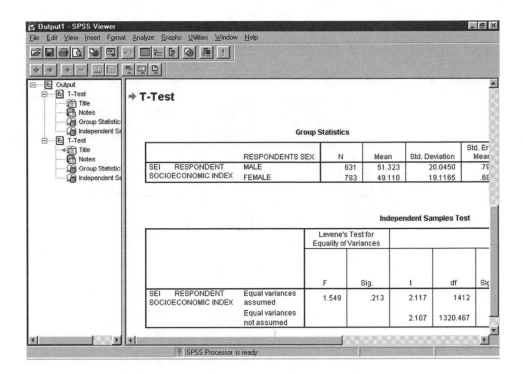

The mean difference in socioeconomic index ratings of men and women is 2.2 on a scale from 0 to 100. Moreover, SPSS tells us that such a difference could be expected as a consequence of sampling error in about 34 samples in 1,000 ($p = .034$). That's evidently not the reason women earn less.

To pursue this line of inquiry further, you will need additional analytic skills, which will be covered shortly in our discussion of multivariate analysis.

If you want to experiment more with T-Test, you might substitute RACE for SEX in the commands we've been sending to SPSS. If you do that, realize that you have asked SPSS to consider only code categories 1 and 2 on SEX; applied to RACE, that will limit the comparison to whites and blacks, omitting the "other" category.

9.3 Analysis of Variance

The t test is limited to the comparison of two groups at a time. If we wanted to compare the levels of education of different religious groups, we'd have to compare Protestants and Catholics, Protestants and Jews, Catholics and Jews, and so forth. And if some of the comparisons found significant differences and other comparisons did not, we'd be hard-pressed to reach an overall conclusion about the nature of the relationship between the two variables.

The **analysis of variance** (ANOVA) is a technique that resolves the shortcoming of the t test. It examines the means of subgroups in the sample and analyzes the variances as well. That is, it examines more than whether the actual values are clustered around the mean or spread out from it.

If we were to ask ANOVA to examine the relationship between RELIGCAT and EDUC, it would determine the mean years of education for each of the different religious groups, noting how they differed from one another. Those "between-group" differences would be compared with the "within-group" differences (variance): how much Protestants differed among themselves, for example. Both sets of comparisons are reconciled by ANOVA to calculate the likelihood that the observed differences are merely the result of sampling error.

To get a clearer picture of ANOVA, ask SPSS to perform the analysis we've been discussing. You can probably figure out how to do that, but here's a hint:

Analyze → Compare Means → One-way ANOVA

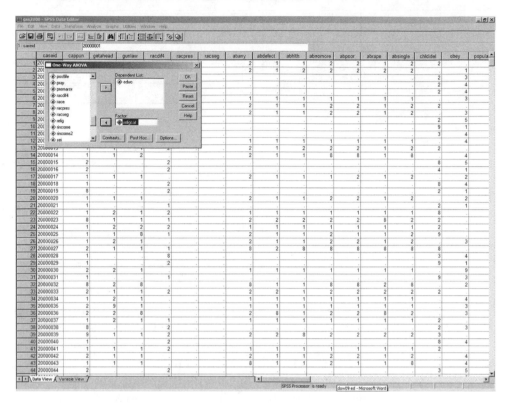

Put EDUC into the "Dependent" list and RELIGCAT in the "Factor" field. Launch the procedure.

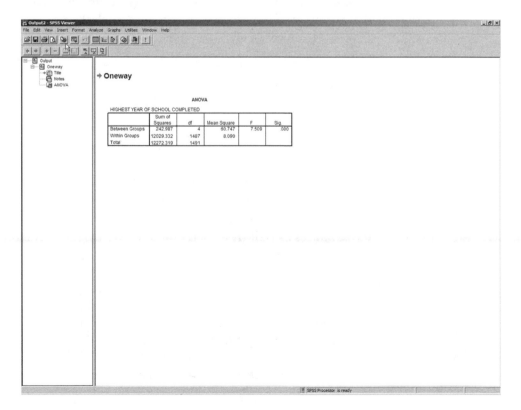

Here's the SPSS report on the analysis. Again, we've gotten more information than we want for our present purposes. For our immediate purposes, let's look simply at the row titled "Between Groups." This refers to the amount of variance in EDUC that can be explained by variations in RELIG. Because our present purpose is to learn about tests of statistical significance, let's move across the row to the statistical significance of the explained variance, the column titled "Sig." If religion and education were unrelated to each other in the population, we might expect samples that would generate this amount of explained variance about once in 1,000 samples.

Perhaps you will find it useful to think of ANOVA as something like a statistical broom. We began by noting a lot of variance in educational levels of our respondents; imagine people's educations spread all over the place. In an attempt to find explanatory patterns in that variance, we use ANOVA to sweep the respondents into subgroups based on religious affiliation (stay with us on this). The questions are whether variations in education are substantially less within each of the piles than we originally observed in the whole sample and whether the mean years of education in each of the subgroups are quite different from one another. Imagine a set of tidy piles that are quite distant from one another. ANOVA provides a statistical test of this imagery. It is also possible for ANOVA to consider two independent variables, but that goes beyond the scope of this book. We have introduced you to ANOVA because we feel it is useful and we wanted to open up for you the possibility of your using this popular technique; however, you will need more specialized training in the performance of analysis of variance to use it effectively.

9.4   Summary

This chapter has taken on the difficult question of whether the observed relationship between two variables is important or not. It is natural that you would want to know whether and when you have discovered something worth writing home about. No one wants to shout, "Look what I've discovered!" and have others say, "That's no big thing."

We've presented several statistics that help resolve whether a relationship exists between two variables. We've also seen that the level of measurement of the variables determines which statistic to use and how much we learn about the association. For nominal-level variables, we can learn only whether or not a relationship exists. For ordinal variables, we can learn whether it exists and in what direction (positive or negative). For interval- and ratio-level variables, we have a lot more information, and we learn not only about existence and direction but also about the strength of the relationship.

Ultimately, there is no simple test of the substantive significance of a relationship between variables. If we found that women earn less than men, who can say if that amounts to a lot less or just a little bit less? In a more precise study, we could calculate exactly how much less in dollars, but we would still not be in a position to say absolutely whether that amount was a lot or a little. If women made a dollar a year less than men on the average, we'd all probably agree that that was not an important difference. Conversely, if we learned that men earned a hundred times as much as women, we'd probably all agree that that was a big difference. Few of the differences we discover in social science research are that dramatic, however.

In this chapter, we've examined a very specific approach that social scientists often take in addressing the issue of significance. As distinct from notions of *substantive significance,* we have examined *statistical significance.* In each of the measures we've examined—chi-square, *t*-test, and analysis of variance—we've asked how likely it would be that sampling error could produce the observed relationship if there were actually no relationship in the population from which the sample was drawn.

This assumption of no relationship is sometimes referred to as the **null hypothesis.** The tests of significance we've examined all deal with the probability that the null hypothesis is correct. If the probability is relatively high, we conclude that there is no relationship between the two variables under study in the whole population. If the probability is small that the null hypothesis could be true, we conclude that the observed relationship reflects a genuine pattern in the population.

Key Terms

analysis of variance (ANOVA)
chi-square
degrees of freedom *(df)*
null hypothesis

sampling error
statistical significance
substantive significance
t-test

Part IV Multivariate Analysis

Now that you've mastered the logic and techniques of bivariate analysis, we are going to take you one step further: to the examination of three or more variables at a time, known as *multivariate analysis*. In Chapter 10, we'll explore how to examine several independent variables. Chapter 11 will pick up some loose threads of our bivariate analysis and pursue them further with our new analytic capability, helping us understand attitudes about guns and capital punishment. Finally, Chapter 12 presents logistic regression, an approach with much promise for criminal justice research, as we examine college student drug and alcohol abuse.

Chapter 10 **Examining Several Independent Variables**

Multivariate analysis is the simultaneous analysis of three or more variables. It is the next step beyond bivariate (two-variable) analysis. In the next few chapters, we will see that using more than one independent variable in predicting some dependent variable can yield a variety of outcomes. We will start with the simplest of outcomes, moving from using just one predictor variable at a time to using several at the same time.

10.1   Age, Sex, and Religiosity

It is often the case with social phenomena that people's attitudes and behaviors are affected by more than one factor. It is the task of the social scientist, then, to discover all the factors that influence the dependent variable in question and discover how those factors work together to produce a result. Consider religiosity: Women appear to be more religious than men, and old people seem more religious than young people. If both age and gender affect religiosity independently, perhaps a combination of the two would predict even better.

To begin our multivariate analysis, let's see how well we can predict religiosity if we consider AGE and SEX simultaneously. Does religiosity increase with age among both men and women separately? Moreover, do the two variables have a cumulative effect on religiosity? That is, are older women the most religious and young men the least religious?

To begin our exploration of this topic, let's use CHATT (church attendance) as the dependent variable; that is, let's see how well we can predict or explain attendance at worship services. To examine simultaneous impact of AGECAT and SEX on CHATT, simply make an additional modification to the now-familiar Crosstabs command: Enter CHATT as the row variable, AGECAT as the column variable. Then select SEX in the list of variables. Notice that the arrows activated would let you transfer SEX as a row variable or as a column variable—or you can transfer it to the third field, near the bottom of the window. Do that.

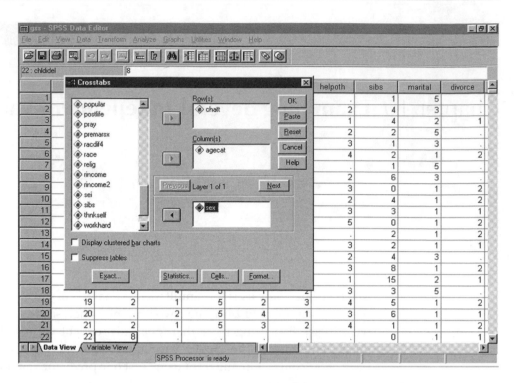

Check that the cells are set to be percentaged by columns, and then execute the command. (You can uncheck "observed" in the cells command.) This command produces a complex table. We have asked SPSS to examine the impact of AGECAT on CHATT separately for men and women. Thus we are rewarded with the following:

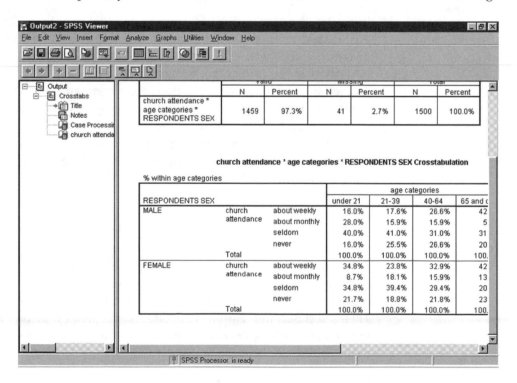

Notice that the first part is labeled "RESPONDENTS SEX MALE." Thus we know that the data are limited to men. The data in the second part, as you'll note, are limited to women.

To view the results more easily, we might create a summary table as follows:

Percentage of respondents who attend worship services about weekly:

	Under 21	21–39	40–64	65 and Over
		Age		
Men	16	18	27	43
Women	35	24	33	42

There are three primary observations to be made regarding this table. First, within each age group, women are more likely than men to attend worship services. Second, with a minor exception, the previously observed relationship between AGE and ATTEND is true for both men and women. Finally, the question we asked earlier about the cumulative effect of the two causal variables is answered with a clear yes. A mere 16% of the youngest men attend worship services weekly, contrasted to 42% of the oldest women.

10.2   Family Status and Religiosity

According to social deprivation theory, "family status" is also related to religiosity. In one study (Glock, Ringer, & Babbie, 1967), people living in "complete families" (two parents and children) were the least religious among Episcopal church members surveyed in 1952, suggesting that those persons who lacked families were turning to the church for emotional support and gratification.

Using Crosstabs, set CHATT as the row variable and MARITAL as the column variable. Here's what you should get:

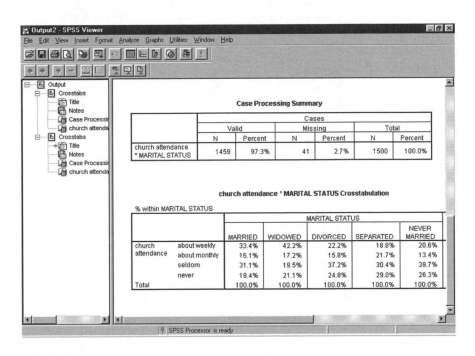

These data do not confirm the earlier finding. Although the widowed are the most religious, the currently married are next. It would not appear that people deprived of conventional family status are turning to the church as an alternative source of emotional support. Perhaps the explanation for this lies in historical changes.

In the 48 years separating these two studies (the 1952 study and this analysis of 2000 GSS data), many changes in family life have occurred in the United States. Divorce, single-parent families, unmarried couples living together—these and other variations on the traditional family have become more common and more acceptable. It would make sense, therefore, that people who lacked regular family status in 2000 would not feel as deprived as such people may have felt in the early 1950s.

Before setting this issue aside, however, we should take a minute to consider whether the table we've just seen is concealing anything. In particular, can you think of any other variable related to both attendance at worship services and marital status? If so, that variable might be clouding the relationship between marital status and religiosity.

The variable we are thinking of is age. We've already seen that age is strongly related to church attendance. It is also probably related to marital status in that young people (low in church attendance) are the most likely to be "never married." And old people (high in church attendance) are the most likely to be widowed. It is therefore possible that the widowed are high in church attendance only because they're mostly older and the never married are low in church attendance only because they're young. This kind of reasoning lies near the heart of multivariate analysis, and the techniques you've mastered allow you to test this possibility.

Return to the Crosstabs window and add AGECAT as the third variable. Once you've reviewed the resulting tables, see if you can construct the following summary table.

Percentage of respondents who attend church about weekly:

Age	Married	Widowed	Divorced	Separated	Never Married
Under 21	—	—	—	—	28
21–39	29	50	16	21	14
40–64	33	41	26	18	29
65 and over	51	42	21	—	50

Dashes in this table indicate that there are too few cases for percentages to be meaningful. We've required at least 10 cases, a common standard.

As it turns out, the original pattern observed in the relationship between marital status and church attendance is maintained at each age level. The widowed are the most religious in the three age groups where there are enough of them for a meaningful comparison. Thus their high frequency of church attendance cannot be explained as simply a function of their being older. By the same token, the never married have a relatively low level of church attendance regardless of their age, except for those 65 and up.

You can also observe in this table that the effect of age on church attendance is mostly maintained regardless of marital status. Among the never married, the original relationship partially disappears, and even there the oldest are the most religious.

Social scientists often use the term *replication* for the analytic outcome we've just observed. Having discovered that church attendance increases with age overall, we've now found that this relationship holds true regardless of marital status. That's an important discovery in terms of the generalizability of what we have learned about the causes of religiosity.

10.3   Social Class and Religiosity

In the earlier study, Glock and his colleagues (1967) found that religiosity increased as social class decreased; that is, people in the lower class were more religious than those in the upper class. This fits nicely into the deprivation thesis that those deprived of status in the secular society would turn to the church as an alternative source of emotional support and gratification. The researchers indicated, however, that this finding might be limited to the Episcopalian church members under study. They suggested that the relationship might not be replicated in the general public. You have the opportunity to check this out.

Let's begin with our measure of subjective social class. Run Crosstabs with CHATT as the row variable and CLASS as the column variable. Here's what you should get:

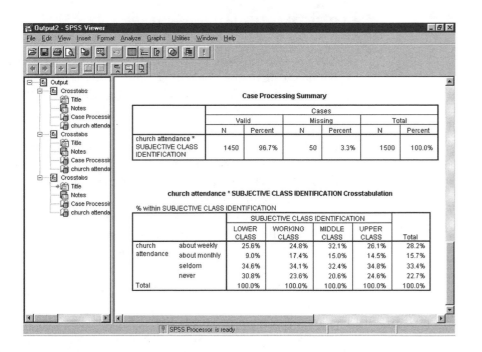

This table suggests that there is no relationship between social class and church attendance. To be sure of this conclusion, you might want to rerun the table, controlling for sex and for age. At the same time, you can test the generalizability of the previously observed effects of sex and age on church attendance. Do they hold up among members of different social classes?

To pursue this issue even further, you might want to examine a different measure of social class. Look through the list of variables and decide which ones offer other views of class standing. Once you've done that, see how they relate to church attendance.

10.4   Other Variables to Explore

Notice that our analyses so far in this chapter have used CHATT as the dependent variable, the measure of religiosity. Recall, however, our earlier comments on the shortcomings of single-item measures of variables. Perhaps our analyses have been misleading by seeking to explain church attendance. Perhaps different conclusions might be drawn if we had studied beliefs in an afterlife or frequency of prayer. Why don't you test some of the earlier conclusions by using other measures of religiosity? If you are really ambitious, you could create a composite index of religiosity and look for causes.

Similarly, we have limited our preceding investigations in this chapter to the variables examined by Glock and his colleagues. Now that you have gotten the idea about how to create and interpret multivariate tables, you should broaden your exploration of variables that might be related to religiosity. What are some other demographic variables that might affect religiosity? Or you might want to explore the multivariate relationships between religiosity and some of the attitudinal variables we've been exploring: political philosophies, sexual attitudes, and so forth. In each instance, you should examine the bivariate relationships first, then move on to the multivariate analyses.

10.5   Multiple Linear Regression

So far, we've introduced the logic of multivariate analysis through the use of Crosstabs. You've already learned some other techniques that can be used in your examination of several variables simultaneously.

First, we should remind you that you may want to use a chi-square test of statistical significance when you use Crosstabs. It's not required, but you may find it useful as an independent assessment of the relationships you discover.

Second, regression can be a powerful technique for exploring multivariate relationships. This is called **multiple regression.** To use regression effectively, you will need more instruction than we propose to offer in this book. Still, we want to give you an introductory look into this technique.

In our previous use of regression, we examined the impact of EDUC on SEI. Now we'll open the possibility that other variables in the data set might also affect socioeconomic status. AGE is another ratio variable and one we might expect to have an impact. (Be sure to return to its original form, so it has a ratio level of measurement.)

We are also going to consider SEX, reasoning that men and women are treated very differently in the labor force. Notice that SEX is a nominal variable, not a ratio variable. However, researchers sometimes treat such dichotomies as so-called **dummy** or **indicator variables** appropriate to a regression analysis. The logic used here transforms gender into a measure of "maleness," for example, with men respondents being 100% and the women 0% male. The following recode statement accomplishes that transformation.

Let's temporarily recode SEX as just described. Take the following steps: Transform → Recode → Into Different Variables. Select SEX as the "Input Variable." Let's call the new variable SEX2. Using the "Old and New Values" field, make these assignments.

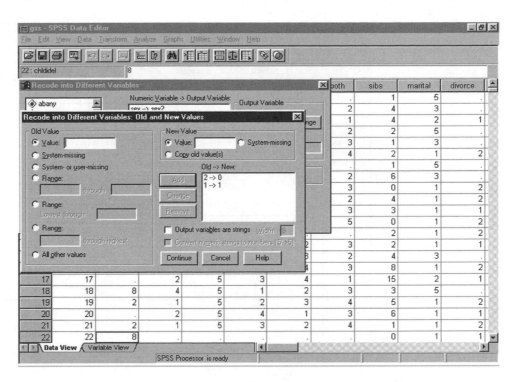

Execute the Recode command, and we are ready to request the multiple regression analysis: Analyze → Regression → Linear Regression takes us to the window we want. Put SEI as the dependent variable and EDUC, SEX2, and AGE as independent variables. In the small box next to "Method," "Enter" should be the default. If it is not, choose the Enter method now.

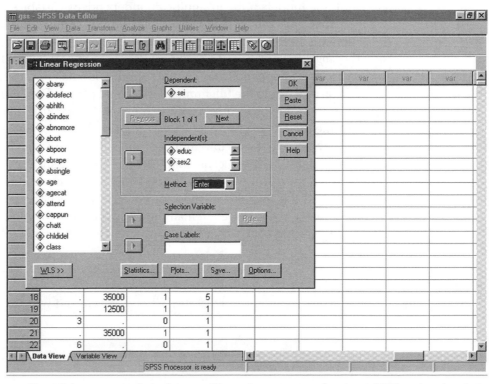

Run this command, and you will receive a mass of output. Without going into all the details, we are simply going to show you how it establishes the equation we asked for. We'll take the output a piece at a time. For our purposes, we'd like you to skip through the output on your screen until you find the "Coefficients" table:

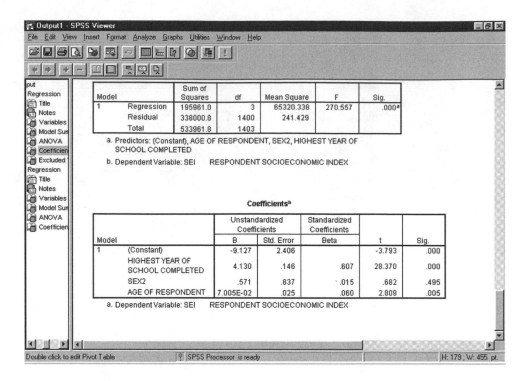

We have given SPSS several variables it might use to predict socioeconomic status. With the Enter regression, all the independent variables are entered in a single step.

This gives us only one "model" to analyze. If we had used the Stepwise method instead, SPSS would enter one independent variable at a time, giving us multiple models until all significant independent variables are entered.

To create our equation from our simple "Enter" model, we locate several numbers in the output: the constant or intercept (−9.127), the **B value** (also called the *slope)* for EDUC (4.130), and the *B* value for AGE (.007005). The notation next to the AGE slope indicates that this number is small and the printout simply does not carry it out to the full number of decimal places. The "E-02" indicates the need for two more zeros in front of the number. Notice also that we are not going to include the *B* value for SEX2. This is because the test of significance (the rightmost column) for that variable indicates nonsignificance (much higher than the .05 cutoff point). This means that there is no statistically significant difference between men and women with regard to their socioeconomic index score. If we had used the Stepwise method for entering independent variables, SEX2 would have never been entered, remaining excluded from the model.

So getting back to our equation, here's what we need to create:

$$SEI = -9.127 + (EDUC \times 4.130) + (AGE \times .007005)$$

Thus we would predict the SEI of a 25-year-old with 10 years of education as follows:

$$SEI = -9.127 + (10 \times 4.130) + (25 \times .007005) = 32.348$$

Let's look at the information for SEX2, even though we will not include it in our equation for predicting SEI. Notice that being a man is worth only about an additional half point (.571) of SEI—when education and age are held constant.

Note the column headed "Beta." **Beta** is a guide to the relative impact of the different variables. Take a minute to consider the little or no impact of the independent variable of SEX on the dependent variable of SEI. The small slope is logically not statistically significant. This means that a person's value on that variable (SEX, in this example) does not make much difference in predicting the dependent variable (SEI, in this example). By the same token, the larger the slope for any given variable, the larger its part in determining the resulting prediction. But why does AGE have a much smaller slope (0.007005) than SEX (.571) when AGE is supposed to be a better predictor?

The solution to this puzzle lies in the different scales used in the different variables. SEX goes only as high as 1 (male), whereas AGE goes to 89. The beta values are the **standardized slopes** for the different variables. These are what the slopes would be if each of the variables used the same scale of variation.

The data presented here, then, indicate that EDUC has the most impact on SEI, followed distantly by AGE and SEX.

Realize that we've given you only a meager introduction to this powerful technique. It is one you may want to study further outside of this book. At the same time, you should feel free to experiment with it.

10.6 Summary

In this chapter, we have given you an initial peek into the logic and techniques of multivariate analysis. As you've seen, the difference between bivariate and multivariate analysis is much more than a matter of degree. Multivariate analysis does more than bring in additional variables: It represents a new logic for understanding social scientific relationships. But multivariate analysis usually makes a number of underlying assumptions about the data, so we suggest that you learn more about these from an advanced statistics book (e.g., Hamilton, 1992).

For this contact, we've looked at how multivariate analysis lets us explore the nature of complex relationships, seeing how two or more independent variables affect a dependent variable statistically. In addition, we've used multivariate techniques for the purpose of testing the generalizability of relationships.

In the latter regard, we have begun using multivariate techniques for the purpose of considering hidden relationships between variables, as when we asked whether the widowed attended church frequently just because they were mostly older people. We'll pursue this kind of detective work further in the chapters to come.

Key Terms

B value	multiple regression
beta	multivariate analysis
dummy variables	replication
indicator variables	standardized slopes

Chapter 11 Exploring What Shapes Attitudes About Guns and Capital Punishment

In Chapter 7, we began exploring some of the causes of political philosophies and party identification. Now you are equipped to dig more deeply, allowing you to examine how these personal values influence attitudes about guns and capital punishment.

Let's start with the relationship between political philosophy and party identification. As you'll recall, our earlier analysis showed a definite relationship, although it was not altogether consistent. Perhaps we can clarify it.

11.1 Political Philosophy and Party Identification

On the whole, Democrats in our sample were more liberal than Independents or Republicans, as you'll recall. Also, Republicans were the most conservative, although there wasn't much distinction between Democrats and Independents in that regard. Here's the basic table from Chapter 7.

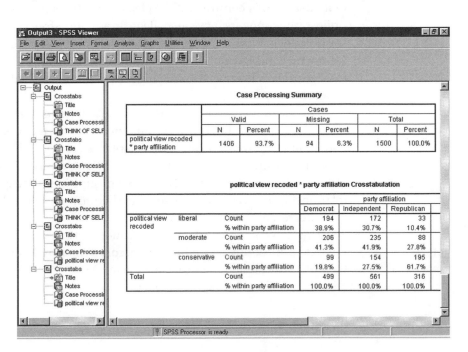

For purposes of this analysis, let's focus on the percentages who identify themselves as "conservative." In the table, the percentage difference separating Democrats and Republicans who call themselves conservative amounts to 42 points. You'll recall, perhaps, that percentage differences are sometimes called epsilon.

If you were to undertake a study of the political party platforms and/or the speeches of political leaders from the two major parties, you would conclude that Democrats are, in fact, somewhat more liberal than Republicans and that Republicans are, in fact, somewhat more conservative than Democrats. If the relationship between political philosophy and party identification is not as clear as we might like, perhaps some of the respondents simply don't know how the two parties are generally regarded.

Who do you suppose would be the least likely to know the philosophical leanings of the two parties? Perhaps those with the least education would be unaware of this. If that were the case, then, we should expect a clearer relationship between political philosophy and party identification among the more educated respondents than among the less educated.

Why don't you run the SPSS command that would let you create the following three-variable summary table?

Percentage of respondents characterizing themselves as conservative:

| Party Identification | Education | | | |
	Less Than High School	High School Grad.	Some College	College Grad.
Democrats	27	19	22	13
Independents	23	27	32	36
Republicans	41	49	66	70
Epsilon	14	30	44	57

Our suspicion is confirmed. The clearest relationship between party and political philosophy appears among college graduates, followed by respondents with some college. Notice that epsilon shows 30 or fewer percentage points separating Democrats and Republicans among the least educated group, and that among the least educated, Democrats score higher than Independents, the reverse of what we expected.

This table reveals something else that relates to our earlier analysis. You may recall that we found only a weak and inconsistent relationship between education and political philosophy in our Chapter 7 analysis. There was a tendency for liberalism to increase with education, although only 17 percentage points separated the least from the most educated groups in that respect. There was no clear relationship between conservatism and education, with the "moderate" point of view decreasing with education.

This new table clarifies the situation somewhat. The relationship between political philosophy and education occurs primarily among Democrats. Although the most educated Republicans are the most conservative, there are few differences among the other three educational groups.

This table represents what social scientists call a **specification.** We have specified the relationship between education and political philosophy: It occurs primarily among Democrats. Or we could say that we have specified the relationship between political philosophy and party identification: It occurs primarily among the better educated.

Specification stands as an alternative to *replication*. You'll recall that replication indicates that a relationship between two variables can be generalized to all kinds of people. Specification indicates that it cannot.

When we look at the relationship between two variables, such as political philosophy and party identification, among subgroups determined by some other variable, such as education, we often say that we are controlling for that third variable. Social scientists use the expression "controlling for" in the sense of simulating the creation of controlled conditions by statistical manipulation: only college graduates, only people with some college, and so on. We also speak of "holding education constant" in the sense that education is no longer a variable when we look only at one educational group at a time; it is a constant.

Why don't you experiment with this logic, testing the generalizability of the relationship between political philosophy and party identification among other subgroups, formed by holding other variables constant?

11.2   The Mystery of Politics and Marital Status

In Chapter 7, we encouraged you to explore the relationship between marital status and politics. If you took us up on the invitation, you should have found an interesting relationship between marital status and political philosophy. Let's look at the table of MARITAL and POLVIEWS. Because relatively few respondents were separated from their spouses, we should combine them with some other group. It would seem to make sense to combine the separated with the divorced, reasoning that separation is often an interim step toward divorce.

Let's recode MARITAL into a new variable, MARITAL2, with Transform Recode → Into Different Variables.

Once in the Recode window, you should enter MARITAL as the input variable and MARITAL2 as the output variable. Then, in the "Old and New Values" field, carry all the old values, except 4, to MARITAL2 (i.e., 1 → 1, 2 → 2, 3 → 3, 4 → 3, and 5 → 5). Don't forget to use "Add" to record the instructions. Then you can "Continue" and "OK" your way to the recoded variable. (By the way, it's usually a good idea to add value labels after recoding; they make it a lot easier to interpret the data.)

Now run Crosstab, with POLREC as the row variable and MARITAL2 as the column variable. Here's what you should get:

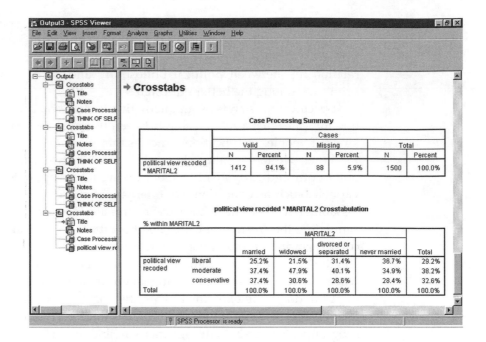

If you had run the chi-square test of statistical significance, you would have found this relationship to exceed the .001 level of significance. So why is it that married and widowed respondents are more conservative than the divorced, separated, or never married? Your multivariate skills will allow you to explore this matter in more depth than was possible before.

Perhaps age is the key. The widowed are likely to be older than others, and the never married are likely to be younger. As we've seen, people tend to become more conservative with age. Here is a summary table created from the results of the crosstab of POLREC by MARITAL2 by AGECAT. See if you can duplicate this yourself.

Percentage of respondents characterizing themselves as conservative:

| | | *Marital Status* | | |
Age	*Married*	*Widowed*	*Divorced or Separated*	*Never Married*
Under 21	50	—	—	24
21-39	37	25	25	29
40-64	35	29	33	28
65 and over	51	32	18	35

This table helps clarify matters. The married are consistently more conservative than the divorced and never married, and the widowed maintain their conservative stance. The never married and divorced and separated are more apt to be liberal.

How about sex? Perhaps it can shed some light on this relationship. Why don't you run the tables that would result in this summary?

Percentage of respondents characterizing themselves as conservative:

	Marital Status			
Sex	Married	Widowed	Divorced or Separated	Never Married
Men	42	39	37	27
Women	33	29	23	30

As before, the married remain relatively conservative, the widowed vary (more conservative among men than women), and the divorced and never married remain relatively less conservative (except maybe divorced men).

To pursue this further, you might want to consider education. Here's the summary table you should generate if you follow this avenue.

Percentage of respondents characterizing themselves as conservative:

	Marital Status			
Education	Married	Widowed	Divorced or Separated	Never Married
Less than high school	28	29	29	25
High school graduate	32	20	29	25
Some college	38	50	33	33
College graduate	48	25	24	38

Education does not seem to clarify the relationship we first observed between marital status and political philosophy. This is the point in an analysis where you sometimes wonder if you should ever have considered this line of inquiry.

See what happens when we introduce race as a control.

Percentage of respondents characterizing themselves as conservative:

	Marital Status			
Race	Married	Widowed	Divorced or Separated	Never Married
White	40	30	30	31
Black	17	31	25	25
Other	33	33	—	20

(As in other tables, the dashes here indicate that there are too few cases for meaningful percentages.)

When we consistently fail to find a clear answer to a question, it is sometimes useful to reconsider the question itself. We have been asking why marital status affects political philosophy. Perhaps we have the question reversed. What if political philosophy affects marital status? Is that a possibility?

Perhaps people who are politically conservative are also socially conservative. Maybe it would be especially important for them to form and keep traditional families. During the presidential election that followed on the heels of this General Social Survey (GSS), the political conservatives made "traditional family values" a centerpiece of their campaign. Let's see what the table would look like if we percentaged it in the opposite direction.

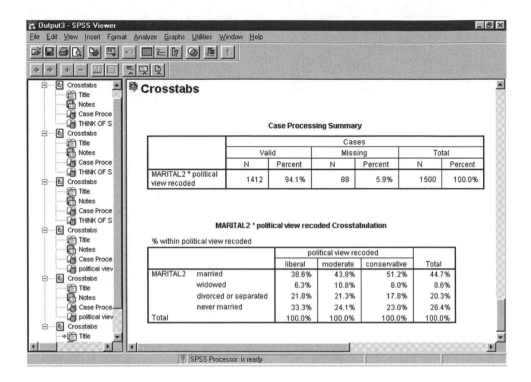

Look at the first row in this table. The percentage married steadily increases with increasing conservatism across the table. Divorce and singlehood decrease just as steadily. Perhaps marital status is more profitably seen as a dependent variable in this context, affected to some extent by worldviews as reflected in political philosophy.

Sometimes the direction of a relationship—which is the dependent and which the independent variable—is clear. If we discover that voting behavior is related to gender, for instance, we can be sure that gender can affect voting, but how you vote can't change your gender. In other situations, such as the present one, the direction of a relationship is somewhat ambiguous. Ultimately, this decision must be based on theoretical reasoning. There is no way the analysis of data can determine which variable is dependent and which is independent.

If you wanted to pursue the present relationship, you might treat marital status as a dependent variable, subjecting its relationship with political philosophies to a multivariate analysis.

One last comment: Although it is important to engage in post hoc (i.e., after you have done the data collection and analysis) hypothesizing about why things turned out the way they did, don't confuse this post hoc hypothesizing with the work of testing hypotheses in the strict sense.

11.3   Guns and Capital Punishment

In Chapter 7, we began looking for the causes of opinions on two political issues:

GUNLAW   Registration of firearms

CAPPUN   Capital punishment

Now that you have the ability to undertake multivariate analysis, you can delve more deeply into the causes of public opinion. Let's think a little about capital punishment for the moment. Here are some variables that might logically affect how people feel about the death penalty.

POLREC and PARTY are obvious candidates. Liberals are generally more opposed to capital punishment than conservatives are. Similarly, Republicans have tended to support it more than Democrats have. You might check to see how these two variables work together on death penalty attitudes.

Given that capital punishment involves the taking of a human life, you might expect some religious effects. How do the different religious affiliations relate to support for or opposition to capital punishment? What about beliefs in an afterlife? Do people who believe in life after death find it easier to support the taking of a life? How do religious and political factors interact in this arena?

Opponents of capital punishment base their opposition in the view that it is wrong to take a human life. The same argument is made by opponents of abortion. Logically, you would expect people opposed to abortion also to oppose capital punishment. Why don't you check it out? You may be surprised by what you find.

Another approach to understanding opinions about capital punishment might focus on what groups in society are the most likely to be the victims of it. Men are more likely to be executed than women. Blacks are executed disproportionately more often, in comparison with their numbers in the population.

11.4   Summary

These few suggestions should launch you on an extended exploration of the nature of political orientation and how it might be associated with attitudes about crime and justice. Whereas people often talk pretty casually about such matters, you are now in a position to check out the facts and to dig deeply into understanding why people feel as they do about politics, crime, and justice.

Multivariate analysis techniques let you uncover some of the complexities that can make human behavior difficult to understand.

Key Term

specification

Chapter 12 Logistic Regression: Understanding College Student Drug and Alcohol Abuse

Many dependent variables in criminal justice research turn out to be ones in which the categories are simple dichotomies—either something happens or something doesn't, or something is or something is not; for example:

- The person is the victim of a crime or isn't a victim.
- The person uses drugs or doesn't use drugs.
- The person is convicted or is acquitted.
- The police department adopts an innovative program or it doesn't.
- The state passes a new law or it doesn't.
- The nation has capital punishment or it doesn't.

In the more technical language we used in Chapter 1, these are all examples of nominal (as opposed to interval or ratio) scale variables or of categorical (as opposed to continuous or quantitative) variables. We have discussed how multiple regression provides a powerful way of understanding how a quantitative dependent variable is associated with several independent variables, both quantitative and even qualitative (transformed into dummy variables). But for several technical reasons, which we won't discuss here, multiple regression usually shouldn't be used with a categorical or qualitative dependent variable.

In contemporary criminal justice research, a statistical technique called *logistic regression* is widely used when the researcher has a qualitative or categorical dependent variable. Although logistic regression is challenging to learn, we'll keep things simple by first discussing the case when there is a dependent variable that is just a yes-no dichotomy and a single independent variable that is also a yes-no dichotomy. We'll talk about how you can interpret any association between these two variables in simple terms, using only techniques available in SPSS for Windows Student Version. Then we'll move on to logistic regression involving these two variables, using the Advanced Statistics module in SPSS for Windows. Finally, we'll talk about how logistic regression can take on even more demanding assignments, such as several independent variables and independent variables that are quantitative as well as being dichotomies.

12.1   Binge Drinking: A Dichotomous Dependent Variable

Let's choose to explore once again binge drinking among college students using the "BINGE.SAV" data set. One of the most important variables in that data set is COLLBING, defined as whether or not a student is a current binge drinker. You'll recall that this variable is given a "gender-specific" definition so that a male who drinks five or more drinks in a row and a female who drinks four or more drinks in a row are both defined as bingers. Let's discuss gender and binge drinking a bit more.

In the "BINGE.SAV" file, both GENDER and COLLBING are examples of **dichotomous variables** in that each cuts the variable into only two values: "male" versus "female" and "binge" versus "nonbinge."

As we noted, many other variables in criminal justice research are "natural" dichotomies. But some are not. For example, if you look through the variables in the General Social Survey [GSS] "GSS.SAV" file or the College Alcohol Survey "BINGE.SAV" file, you'll find many variables (such as a person's occupational prestige score in the GSS or the number of drinks it takes to get drunk in the BINGE data file) that take on many values.

Age, for example, is a variable that could be recoded into just two categories: Students who are 21 and over and those who are under 21. Or we could set the criterion to be 24 years and older and create a somewhat different variable that indicates whether the student is or is not in the traditional college age group. In either case, we would carry out the same steps in SPSS, changing only the value we use to create the dichotomy. In general, we create a *dummy* (or *indicator) variable* when we recode a variable into just two categories, usually giving a 1 to cases that have the trait or characteristic (e.g., a person who is 21 or older) and a 0 to cases without the characteristic (e.g., a person under 21). (You could even have a series of dummy variables indicating specific age groups.)

When you recode a continuous variable such as age into a dummy variable, you should be aware that you have taken a variable measured at the interval or ratio level of measurement and recoded it into a variable at the nominal level of measurement. If you do this type of recoding, it's probably a good idea to perform it in such a way that you keep the old variable (e.g., AGE) while recoding it into a new variable (e.g., AGELT24, a name that might indicate "age less than 24"). It's also a good idea always to use SPSS to give labels to both the new variable and its values.

Let's begin our exploration of logistic regression by considering an example of a dichotomous dependent variable and just one dichotomous independent variable. Open the "BINGE.SAV" file by issuing the command File → Open → Data and then specifying "BINGE.SAV."

Let's return to an issue we discussed once before: Do men and women differ in terms of their binge drinking? First, let's run Crosstabs, using COLLBING as the dependent (row) variable and GENDER as the independent (column) variable by following the familiar Analyze à Descriptive Statistics à Crosstabs sequence. In the "Crosstabs" dialog box, click on "Cells," make sure the "Observed" choice is checked under the "Counts" option, and ask for nothing else this time. Launch the crosstabulation, and here's what we get:

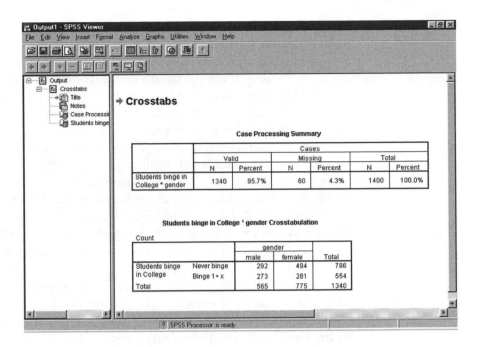

12.2 The Odds Ratio: Gender and Binge Drinking

In addition to the measures of association we've discussed in Chapter 8, several other options are available for us to understand the association between gender and binge drinking.

Let's begin by noting that 41.3% of the *nonabstaining* college students (554 divided by 1,340 valid cases) in the sample binge drink. (Bear in mind that only students who drink at any level are being compared; the original questionnaire eliminated any student who never drank anything from answering specific questions about the amount he or she drank.) What, then, are the odds of a male or a female student's binge drinking? Well, the **odds** of something happening are simply the number of events compared with (or divided by) the number of non-events. So the odds of bingeing are the number of students who binge divided by the number who don't binge. For the total sample, that is 554/786 = .7048; for men, 273/292 = . 9349; and for women, 281/494 = .5688. Odds are sometimes expressed in terms of how much more or less favored the event is compared with the non-event, so for the total sample we would say the odds of bingeing are roughly .7 to 1; for men, roughly .9 to 1; and for women, roughly .6 to 1. (It may be easier to picture these odds by expressing them as 7 to 10, 9 to 10, or 6 to 10.)

How could we compare the odds of bingeing for men and women? We could simply take the odds for men and divide them by the odds for women. If we did that, we'd create an **odds ratio** (odds for men = .9349, odds for women = .5688; odds ratio = .9349/.5688, or 1.6436). (If we compared the odds of women's bingeing compared with the odds of men's bingeing, the odds ratio would be .5688/.9349 = 0.6084. It's important to see that it makes a big difference which group is compared to which group. The group or category with which the comparison is made is called the **reference category** and is the denominator in the ratio.)

What does the odds ratio tell us? It tells us that the odds of men's bingeing are 1.6 times greater than the odds of women's bingeing. Put another way, it is a measure of the association between bingeing and gender, indicating how much higher the odds of men's bingeing are relative to the odds for women.

So the odds ratio is another measure of association, a topic we discussed back in Chapter 8. To be more precise, the odds ratio tells us about the *existence, direction,* and *strength* of an association between two dichotomous variables.

Let's first discuss *existence:* If there was no association, there wouldn't be a difference in the odds for men and the odds for women, so the ratio of those odds would be 1.0. But if the association exists, so that one gender had relatively higher (or relatively lower) odds of bingeing than the other gender, the odds ratio would go below or above 1.0. (We'll discuss shortly how to calculate the statistical significance of an odds ratio that has been estimated from sample data.)

What about *direction?* If we're calculating the odds ratio of men's bingeing (relative to women's), if the odds ratio goes above 1.0, we know that the odds of men's bingeing are higher than the odds of women's bingeing. By contrast, if that odds ratio fell below 1.0, it would tell us that the odds for men's bingeing were lower than the odds for women's bingeing. When we compare women's odds with men's odds in this example, the direction is reversed, and the odds ratio falls below 1.0.

Finally, how about the *strength* of association? Just as for correlation, there are no hard-and-fast rules for judging strength. But the greater the odds ratio rises above 1.0 or the more it falls below 1.0, the stronger the association.

Before we go further, let's clarify a few more points. First, if you can crosstabulate two dichotomous variables and record the frequency falling into each cell of the four cells, you can calculate the odds and odds ratio for the occurrence of either category of the dependent variable for either category of the independent variable quite easily by hand. To take our binge-drinking example, you could calculate the odds ratio of males (relative to the referent category females) for binge drinking (relative to the reference category nonbinge drinking) or the odds ratio of females (relative to males) for nonbinge drinking (relative to binge drinking).

But usually we just calculate the odds for one category of the dependent variable, the event or "happening"—in this example, binge drinking—and compare the odds for the two categories of the independent variable—in this case, men versus women. Let's just take the cell frequencies out of the crosstabulation we ran before and enter them into the following matrix by hand.

	Gender (Male)	
Binge Drinker	Yes	No
Yes	Cell A: Male bingers (n = 273)	Cell B: Female bingers (n = 281)
No	Cell C: Male nonbingers (n = 292)	Cell D: Female nonbingers (n = 494)

Once you have the matrix, just take the numbers right out of the cell frequencies and calculate the numbers by hand or with a calculator.

$$\text{The odds of men bingeing} = \frac{273}{292} = .9349$$

$$\text{The odds of women bingeing} = \frac{281}{494} = .5688$$

$$\text{The odds ratio of men's odds to women's odds} = \frac{.9349}{.5688} = 1.64$$

Convince yourself that all you need to know to calculate the odds ratio is in a crosstabulation with cell frequencies shown. You don't always need a computer!

But why would you want to do these calculations? In part, to understand your own data better. Odds ratios are intuitively appealing because they can tell you how much more the odds of an outcome such as bingeing are for two different groups such as men and women. And you really don't need a computer to calculate odds ratios, once you know how many cases fall into each cell.

12.3   Using SPSS for Windows Student Version for the Odds Ratio

But wait a minute. You've read this book so far just so that you could use a computer to do things like this, so let's discuss how to use SPSS to help you assess your data.

If all you need to do is to get the odds ratio for two crosstabulated dichotomous variables in your data, SPSS for Windows Student Version can provide you with this. But you have to make sure your variables meet the precise requirements of SPSS. For SPSS, the trick is that the two variables have to be arranged so that the yes/yes cell is in the upper left corner and the no/no cell is in the lower right corner, as in the matrix we created.

If you use the variables COLLBING and GENDER, the output does not conform to what you need because COLLBING placed its "no" responses in the upper boxes and the "yes" responses in the lower boxes. So we had to rearrange the results of the crosstabulation into that table by hand before calculating the odds ratio by hand.

To have SPSS calculate the odds ratio, recode COLLBING into a variable called BINGE (with 1 = yes, binge; 1 + x, one or more times; and 2 = no, never binge), and then you can crosstabulate BINGE with GENDER.

(Here's a detailed hint: Follow the Transform   Recode   Into Different Variables route. Move COLLBING into the "Numeric Variable" box. Fill the "Output Variable" box with BINGE, and fill the label box with "Binge 1 = yes, binge 1 + x; 2 = no, never binge." Click on "Change." Then click on "Old and New Values." Enter "1" as an old value, and click "Copy Old Value" under "New Value." Click "Add." Then make the old value "0" into the new value "2." Click "Add." Set "System-missing" to "System-missing" and click "Add" again. Click "Continue" and then "OK." How's that for a detailed hint?)

After you've carefully selected the row (BINGE) and column (GENDER) variables in Crosstabs, make sure you click on the box marked "Statistics" and then on the box marked "Risk," as shown in the following figure:

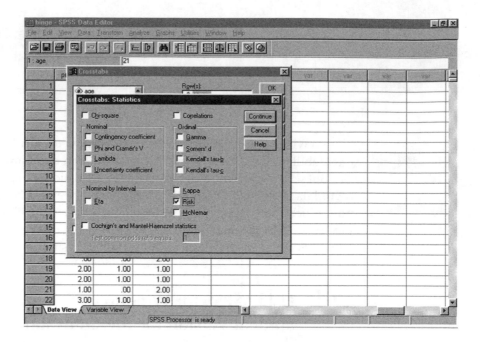

After you run Crosstabs, scroll down until you have the following on your screen:

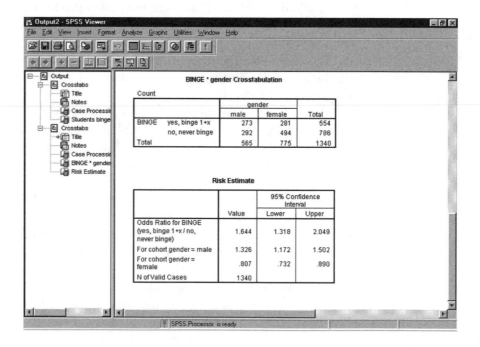

Examine the part of the output that appears below the familiar crosstabulation table. The value of 1.644 is the odds ratio, and the two numbers to its right are the lower and upper bounds of the 95% confidence interval.

The odds ratio can be interpreted readily: It's the same value that you were able to calculate by hand earlier. But what if you're working with data from a random sample? How can you be sure that the odds ratio you observe in your sample data isn't just due to the luck of the sample you drew? Yes, it's the same question you had to ask about your results back when we discussed tests of significance in Chapter 9. You don't want to reach an erroneous conclusion about the entire universe based only on your one set of sample data, so you want some way of checking out how likely these sample results would be if the null hypothesis of no relationship between the two variables were true in the entire universe or population.

For odds ratios, the way to answer this question is to estimate a confidence interval around the odds ratios you observe. The **confidence interval** tells you that some proportion of the time in repeated tests of different samples (usually 95 times out of every 100 times) the population odds ratio should be captured between the lower and upper bounds of the intervals. So the confidence interval is a way of indicating sampling error. If the confidence interval's boundaries include the odds ratio 1.0, it means that the odds ratio isn't statistically significantly different from 1.0, so the association isn't statistically significant. The lower bound of this interval is 1.318 and the higher is 2.049, so we can be reasonably certain that the odds ratio of the population of men versus women college students who drink is between those two bounds.

You can create odds ratios and their confidence intervals by hand with a calculator, although the computations involve using natural logs and thus get a bit more complex. A good advanced statistics book shows you how. So we've found that using either a hand calculator and the crosstabulated output or SPSS for Windows Student Version, we can calculate the bivariate odds ratio and the 95% confidence interval.

12.4   Logistic Regression in SPSS for Windows

But what if we want to proceed beyond estimating the bivariate odds ratio to **logistic regression,** regression analysis involving a dichotomous dependent variable? It turns out that the Advanced Statistics Module for SPSS for Windows contains a very useful Logistic Regression module, so this section will discuss several procedures available only with that module and the full-product version.

Everything in this book up until this point has been obtainable using only SPSS for Windows Student Version, a tribute to how useful for criminal justice researchers it is! If you have access to the Advanced Statistics Module and the Base System of SPSS for Windows, you'll be able to complete this section as well. If not, the section can be a preview of what awaits you when you acquire the use of these advanced features.

How do you know what version or what modules are available to you? Perform the following:

Help → About . . .

You will get a screen that announces what version of SPSS you have (e.g., "SPSS for Windows Student Version Release 11.0") and to whom it's licensed. You can tell if you have the Advanced Statistics module and its logistic regression feature by clicking the following sequence:

Analyze → Regression

If you have the Student Version, the only choices available under "Regression" will be

Linear . . .

Curve Estimation . . .

If this is the case, you won't be able to carry out the actual steps discussed here. But we invite you to come along with us. That way, when you are able to use another version of SPSS that has logistic regression, you'll be ready for this part of your adventure in criminal justice research.

If you have the Standard Version and the Advanced Statistics Module, there will be additional choices under "Regression," including

Binary Logistic . . .

We'll ignore any other choices available so that we can concentrate on Binary Logistic . . .

Let's begin by redoing the analysis of whether gender predicts binge drinking that we did earlier by using crosstabulation and hand calculation.

Enter the following set of commands:

Analyze → Regression → Binary Logistic

and you will be looking at the following screen:

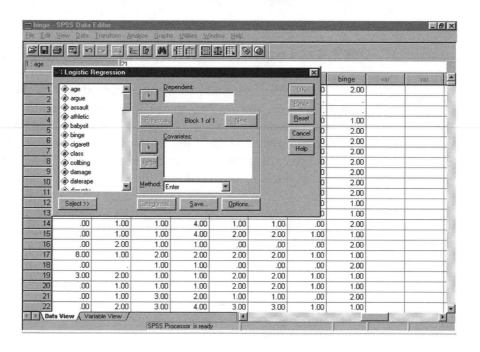

The first step is to find the dependent variable COLLBING in the box of variables on the left of the Logistic Regression window. Select it, and then click on the right-pointing arrow toward the top middle of the screen to move COLLBING into the "Dependent" box.

Next, select the variable GENDER, and click on the right-pointing arrow in the center middle of the screen to move GENDER into the "Covariates" box. Your screen should now look like this:

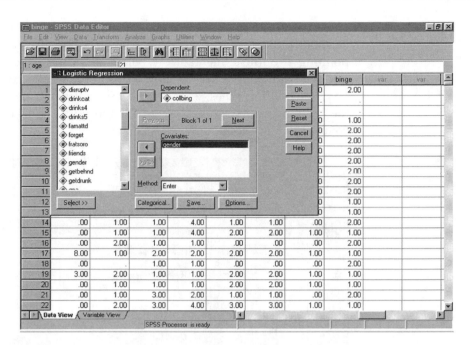

SPSS includes a very useful feature in its logistic regression routines, a way of transforming variables into dichotomies without going through the slightly more elaborate recoding we've discussed earlier. Here's how to use it on GENDER, a variable whose original coding was 1 = male and 2 = female. We know that males binge more than females, so we probably want to show how being male elevates the odds of bingeing relative to the female odds of bingeing (that is, we want to think of being male as a "risk factor" for bingeing). That means that we want to construct a variable in which being female is the reference category, against which the elevated odds associated with being male are compared. While in the Logistic Regression window, click "Categorical" at the bottom of the box and you will be looking at the following:

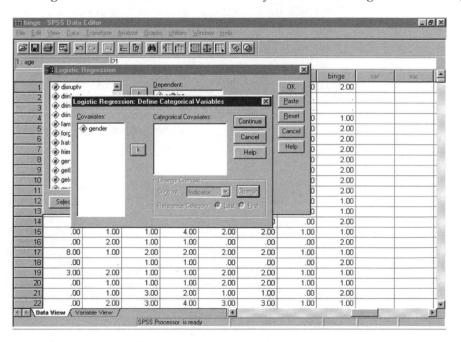

In the Logistic Regression: Define Categorical Variables window, click to select "GENDER" in the "Covariates" box on the left. Click on the right-pointing arrow to move "GENDER" into the "Categorical Covariates" box. On your screen, "Gender(Indicator)" appears. Now click in "Change Contrast" on the downward-pointing "Contrast" menu arrow. Select "Indicator" and then click on "Change" just to its right. Leave the "Reference Category" selected on "Last"; remember that 1 is the code for males, 2 for females, so you want the "last" (females) used as the reference category against which the odds associated with being male is compared. You should now see this:

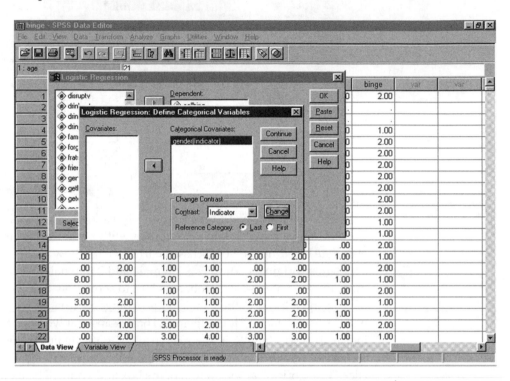

Click on "Continue" to return to the Logistic Regression window. Although there are many other choices you can make, let's keep this as simple as possible. You should see the following:

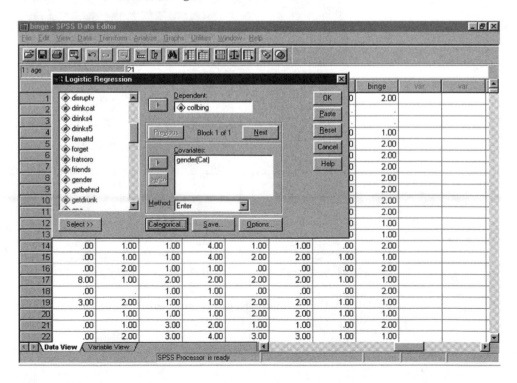

Click on "OK," and you have launched your first logistic regression! You'll get the following new output, which we'll scroll through a little bit at a time.

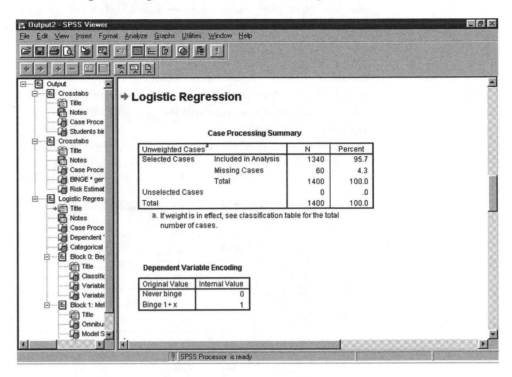

This tells you that you have 1,400 cases, of which 60 were rejected because of missing values, leaving you with 1,340 cases in the analysis. Toward the middle of the page, you learn that your dependent variable has the same values (0 and 1) as you thought it had—no surprises here, fortunately. Let's scroll down the output two more screens' worth:

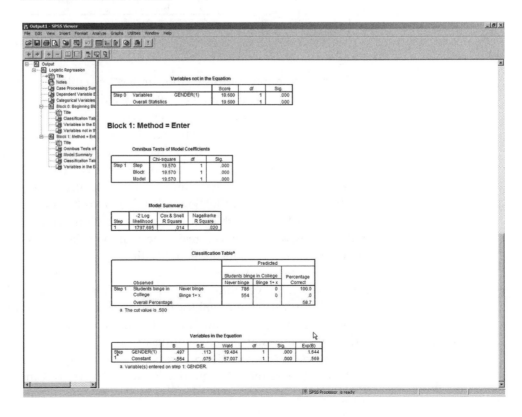

We'll offer interpretations of only what you absolutely need to know. You'll see information for "Block 1: Method = Enter." The "Model Summary" box tells you the fit of the model: The "–2 Log Likelihood" is a measure of fit when the model contains both the intercept and the covariate GENDER.

The output also includes a box called "Omnibus Tests of Model Coefficients." This is a model chi-square test of the null hypothesis that the logistic regression model with a covariate and an intercept is not statistically different from the one with just the intercept. If this model chi-square (with its degrees of freedom specified) is statistically significant, we can reject the null hypothesis that the regression coefficients equal zero.

We will not discuss here how to interpret the next part of the output, the "Classification Table for COLLBING." So let's look at the next part of the output:

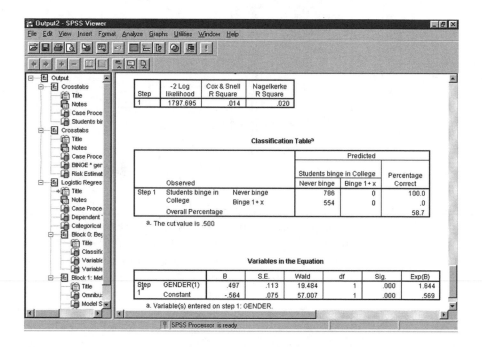

Examine the part of this output under "Variables in the Equation" carefully, and you should find the same results as we discussed earlier. You find the odds ratio stated once again, except it is labeled "Exp(B)" and is found at the far right of the first line, which presents the results for the covariate GENDER. This means exactly what it meant before. But you also find the logistic regression coefficient B, which has a value of .497. If you take out your trusty (rusty?) calculator, you'll find that raising the natural logarithm base e (2.71828) to this power ends up giving you the odds ratio of 1.6436! So that's what "Exp(B)" stands for!

You also find that this coefficient has a significance test run on it—if the p value is below .05, you can reject the null hypothesis that says the coefficient is equal to zero in the underlying population.

What's the confidence interval around this value of the odds ratio? Unfortunately, the versions of logistic regression for SPSS for Windows don't calculate the confidence interval for the odds ratio directly. But if the p value of the coefficient is below .05, you know that the confidence interval doesn't include 1 and is therefore statistically significant.

If you need the confidence interval of the odds ratio, you can calculate it by hand. To estimate the 95% confidence interval, carry out the following steps:

- Multiply 1.96 to the standard error (*SE*) of *B*
- Subtract (add) that quantity from (to) *B*
- Exponentiate (raise the natural logarithm *e* to this power) to estimate the lower (upper) boundaries of the interval.

So in our example, the lower and upper boundaries are given by:

$$(e^{0.4969 - (1.96 \times .1126)}, e^{0.4969 + (1.96 \times .1126)})$$

and the 95% confidence interval of the odds ratio is (1.318, 2.049). For further discussion of this calculation, see a statistics text.

Want to try another logistic regression, this time exploring student drug use? Why don't you explore the association between gender and use of marijuana in the past 30 days? First, formulate a hypothesis about what you expect to find: Men are more likely to use marijuana than women. Next, use the same approach we discussed before to estimate the odds ratio of using marijuana (as indicated by the variable USEGRASS). Examine the odds ratio, and use the confidence interval to judge whether to reject the null hypothesis that the odds ratio equals 1 in the population.

Enter once again the following commands:

Analyze → Regression → Binary Logistic

Use USEGRASS as the dependent variable, and choose GENDER as "Covariates." (If you need to change the whole screen, remember that the "Reset" button will clear all the boxes.)

12.5   Multiple Logistic Regression

Logistic regression is now in widespread use in criminal justice research, in part because it helps us understand the kind of dichotomous dependent variable often encountered in such research. It also sheds light on making decisions that can have only one of two possible outcomes, again similar to many decisions in the real criminal justice system, such as deciding to release on parole or not, deciding to convict or not, or deciding to incarcerate or not.

Multiple logistic regression is particularly useful in criminal justice research. Just as was the case in multiple linear regression, once you understand bivariate logistic regression, **multiple logistic regression,** or logistic regression with a single dichotomous dependent variable and two or more independent variables, is a relatively straightforward next step. But it's a step with big payoffs for the researcher. Multiple logistic regression produces estimates of the odds ratio for each independent variable, taking into account the presence of the other independent variables. In SPSS, it's as simple as adding two or more variables into the "Covariates" box.

There are examples of the use of both bivariate and multiple logistic regression in the paper by Henry Wechsler, George Dowdall, Andrea Davenport, and Sonia Castillo (1995), "Correlates of College Student Binge Drinking" in the *American Journal of Public Health.* To keep things simple, that article recoded several independent variables that were quantitative (such as age and number of hours spent studying) into dichotomies. Other independent variables (such as the items about experiencing the secondhand effects of alcohol use) were qualitative variables with more than two levels, and those too were recoded into dichotomies. Moreover, the dichotomies were recoded if necessary so that the odds ratios are all above 1.0; that is to say, each independent variable is recoded so that its association with bingeing is expressed in terms of raising the odds of bingeing. The result is a set of findings that should be readily interpreted.

You can use the "BINGE.SAV" data set to generate your own set of findings, going beyond that article to explore new variables. Keep in mind that "BINGE.SAV" is a subset of the data used to write the article in the *American Journal of Public Health*; your CD has 1,400 randomly selected cases from the 17,592 cases in the original College Alcohol Study. Your results will almost certainly differ from those for the entire study, although not by much.

Let's begin by estimating the odds ratios of binge drinking for gender (male) and marijuana (use). Just as was the case with multiple linear regression, multiple logistic regression allows us to understand how one independent variable (e.g., gender) is related to the dependent variable (binge drinking), taking into account or controlling for another independent variable (marijuana use). Because each odds ratio takes into account one or more other independent variables, the odds ratio produced in multiple logistic regression is called a **conditional** or **adjusted odds ratio.** To find out the conditional odds ratios for GENDER and USEGRASS, follow the steps we outlined, but enter USEGRASS as the second covariate, with the reference category "did not use marijuana in the past 30 days."

We've introduced logistic regression in what we think of as its simplest form. We've presented examples of dichotomous independent variables because they are simple to interpret in terms of change in the odds ratio. As we've seen, the odds ratio is easy to interpret into understandable terms—perhaps even easier than multiple regression B values and betas.

But logistic regression can also be presented in terms of how a covariate raises or lowers the probability of an outcome, although this is a bit more complex than our presentation. So logistic regression can also be used with quantitative independent variables. Talking about logistic regression beyond its odds ratio form can get complex, so we'll leave that for your future study. Logistic regression is a very powerful set of techniques with great promise for helping criminal justice researchers. If you want to explore this side of the logistic regression story, we can suggest a clear presentation (with criminal justice examples) by Walsh (1987) and even more extensive presentations by Lottes, Adler, and De Maris (1996); Norusis/SPSS (1994, ch. 1); Hamilton (1992, ch. 7); Menard (1995); and Hosmer and Lemeshow (1989), ordered from briefest and simplest to longest and most complex.

12.6   Summary

Logistic regression is widely used in criminal justice research. It helps us understand the kind of dichotomous dependent variable often encountered in such research. It also sheds light on making decisions in the real criminal justice system, such as deciding to release on parole or not, deciding to convict or not, or deciding to incarcerate or not. Multiple logistic regression is particularly useful in producing estimates of conditional or adjusted odds ratios, taking into account several independent variables at the same time.

We've presented just the very basics of both multiple linear regression (in Chapter 10) and logistic regression (in this chapter), to demonstrate how SPSS for

Windows makes the calculation of even these powerful multivariate statistical approaches a straightforward operation. Multiple linear regression demands a quantitative dependent variable, and multiple logistic regression is usually used on a dichotomous dependent variable. Both types can adjust results to take into account the presence of several independent variables, controlling for their impact on the dependent variable. There is much more to be said about both approaches. But you've learned the basics of doing both forms of regression: how to select variables for the models, how to interpret coefficients, how to assess statistical significance or use confidence levels, and how to understand model fit. You're ready to continue your adventure in criminal justice research!

Key Terms

conditional or adjusted odds ratio	multiple logistic regression
confidence interval	odds
dichotomous variables	odds ratio
logistic regression	reference category

Appendix A: Sample Journal Article

Health and Behavioral Consequences of Binge Drinking in College

A National Survey of Students at 140 Campuses

Henry Wechsler, PhD; Andrea Davenport, MPH;
George Dowdall, PhD; Barbara Moeykens, MS; Sonia Castillo, PhD

Objective.—To examine the extent of binge drinking by college students and the ensuing health and behavioral problems that binge drinkers create for themselves and others on their campus.

Design.—Self-administered survey mailed to a national representative sample of US 4-year college students.

Setting.—One hundred forty US 4-year colleges in 1993.

Participants.—A total of 17,592 college students.

Main Outcome Measures.—Self-reports of drinking behavior, alcohol-related health problems, and other problems.

Results.—Almost half (44%) of college students responding to the survey were binge drinkers, including almost one fifth (19%) of the students who were frequent binge drinkers. Frequent binge drinkers are more likely to experience serious health and other consequences of their drinking behavior than other students. Almost half (47%) of the frequent binge drinkers experienced five or more different drinking-related problems, including injuries and engaging in unplanned sex, since the beginning of the school year. Most binge drinkers do not consider themselves to be problem drinkers and have not sought treatment for an alcohol problem. Binge drinkers create problems for classmates who are not binge drinkers. Students who are not binge drinkers at schools with higher binge rates were more likely than students at schools with lower binge rates to experience problems such as being pushed, hit, or assaulted or experiencing an unwanted sexual advance.

Conclusions.—Binge drinking is widespread on college campuses. Programs aimed at reducing this problem should focus on frequent binge drinkers, refer them to treatment or educational programs, and emphasize the harm they cause for students who are not binge drinkers.

—(JAMA. 1994;272:1672-1677)

Heavy episodic or binge drinking poses a danger of serious health and other consequences for alcohol abusers and for others in the immediate environment. Alcohol contributes to the leading causes of accidental death in the United States, such as motor vehicle crashes and falls.[1] Alcohol abuse is seen as contributing to almost half of motor vehicle fatalities, the most important cause of death among young Americans.[2] Unsafe sex—a growing threat with the spread of acquired immunodeficiency syndrome (AIDS) and other sexually transmitted diseases— and unintentional injuries have been associated with alcohol intoxication.[3-5] These findings support the view of college presidents who believe that alcohol abuse is the No. 1 problem on campus.[6]

Despite the fact that alcohol is illegal for most undergraduates, alcohol continues to be widely used on most college campuses today. Since the national study by Straus and Bacon in 1949,[7] numerous subsequent surveys have documented the overwhelming use of alcohol by college students and have pointed to problem drinking among this group.[8-10] Most previous studies of drinking by college students have been conducted on single college campuses and have not used random sampling of students.[9-12] While these studies are in general agreement about the prevalence and consequences of binge drinking, they do not provide a national representative sample of college drinking.

A few large-scale, multicollege surveys have been conducted in recent years. However, these have not selected a representative national sample of colleges, but have used colleges in one state[3] or those participating in a federal program,[5] or have followed a sample of high school seniors through college.[13]

In general, studies of college alcohol use have consistently found higher rates of binge drinking among men than women. However, these studies used the same definition of binge drinking for men and women, without taking into account sex differences in metabolism of ethanol or in body mass.[3,5,9-12,14-17]

The consequences of binge drinking often pose serious risks for drinkers and for others in the college environment. Binge drinking has been associated with unplanned and unsafe sexual activity, physical and sexual assault, unintentional injuries, other criminal violations, interpersonal problems, physical or cognitive impairment, and poor academic performance.[3-5]

This study examines the nature and extent of binge drinking among a representative national sample of students at 140 US 4-year colleges and details the problems such drinking causes for drinkers themselves and for others on their college campus. Binge drinking is defined through a sex-specific measure to take into account sex differences in the dosage effects of ethanol.

Methods

The Colleges

A national sample of 179 colleges was selected from the American Council on Education's list of 4-year colleges and universities accredited by one of the six regional bodies covering the United States. The sample was selected using probability proportionate to enrollment size sampling. All full-time undergraduate students at a university were eligible to be chosen for this study, regardless of the college in which they were enrolled. This sample contained few women-only colleges and few colleges with less than 1000 students. To correct for this problem, an oversample of 15 additional colleges with enrollments of less than 1000 students and 10 all-women's colleges were added to the sample. Nine colleges were subsequently dropped because they were considered inappropriate. These included seminary schools, military schools, and allied health schools.

One hundred forty (72%) of the final sample of 195 colleges agreed to participate. The primary reason stated for nonparticipation by college administrators was inability to provide a random sample of students and their addresses within the time requirements of the study. The 140 participating colleges are located in 40 states and the District of Columbia. They represent a cross-section of US higher education. Two thirds of the colleges sampled are public and one third are private. Approximately two thirds are located in a suburban or urban setting and one third in a small town/rural setting. Four percent are women-only, and 4% are predominantly black institutions.

When the 55 nonparticipating schools were compared with the 140 in the study, the only statistically significant difference found was in terms of enrollment size. Proportionately fewer small colleges (fewer than 1000 students) participated in the study. Since these were oversampled, sufficient numbers are present for statistical analysis.

Sampling Procedures

Colleges were sent a set of specific guidelines for drawing a random sample of students based on the total enrollment of full-time undergraduates. Depending on enrollment size, every xth student was selected from the student registry using a random starting point. A sample of undergraduate students was provided by each of the 140 participating colleges: 215 students at each of 127 colleges, and 108 at each of 13 colleges (12 of which were in the oversample). The final student sample included 28,709 students.

The Questionnaire

The 20-page survey instrument asked students a number of questions about their drinking behavior as well as other health issues. Whenever possible, the survey instrument included questions that had been used previously in other national or large-scale epidemiological studies.[13,14] A drink was defined as a 12-oz (360-mL) can (or bottle) of beer, a 4-oz (120-mL) glass of wine, a 12-oz (360-mL) bottle (or can) of wine cooler, or a shot (1.25 oz [37mL]) of liquor straight or in a mixed drink. The following four questions were used to assess binge drinking: (1) sex; (2) recency of last drink ("never," "not in past year," "within last year but more than 30 days ago," "within 30 days but more than 1 week ago," or "within week"); (3) "Think back over the last two weeks. How many times have you had five or more drinks in a row?" (The use of this question, without specification of time elapsed in a drinking episode, is consistent with standard practice in recent research on alcohol use among this population.[3,5,13,18]); and (4) "During the last two weeks, how many times have you had four drinks in a row (but no more than that) (for women)?" Missing responses to any of these four questions excluded the student from the binging analyses.

Students were also asked the extent to which they had experienced any of the following 12 problems as a consequence of their drinking since the beginning of the school year: have a hang-over; miss a class; get behind in school-work; do something you later regretted; forget where you were or what you did; argue with friends; engage in unplanned sexual activity; not use protection when you had sex; damage property; get into trouble with campus or local police; get hurt or injured; or require medical treatment for an alcohol overdose. They were also asked if, since the beginning of the school year, they had experienced any of the following eight problems caused by other students' drinking: been insulted or humiliated; had a serious argument or quarrel; been pushed, hit, or assaulted; had your property damaged; had to "babysit" or take care of another student who drank too much; had your studying or sleep interrupted; experienced an unwanted sexual advance; or had been a victim of sexual assault or date rape.

The Mailing

The initial mailing of questionnaires to students began on February 5, 1993. By the end of March, 87% of the final group of questionnaires had been received, with another 10% in April and 2% in May and June. There are no discernible differences in binging rates among questionnaires received in each of the 5 months of the survey. Mailings were modified to take into account spring break, so that students would be responding about their binge drinking behavior during a 2-week time on campus. Responses were voluntary and anonymous. Four separate mailings, usually 10 days apart, were sent at each college: a questionnaire, a reminder postcard, a second questionnaire, and a second reminder postcard. To encourage students to respond, the following cash awards were offered: one $1000 award to a student whose name was drawn from among students responding within 1 week, and one $500 award and ten $100 awards to students selected from all those who responded.

The Response Rate

The questionnaires were mailed to 28,709 students. Overall, 3082 students were eliminated from the sample because of school reports of incorrect addresses, withdrawal from school, or leaves of absence, reducing the sample size to 25,627. A total of 17,592 students returned questionnaires, yielding an overall student response rate of approximately 69%. The response rate is likely to be underestimated since it does not take into account all of the students who may not have received questionnaires. At 104 of the colleges, response rates were between 60% and 80%, and only six colleges had response rates less than 50%. Response rate was not associated with the binging rate (ie, the Pearson correlation coefficient between the binge drinking rate at the college and the response rate was 0.06 with a P value of .46).

When responses of early and late responders to the survey were compared, there were no significant differences in the percent of nondrinkers, nonbinge drinkers, and binge drinkers. In the case of 11,557 students who could be classified as early or late responders, there was no significant difference in terms of binge drinking (43% for the early responders vs 42% for the late responders). An additional short form of the questionnaire was mailed to a segment of students who had failed to return the questionnaire. The rate of binge drinking of these nonresponders did not differ from that of responders to the original student survey.

Data Analysis

All statistical analyses were carried out using the current version of SAS.[19] Comparisons of unweighted and weighted sample results suggested little difference between them, so unweighted results are reported here. Chi-square analyses among students who had a drink in the past year were used to compare nonbinge drinkers, infrequent binge drinkers, and binge drinkers. Binge drinking was defined as the consumption of five or more drinks in a row for men and four or more drinks in a row for women during the 2 weeks prior to the survey. An extensive analysis showed that this sex-specific measure accurately indicates an equivalent likelihood of alcohol-related problems. In this article, the term "binge drinker" is used to refer to students who binged at least once in the previous 2 weeks. Frequent binge drinkers were defined as those who binged three or more times in the past 2 weeks and infrequent binge drinkers as those who binged one or two times in the past 2 weeks. Nonbinge drinkers were those who had consumed alcohol in the past year, but had not binged.

Logistic regression analyses were used to examine how much more likely frequent binge drinkers were to experience an alcohol-related problem or driving behavior compared with nonbinge drinkers, and to compare infrequent binge drinkers with nonbinge drinkers. Odds ratios were adjusted for age, sex, race, marital status, and parents' college education.

In examining secondary binge effects, schools were divided into three groups on the basis of the percentage of students who were binge drinkers at each school. The responses of students who had not binged in the past 2 weeks (including those who had never had a drink) and who resided in dormitories, fraternities, or sororities were compared through χ^2 analyses across the three school types. High-level binge schools (where 51% or more students were binge drinkers) included 44 schools with 6084 students; middle-level binge schools (36% to 50% of students were binge drinkers) included 53 schools with 6455 students; and low-level binge schools (35% or less of students were binge drinkers) included 43 schools with 5043 students (for 10 students, information regarding school of attendance was missing). For two of the problems that occurred primarily or almost exclusively to women (sexual assault and experiencing an unwanted sexual advance), only women were included in the analyses.

Results

Characteristics of the Student Sample

This analysis is based on data from 17,592 undergraduate students at 140 US 4-year colleges. The student sample includes more women (58%) than men (42%), due in part to the inclusion of six all-women's institutions. This compares with national 1991 data that report 51% of undergraduates at 4-year institutions are women.[20] The sample is predominantly white (81%). This coincides exactly with national 1991 data that report 81% of undergraduates at 4-year institutions are white.[20] Minority groups included Asian/Pacific Islander (7%), Spanish/ Hispanic (7%), black/African American (6%), and Native American (1%). The age of the students was distributed as follows: 45% younger than 21 years, 38% aged 21 to 23 years, and 17% aged 24 years or more. There were slightly more juniors (25%) and seniors (26%) in the sample than freshmen (20%) and sophomores (19%), probably because 30% of the students were transfers from other institutions.

Distribution of Colleges by Percentage of Binge Drinkers [Figure 1]

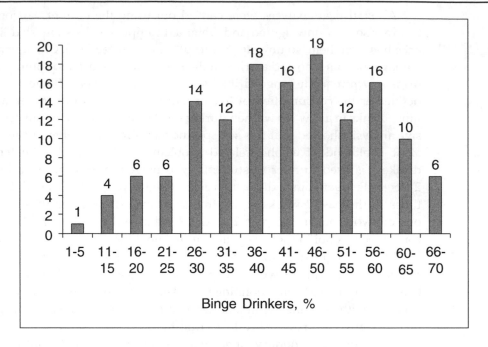

Binge Drinkers, %

Ten percent of the students were in their fifth undergraduate year of school or beyond. Religious affiliation was discerned by asking students in which of the following religions they were raised: Protestant (44%), Catholic (36%), Jewish (3%), Muslim (1%), other (4%), and none (12%). Religion was cited as an important to very important activity among 36% of the students. Approximately three of five students (59%) worked for pay. Approximately half (49%) of the students had a grade-point average of A, A−, or B+.

Extent of Binge Drinking

Because of missing responses, there were 496 students excluded from binging analyses (ie, 17,096 were included). Most students drank alcohol during the past year. Only about one of six (16%) were nondrinkers (15% of the men and 16% of the women). About two of five students (41%) drank but were nonbinge drinkers (35% of the men and 45% of the women). Slightly fewer than half (44%) of the students were binge drinkers (50% of the men and 39% of the women). About half of this group of binge drinkers, or about one in five students (19%) overall, were frequent binge drinkers (overall, 23% of the men and 17% of the women).

Binge Drinking Rates at Colleges

Figure [1] shows that binge drinking rates vary extensively among the 140 colleges in the study. While 1% of the students were binge drinkers at the school with the lowest rate of binge drinkers, 70% of students were binge drinkers at the school with the highest rate. At 44 schools, more than half of the responding students were binge drinkers.

When the 140 colleges were divided into levels of binging rate, χ^2 analyses showed that several college characteristics were individually associated

Table 1   Drinking Styles of Students Who Were Nonbinge Drinkers, Infrequent Binge Drinkers, or Frequent Binge Drinkers*

Drinking Styles	Nonbinge Drinkers, %†		Infrequent Binge Drinkers, %‡		Frequent Binge Drinkers, %§	
	Men (n = 2539)	Women (n = 4400)	Men (n = 1968)	Women (n = 2130)	Men (n = 1630)	Women (n = 1684)
Drank on 10 or more occasions in the past 30 d‖	3	1	11	6	61	39
Usually binges when drinks	4	4	43	45	83	82
Was drunk three or more times in the past month	2	1	17	13	70	55
Drinks to get drunk¶	22	18	49	44	73	68

* Chi-square comparisons of students who were nonbinge drinkers, infrequent binge drinkers, and frequent binge drinkers and each of the four drinking styles were significant for men and women separately at $P < .001$. Sample sizes vary slightly for each question because of missing values. Binging is defined as four or more drinks for women and five or more drinks for men.
† Students who consumed alcohol in the past year, but did not binge.
‡ Students who binged one or two times in a 2-week period.
§ Students who binged three or more times in a 2-week period.
‖ Question asked, "On how many occasions have you had a drink of alcohol in the past 30 days?" Response categories were 1 to 2 occasions, 3 to 5 occasions, 6 to 9 occasions, 10 to 19 occasions, 20 to 39 occasions, and 40 or more occasions.
¶ Says that to get drunk is an important reason for drinking.

(at $P < .05$) with binging rate. Colleges located in the Northeast or North Central regions of the United States (compared with those in the West or South) or those that were residential (compared with commuter schools, where 90% or more of the students lived off campus)[21] tended to have higher rates of binging. In addition, traditionally black institutions and women's colleges had lower binge rates than schools that were not traditionally black or were coeducational colleges. Other characteristics, such as whether the college was public or private and its enrollment size, were not related to binge drinker rates.

Examination of whether college alcohol programs and policies have any association with binge drinking will be presented in a separate publication. There is little evidence to conclude that current policies have had strong impacts on overall drinking levels. Preliminary analyses suggest that individual binge drinking is less likely if the institution does not have any alcohol outlets within 1 mile of campus, or if it prohibits alcohol use for all persons (even those older than 21 years) on campus.

Drinking Patterns of Binge Drinkers

Table 1 indicates that our designations of binge drinker and frequent binge drinker are strongly indicative of a drinking style that involves more frequent and heavier drinking. Furthermore, intoxication (often intentional) is associated with binge drinking in men and women.

Binge drinking is related to age. Students who are in the predominant college age group (between 17 and 23 years) have much higher binging rates than older students. However, within the predominant college age group, students who are younger than the legal drinking age of 21 years do not differ in binging rates from students aged 21 to 23 years. In contrast to the modest effects of age, there is no relationship between year in school and binging, with rates of binge drinking virtually identical among students across the years of college attendance.

Alcohol-Related Health and Other Problems

There is a strong, positive relationship between the frequency of binge drinking and alcohol-related health and other problems reported by the students (Table 2). Among the more serious alcohol-related problems, the frequent binge drinkers were seven to 10 times more likely than the nonbinge drinkers to not use protection when having sex, to engage in unplanned sexual activity, to get into trouble with campus police, to damage property, or to get hurt or injured. A similar comparison between the infrequent binge drinkers and nonbinge drinkers also shows a strong relationship.

Men and women reported similar frequencies for most of the problems, except for damaging property or getting into trouble with the campus police. Among the frequent binge drinkers, 35% of the men and 9% of the women reported damaging property, and 16% of the men and 6% of the women reported getting into trouble with the campus police.

Drinking and Driving

There is also a positive relationship between binge drinking and driving under the influence of alcohol (Table 3). A large proportion of the student population reported driving after drinking alcohol. Binge drinkers, particularly frequent binge drinkers, reported significantly ($P < .001$) higher frequencies of dangerous driving behaviors than non-binge drinkers.

Number of Problems

Nearly half (47%) of the frequent binge drinkers reported having experienced five or more of the 12 problems listed in Table 2 (omitting hangover and including driving after drinking) since the beginning of the school year, compared with 14% of infrequent binge drinkers and 3% of nonbinge drinkers. The adjusted odds ratios indicate that frequent binge drinkers were 25 times more likely than nonbinge drinkers to experience five or more of these problems, while the infrequent binge drinkers were five times more likely than nonbinge drinkers to experience five or more problems.

Self-Assessment of Drinking Problem

Few students describe themselves as having a drinking problem. When asked to classify themselves in terms of their current alcohol use, less than 1% of the total sample (0.2%), including only 0.6% of the frequent binge drinkers, designated

Table 2   Risk of Alcohol-Related Problems Comparing Students Who Were Infrequent Binge Drinkers or Frequent Binge Drinkers With Students Who Were Nonbinge Drinkers Among College Students Who Had a Drink in the Past Year*

Reporting Problem	Nonbinge Drinkers, % (n = 6894)	Infrequent Binge Drinkers		Frequent Binge Drinkers	
		% (n = 4090)	Adjusted OR (95% CI)†	% (n = 3291)	Adjusted OR (95% CI)‡
Have a hangover	30	75	6.28 (5.73-6.87)	90	17.62 (15.50-20.04)
Do something you regret	14	37	3.31 (3.00-3.64)	63	8.98 (8.11-9.95)
Miss a class	8	30	4.66 (4.15-5.24)	61	16.58 (14.73-18.65)
Forget where you were or what you did	8	26	3.62 (3.22-4.06)	54	11.23 (10.05-12.65)
Get behind in school work	6	21	3.70 (3.26-4.20)	46	11.43 (10.09-12.94)
Argue with friends	8	22	3.06 (2.72-3.46)	42	7.77 (6.90-8.74)
Engage in unplanned sexual activity	8	20	2.78 (2.46-3.13)	41	7.17 (6.37-8.06)
Get hurt or injured	2	9	3.65 (3.01-4.43)	23	10.43 (8.70-12.52)
Damage property	2	8	3.09 (2.53-3.77)	22	9.48 (7.86-11.43)
Not use protection when having sex	4	10	2.90 (2.45-3.42)	22	7.11 (6.07-8.34)
Get into trouble with campus or local police	1	4	2.50 (1.92-3.26)	11	6.92 (5.44-8.81)
Require medical treatment of alcohol overdose	<1	<1	NS	1	2.81 (1.39-5.68)
Have five or more alcohol-related problems since the beginning of the school year§	3	14	4.95 (4.17-5.89)	47	25.10 (21.30-29.58)

*Problem occurred not at all or one or more times. Chi-square comparisons of nonbinge drinkers, infrequent binge drinkers, and frequent binge drinkers and each of the problems are significant at $P < .001$, except for alcohol overdose ($P = .002$). Sample sizes vary slightly for each problem because of missing values. OR indicates odds ratio; CI, confidence interval. See Table 1 for explanation of drinking classification.
†Adjusted ORs of infrequent binge drinkers vs nonbinge drinkers are significant at $P < .001$.
‡Adjusted ORs of frequent binge drinkers vs nonbinge drinkers are significant at $P < .001$, except for alcohol overdose, $P < .01$.
§Excludes hangover and includes driving after drinking as one of the problems.

themselves as problem drinkers. In addition, few students have ever sought treatment for a problem with alcohol.

A somewhat larger proportion of students indicated that they had ever had a drinking problem. Slightly more than one fifth (22%) of the frequent binge drinkers thought that they ever had a drinking problem, compared with 12% of the infrequent binge drinkers and 7% of the nonbinge drinkers.

Table 3 Alcohol-Related Driving Behavior for a 30-Day Period Comparing Students Who Were Infrequent Binge Drinkers or Frequent Binge Drinkers With Students Who Were Nonbinge Drinkers*

Driving Behavior	Nonbinge Drinkers		Infrequent Binge Drinkers			Frequent Binge Drinkers		
	Men, % (n = 2531)	Women, % (n = 4393)	Men, % (n = 1975)	Women, % (n = 2132)	Adjusted OR (95% CI)†	Men, % (n = 1630)	Women, % (n = 1684)	Adjusted OR (95% CI)‡
Drove after drinking alcohol	20	13	47	33	5.13 (4.67-5.64)	62	49	10.33 (9.34-11.42)
Drove after having five or more drinks	2	1	18	7	22.23 (16.89-29.26)	40	21	74.30 (56.56-97.58)
Rode with a driver who was high or drunk	7	7	23	22	4.73 (4.20-5.32)	53	48	15.97 (14.22-17.95)

*Chi-square comparisons of nonbinge drinkers, infrequent binge drinkers, and frequent binge drinkers and each of the three driving behaviors were all significant for men and women separately at $P < .001$. Sample sizes vary slightly for each question because of missing values. OR indicates odds ratio; CI, confidence interval. See Table 1 for explanation of drinking classification.

†Adjusted OR of infrequent binge drinkers vs nonbinge drinkers (sex combined) are significant at $P < .001$.

‡Adjusted OR of frequent binge drinkers vs nonbinge drinkers (sex combined) are significant at $P < .001$.

Table 4   Students Experiencing Secondary Binge Effects (Based on Students Who Were Not Binge Drinkers and Living in Dormitories, Fraternities, or Soronties)*

| Secondary Binge Effect | Low, % (n = 801) | School's Binging Level | | | |
| | | Middle | | High | |
		% (n = 1115)	Adjusted OR (95% CI)†	% (n = 1064)	Adjusted OR (95% CI)‡
Been insulted or humiliated	21	30	1.6 (1.3-2.1)	34	1.9 (1.5-2.3)
Had a serious argument or quarrel	13	18	1.3 (1.0-1.7)	20	1.5 (1.1-2.0)
Been pushed, hit, or assaulted	7	10	1.4 (1.0-2.1)	13	2.0 (1.4-2.8)
Had your property damaged	6	13	2.0 (1.4-2.8)	15	2.3 (1.6-3.2)
Had to take care of drunken student	31	47	1.9 (1.6-2.3)	54	2.5 (2.0-3.0)
Had your studying/ sleep interrupted	42	64	2.3 (1.9-2.8)	68	2.6 (2.2-3.2)
Expenenced an unwanted sexual advance§	15	21	1.7 (1.2-2.3)	26	2.1 (1.5-2.8)
Been a victim of sexual assault or date rape§	2	1	NS	2	NS
Experienced at least one of the above problems	62	82	2.8 (2.3-3.5)	87	4.1 (3.2-5.2)

*OR indicates odds ratio; CI, confidence interval.
†Adjusted ORs of students at schools with middle levels of binging vs students at schools with low levels are significant at $P < .05$.
‡Adjusted ORs of students at schools with high levels of binging vs students at schools with low levels are significant at $P < .05$.
§Based on women only.

Secondary Binge Effects

Table 4 reports on the percentage of nonbinging students who experienced "secondary binge effects," each of eight types of problems due to other students' drinking at each of the three different school types (ie, schools with high, middle, and low binge levels). For seven of the eight problems studied, students at schools with high and middle binge levels were more likely than students at schools with low binge levels to experience problems as a result of the drinking behaviors of others. Odds ratios (adjusted for age, sex, race, marital status, and parents' college education) indicated that nonbinging students at schools with the high binge levels were more likely than nonbinging students at schools with low binge levels to experience secondary binge effects.

The odds of experiencing at least one of the eight problems was roughly 4:1 when students at schools with high binge levels were compared with students at schools with low binge levels.

Binge Drinking in High School

Most students reported the same drinking behavior in high school as in college. Almost half (47%) had not been binge drinkers in high school and did not binge in college, while one fifth (22%) binged in high school and in college. One fifth (22%) of the students were binge drinkers in college but not in high school, while 10% were not binge drinkers at the time of the survey in college, but reported having been binge drinkers in high school.

Comment

To our knowledge, this is the first study that has used a representative national sample, and the first large-scale study to measure binge drinking under a sex-specific definition. Forty-four percent of the college students in this study were classified as binge drinkers. This finding is consistent with the findings of other national studies such as the University of Michigan's Monitoring the Future Project, which found that 41% of college students were binge drinkers,[13] and the Core Alcohol and Drug Survey, which found that 42% of college students were binge drinkers.[5] All three studies used a definition of binging over a 2-week period, but the other studies used the same five-drink measure for both sexes. Binge drinking was defined in terms of the number of drinks consumed in a single episode. No attempt was made to specify the duration of time for each episode. Future research might examine whether subgroup differences exist in duration and whether such differences are linked to outcomes.

A possible limitation of surveys using self-reports of drinking behavior pertains to the validity of responses; however, a number of studies have confirmed the validity of self-reports of alcohol and substance use.[22-24] Findings indicate that if a self-report bias exists, it is largely limited to the heaviest use group[25] and should not affect such a conservative estimate of heavy volume as five drinks.

The results confirm that binge drinking is widespread on college campuses. Overall, almost half of all students were binge drinkers. One fifth of all students were frequent binge drinkers (had three or more binge drinking occasions in the past 2 weeks) and were deeply involved in a lifestyle characterized by frequent and deliberate intoxication. Frequent binge drinkers are much more likely to experience serious health and other consequences of their drinking behavior than other students. Almost half of them have experienced five or more alcohol-related problems since the beginning of the school year, one of three report they were hurt or injured, and two in five engaged in unplanned sexual activity. Frequent binge drinkers also report drinking and driving: Three of five male frequent binge drinkers drove after drinking some alcohol in the 30 days prior to the survey, and two of five drove after having five or more drinks. A recent national report that reviewed published studies concluded that alcohol was involved in two thirds of college student suicides, in 90% of campus rapes, and in 95% of violent crime on campus.[26]

Almost a third of the colleges in the study have a majority of students who binge. Not only do these binge drinkers put themselves at risk, they also create problems for their fellow students who are not binge drinking. Students who did not binge and who reside at schools with high levels of binge drinkers were up to three times as likely to report being bothered by the drinking-related behaviors of other students than students who did not binge and who reside at schools with lower levels of binge drinkers. These problems included being pushed, hit, or assaulted and experiencing an unwanted sexual advance.

Effective interventions face a number of challenges. Drinking is not typically a behavior learned in college and often continues patterns established earlier. In fact, one of three students in the present study was already a binge drinker in the year before college.

The prominence of drinking on college campuses reflects its importance in the wider society, but drinking has traditionally occupied a unique place in campus life. Despite the overall decline in drinking in US society, recent time-trend studies have failed to show a corresponding decrease in binge drinking on college campuses.[3,13] The variation in binge drinking rates among the colleges in this study suggest that colleges may create and unwittingly perpetuate their own drinking cultures through selection, tradition, policy, and other strategies. On many campuses, drinking behavior that would elsewhere be classified as alcohol abuse may be socially acceptable, or even socially attractive, despite its documented implication in automobile crashes, other injury, violence, suicide, and high-risk sexual behavior.

The scope of the problem makes immediate results of any interventions highly unlikely. Colleges need to be committed to large-scale and long-term behavior change strategies, including referral of alcohol abusers to appropriate treatment. Frequent binge drinkers on college campuses are similar to other alcohol abusers elsewhere in their tendency to deny that they have a problem. Indeed, their youth, the visibility of others who drink the same way, and the shelter of the college community may make them less likely to recognize the problem. In addition to addressing the health problems of alcohol abusers, a major effort should address the large group of students who are not binge drinkers on campus who are adversely affected by the alcohol-related behavior of binge drinkers.

This study was supported by the Robert Wood Johnson Foundation. We wish to thank the following persons who assisted with the project: Lloyd Johnston, PhD, Thomas J. Mangione, PhD, Anthony M. Roman, MD, Nan Laird, PhD, Jeffrey Hansen, Avtar Khalsa, MSW, and Marianne Lee, MPA.

References

1. US Dept of Health and Human Services. *Alcohol and Health.* Rockville, Md: National Institute on Alcohol Abuse and Alcoholism; 1990.

2. Robert Wood Johnson Foundation. *Substance Abuse: The Nation's Number One Health Problem. Key Indicators for Policy.* Princeton, NJ: Robert Wood Johnson Foundation; October 1993.

3. Wechsler H, Issac N. 'Binge' drinkers at Massachusetts colleges: prevalence, drinking styles, time trends, and associated problems. *JAMA*, 1992:267:2929-2931.

4. Hanson DJ, Engs RC. College students' drinking problems: a national study, 1982-1991. *Psychol Rep.* 1992;71:39-42.

5. Presley CA, Meilman PW, Lyerla R. *Alcohol and Drugs on American College Campuses: Use, Consequence, and Perceptions of the Campus Environment, Volume I: 1989-1991.* Carbondale, Ill: The Core Institute, 1993.

6. The Carnegie Foundation for the Advancement of Teaching. *Campus Life: In Search of Community.* Princeton, NJ: Princeton University Press: 1990.

7. Straus R, Bacon SD. *Drinking in College.* New Haven, Conn: Yale University Press: 1953.

8. Berkowitz AD, Perkins HW. Problem drinking among college students: a review of recent research. *J Am Coll Health.* 1986;35:21-28.

9. Saitz R, Elandt D. College student drinking studies: 1976-1985. *Contemp Drug Probl.* 1986;13:117-157.

10. Haworth-Hoeppner S, Globetti G, Stem J, Morasco F. The quantity and frequency of drinking among undergraduates at a southern university. *Int J Addict.* 1989;24:829-857.

11. Liljestrand P. Quality in college student drinking research: conceptual and methodological issues. *J Alcohol Drug Educ.* 1993;38:1-36.

12. Hughes S, Dodder R. Alcohol consumption patterns among college populations. *J Coll Student Personnel.* 1983;20:257-264.

13. Johnston LD, O'Malley PM, Bachman JG. *Drug Use Among American High School Seniors, College Students, and Young Adults, 1975-1990, Volume 2.* Washington, DC: Government Printing Office; 1991. US Dept of Health and Human Services publication ADM 91-1835.

14. Wechsler H, McFadden M. Drinking among college students in New England. *J Stud Alcohol.* 1979;40:969-996.

15. O'Hare TM. Drinking in college: consumption patterns, problems, sex differences, and legal drinking age. *J Stud Alcohol.* 1990;51:536-541.

16. Engs RC, Hanson DJ. The drinking patterns and problems of college students: 1983. *J Alcohol Drug Educ.* 1985;31:65-83.

17. Brennan AF, Walfish S, AuBuchon P. Alcohol use and abuse in college students, I: a review of individual and personality correlates. *Int J Addict.* 1986;21:449-474.

18. Room R. Measuring alcohol consumption in the US: methods and rationales. In: Clark WB, Hilton ME, eds. *Alcohol in America: Drinking Practices and Problems.* Albany: State University of New York Press; 1991:26-50.

19. SAS Institute Inc. *SAS/STAT User's Guide Release 6.03 ed.* Cary, NC: SAS Institute Inc; 1988.

20. US Dept of Education. *Digest of Educational Statistics.* Washington, DC: National Center of Educational Statistics; 1993;180,205.

21. *Barron's Profiles of American Colleges.* Hauppauge, NY: Barron's Educational Series Inc; 1992.

22. Midanik L. Validity of self-reported alcohol use: a literature review and assessment. *Br J Addict.* 1988;83:1019-1030.

23. Cooper AM, Sobell MB, Sobell LC, Maisto SA. Validity of alcoholics' self-reports: duration data. *Int J Addict.* 1981;16:401-406.

24. Reinisch OJ, Bell RM, Ellickson PL. *How Accurate Are Adolescent Reports of Drug Use?* Santa Monica, Calif: RAND: 1991. RAND publication N-3189-CHF.

25. Room R. Survey vs sales data for the US. *Drink Drug Pract Surv.* 1971;3:15-16.

26. CASA Commission on Substance Abuse at Colleges and Universities. *Rethinking Rites of Passage: Substance Abuse on America's Campuses.* New York, NY: Columbia University: June 1994.

Appendix B: College Alcohol Study Questionnaire

Please complete the questionnaire as soon as possible.

Indicate your answers by checking off your responses.

Your answers are anonymous. Do not write your name on the questionnaire.

Your participation is, of course, voluntary. You do not need to answer any question which makes you feel uncomfortable.

Thank you for your help. We do hope you will take part and let your views be represented.

Respondent identification number   **CODE LEADING ZEROES—ID:** ____

1. How old are you?   **AGE:** ____
  [ ] 15
  [ ] 16
  [ ] 17
  [ ] 18
  [ ] 19
  [J 20
  [ ] 21
  [ ] 22
  [ ] 23
  [ ] 24
  [ ] 25
  [ ] 26 or older

2. Are you male or female?   **GENDER:** ____
  [ ] Male
  [ ] Female

3. What is your current year in school?   **CLASS:** ____
  [ ] Freshman (I st year)
  [ ] Sophomore (2nd year)

Questionnaire taken from the Harvard School of Public Health College Alcohol Study.

[ ] Junior (3rd year)
[ ] Senior (4th year)
[ ] 5th year or beyond

4. **Where do you currently live? (Choose one answer)**   **LIVEWITH:** ____
   [ ] Single sex residence hall or dormitory
   [ ] Co-ed residence hall or dormitory
   [ ] Fraternity or sorority
   [ ] Other university housing
   [ ] Co-op or university affiliated group house
   [ ] Off-campus house or apartment

5. **Are you a member of a fraternity or sorority?**   **FRATSORO:** ____
   [ ] Yes
   [ ] No

6. **How important is it for you to participate in the following activities at college? (Choose one answer in each row.)**

		Very Important	Important	Somewhat Important	Not at all Important	
a.	Athletics	[ ]	[ ]	[ ]	[ ]	**ATHLETIC:** ____
e.	Religion	[ ]	[ ]	[ ]	[ ]	**RELIGION:** ____
h.	Parties	[ ]	[ ]	[ ]	[ ]	**PARTIES:** ____

The following questions ask about how much you drink. A "drink" means any of the following:
   A 12-ounce can (or bottle) of beer
   A 4-ounce glass of wine
   A 12-ounce bottle (or can) of wine cooler
   A shot of liquor straight or in a mixed drink

7. **Think back over the last two weeks:**   **DRINKS5:** ____
   How many times have you had 5 or more drinks in a row?
   [ ] None   **SKIP TO QUESTION C3**
   [ ] Once
   [ ] Twice
   [ ] 3 to 5 times
   [ ] 6 to 9 times
   [ ] 10 or more times

8. **During the last two weeks:**   **DRINKS4:** ____
   How many times have you had four drinks in a row (but no more than that)?
   [ ] None
   [ ] Once
   [ ] Twice
   [ ] 3 to 5 times
   [ ] 6 to 9 times
   [ ] 10 or more times

9. **When did you last have a drink**   **LASTDRNK:** ____
   (that is more than just a few sips)?
   (Exclude use in religious ceremonies)
   [ ] I have never had a drink
   [ ] Not in the past year
   [ ] More than 30 days ago, but less than a year ago
   [ ] More than a week ago, but less than 30 days ago
   [ ] Within the last week

**Answer question 10 and 11 only if
you have had a drink in the <u>past 30 days.</u>**

10. **How many drinks in a row does it usually**   **GETDRUNK:** ____
    take you to get drunk? (By drunk we mean
    unsteady, dizzy or sick to your stomach.)
    (Choose one answer)

    [ ] 1 drink or less   [ ] 6 drinks
    [ ] 2 drinks   [ ] 7 drinks
    [ ] 3 drinks   [ ] 8 drinks
    [ ] 4 drinks   [ ] 9 drinks or more
    [ ] 5 drinks   [ ] Don't know or don't get drunk

11. **Since the <u>beginning of the school year,</u> how often has your drinking caused**
    you to . . . (Choose one answer in each row)

		Not at All	Once	Twice or More		
a.	have a hangover	[ ]	[ ]	[ ]	**HANGOVER:**	____
b.	miss a class	[ ]	[ ]	[ ]	**MSSCLASS:**	____
c.	get behind in school work	[ ]	[ ]	[ ]	**GETBEHND:**	____
d.	do something you later regretted	[ ]	[ ]	[ ]	**REGRET:**	____
e.	forget where you were or what you did	[ ]	[ ]	[ ]	**FORGET:**	____
f.	argue with friends	[ ]	[ ]	[ ]	**ARGUE:**	____
g.	engage in unplanned sexual activity	[ ]	[ ]	[ ]	**UNPLANSX:**	____
h.	not use protection when you had sex	[ ]	[ ]	[ ]	**UNSAFESX:**	____
i.	damage property	[ ]	[ ]	[ ]	**DAMAGE:**	____
j.	get into trouble with the campus or local police	[ ]	[ ]	[ ]	**POLICE:**	____
k.	get hurt or injured	[ ]	[ ]	[ ]	**INJURY:**	____
l.	require medical treatment for an alcohol overdose	[ ]	[ ]	[ ]	**OVERDOSE:**	____

12. How would you best describe yourself in terms of your current use of alcohol?

SELFRATE: ____

[ ] Abstainer
[ ] Abstainer-former problem drinker in recovery
[ ] Infrequent drinking
[ ] Light drinker
[ ] Moderate drinker
[ ] Heavy drinker
[ ] Problem drinker

13. Since the <u>beginning of the school year</u>, how often have you experienced any of the following <u>because of other</u> <u>students' drinking?</u> (Choose one answer in each row)

	Not at All	Once	Twice or More		
a. Been insulted or humiliated	[ ]	[ ]	[ ]	INSULT:	____
b. Had a serious argument or quarrel	[ ]	[ ]	[ ]	QUARREL:	____
c. Been pushed, hit or assaulted	[ ]	[ ]	[ ]	ASSAULT:	____
d. Had your property damaged	[ ]	[ ]	[ ]	VANDAL:	____
e. Had to "babysit" or take care of another student who drank too much	[ ]	[ ]	[ ]	BABYSIT:	____
f. Had your studying or sleep interrupted	[ ]	[ ]	[ ]	DISRUPTV:	____
g. Experienced an unwanted sexual advance	[ ]	[ ]	[ ]	PROPOSTN:	____
h. Been a victim of sexual assault or "date rape"	[ ]	[ ]	[ ]	DATERAPE:	____

14. How often, if ever, have you used any of the drugs listed below. Do not include anything you used under a doctor's orders. (Choose one answer in each row)

	Never Used	Used, but NOT In Past 12 Months	Used, But NOT In Past 30 Days	Used in Past 30 Days		
a. Marijuana (or hashish)	[ ]	[ ]	[ ]	[ ]	USEGRASS:	____
m. Cigarettes	[1	[1	[ ]	[1	CIGARETT:	____

15. Have you ever had sexual intercourse?

HADSEX: ____

[ ] Yes
[ ] No   **SKIP TO QUESTION 17**

16. **How many people have you had sexual intercourse with in the <u>past 30 days?</u>**   **SEXPARTN:** ____
    [ ] 0
    [ ] 1
    [ ] 2 or more

17. **How many close student friends do you have?**   **FRIENDS:** ____
    [ ] None
    [ ] One
    [ ] Two
    [ ] Three
    [ ] Four
    [ ] Five or more

18. **Which of the following best describes your grade point average so far this year?**   **GPA:** ____
    [ ] A
    [ ] A–
    [ ] B+
    [ ] B–
    [ ] B
    [ ] C+
    [ ] C
    [ ] C–
    [ ] D
    [ ] No grade or don't know

19. **In the <u>past 30 days</u>, how many hours per day on average have you spent on each of the following activities? (Choose one answer in each row)**

    Average # Hours per day

	0	1	2	3	4	5	6	7	8+	
b. Studying outside of class	[]	[]	[]	[]	[]	[]	[]	[]	[]	**HRSTUDY:** ____
e. Socializing with friends	[]	[]	[]	[]	[]	[]	[]	[]	[]	**HRSSOCLZ:** ____
g. Intercollegiate athletics	[]	[]	[]	[]	[]	[]	[]	[]	[]	**HRSSPORT:** ____

20. **Which of these racial or ethnic groups describes you best? (Choose one answer)**   **RACE:** ____
    [ ] White
    [ ] Black/African American
    [ ] Asian/Pacific Islander
    [ ] Native American Indian/Native Alaskan
    [ ] Other

21. **During your <u>last year in high school</u>, on how many occasions did you have five or more drinks in a row? (Choose one answer)**   **HSBINGE:** ____
    [ ] Never
    [ ] 1-2 occasions

[ ] 3-5 occasions
[ ] 6-9 occasions
[ ] 10-19 occasions
[ ] 20-39 occasions
[ ] 40 or more occasions

**22. How did your family feel about drinking
alcohol when you were growing up?**   **FAMATTD:** ____
[ ] My family did not approve of drinking.
[ ] They accepted light drinking but disapproved of heavy drinking.
[ ] They accepted heavy drinking.
[ ] There was no agreement about drinking in the family.

THANK YOU VERY MUCH FOR YOUR COOPERATION.

Appendix C: Chapter Review Quizzes and Independent Projects

NAME _____

INSTRUCTOR _____

DATE _____

(1) SPSS stands for _____.

(2) _____ research tests and extends theories for better understanding, whereas research improves the operation of criminal justice agencies by studying what works and what does not work.

(3) A _____ is a set of propositions (or statements) that explain how events or factors are related to one another.

(4) A hypothesis is a statement about the relationship between two _____.

(5) Hypotheses are predictions of _____ relationships. In other words, they predict the average outcome and not necessarily the outcome for every individual case.

(6) A researcher starts with a theory, establishes a hypothesis, and uses variables to check the hypothesis. The researcher is using the process of _____ reasoning.

(7) A researcher collects data, uncovers patterns of findings, and then develops a theoretical explanation for his/her observations. This is an example of the _____ type of reasoning.

(8) To measure the concept of marital satisfaction, a researcher asked subjects "How many children do you have?" This measure lacks _____.

(9) On a questionnaire administered to adult professionals, a researcher asked the respondents how many miles they have driven in their lifetime. The responses range from a very low number to a very high number. When the researchers ask again at the end of the survey, people's responses differ from the first time. This illustrates that the measure for number of miles driven is not _____.

(10) You believe cigarette use may be influenced by social class. Social class is measured using income, years of education, and occupation. Social class is now a composite measure, using _____ to measure the concept.

(11) Your measure of daily cigarette use asks: How many cigarettes do you typically have in a day? 0, 1, 2, 3, 4, 5, 6, 7, 8, 9, 10, 11, 12, etc. Daily cigarette use is a _____ level of measurement.

(12) Your composite measure of class categorizes respondents as lower class, middle class, and upper class. This variable has a(n) _____ level of measurement.

NAME _____

INSTRUCTOR _____

DATE _____

(13) The interval level of measurement has all the properties of the ratio level of measurement except a(n) _____.

(14) A research project wants to compare gun ownership in cities with high rates of crime and cities with low rates of crime. The researcher gathers city statistics about crime rates and gun licensing. The units of analysis are _____ in this project.

INDEPENDENT PROJECT A

CHAPTER ONE

NAME _____

INSTRUCTOR _____

DATE _____

Visit the World Wide Web page for Dr. George Dowdall, the coauthor of this textbook (http://www.sju.edu/-gdowdall). Look under the heading "Substance Abuse Among College Students," click on any of the articles, and read about research in this area.

INDEPENDENT PROJECT B

CHAPTER ONE

NAME _____

INSTRUCTOR _____

DATE _____

Use the World Wide Web page for this book and access the *NIJ Research Plan*. Read through the goals of the *NIJ* and write a brief description of the goals.

NAME _____

INSTRUCTOR _____

DATE _____

(1) As students in this class, we will use the General Social Survey (GSS) to test hypotheses. We are conducting _____ analysis.

(2) Sally wants to research the relationship between gender and marijuana use. She designs a survey questionnaire, administers it, collects the data, enters the data into SPSS, and conducts _____ analysis.

(3) The Inter-university Consortium for Political and Social Research (ICPSR) is a large _____ , located at the University of Michigan.

(4) The subjects for the General Social Survey were selected by first selecting cities or counties, then selecting blocks or their rural equivalents, then selecting households, and finally selecting a respondent age 18 or older. This is called _____ sampling.

(5) When respondents were not asked a particular question in a survey or did not answer the question, they are typically marked _____.

INDEPENDENT PROJECT A

CHAPTER TWO

NAME _____

INSTRUCTOR _____

DATE _____

Using the World Wide Web, go to the website for this book
(http://www.sju.edu/- gdowdall). Go to the General Social Survey
site and search for variables that interest you. Choose five (5) variables
and report their variable name, variable label, and level of measurement.

VARIABLE NAME #1:
VARIABLE LABEL:
LEVEL OF MEASUREMENT:

VARIABLE NAME #2:
VARIABLE LABEL:
LEVEL OF MEASUREMENT:

VARIABLE NAME #3:
VARIABLE LABEL:
LEVEL OF MEASUREMENT:

VARIABLE NAME #4:
VARIABLE LABEL:
LEVEL OF MEASUREMENT:

VARIABLE NAME #5:
VARIABLE LABEL:
LEVEL OF MEASUREMENT:

REVIEW QUIZ

CHAPTER THREE

NAME _____

INSTRUCTOR _____

DATE _____

(1) To open a data file, the sequence of SPSS steps is
file → _open_ → _data_ .

(2) When creating your own data set, you want to be sure to enter value labels to all the codes you put in. To do this in SPSS, you want to click on the _variable view_ tab at the bottom of the screen.

(3) In SPSS for Windows, the data editor cells are arranged so that the rows represent _respondents (cases)_ and the columns represent _variables_ .

(4) To save your work, go under the _____ menu to "Save As."

(5) In addition to the Variable View screen, you can also go under the _utilities_ menu to look up what a particular code for a particular variable represents.

• sav = data file (saved)
• spo = output window (saved)

INDEPENDENT PROJECT A

CHAPTER THREE

NAME _____

INSTRUCTOR _____

DATE _____

Photocopy the sample College Alcohol Survey questionnaire in Appendix B of this book, and have two (2) friends complete the survey. Use the LOCAL.SAV file on your disk and start entering the data for both respondents.

Your first respondent is coded as _____ for GENDER, meaning this respondent is a _____.

What grade in school is your second respondent? What code does this respondent get?

What variables were not answered by your respondents?

What codes were entered for your respondents on the GETDRUNK variable?

NAME   _____

INSTRUCTOR   _____

DATE   _____

(1) "R's Religious Preference" is the _____ for **RELIG.**

(2) Of the 1,500 respondents, _____ report they are Catholic.

(3) "Once a month" and "Never" are _____ for the variable ATTEND.

(4) _____ respondents did not answer the question about how often they attend religious services and are considered "missing."

(5) Just over twelve percent of the sample report attending religious services once a year. This is the _____ based on _____ cases.

(6) The cumulative percent of ATTEND shows that about fifty-six percent of respondents attend church _____ or less.

(7) _____ percent of respondents report that they believe in life after death and _____ percent do not believe. [Use valid percent.]

(8) For the variable PRAY, there are _____ missing cases.

(9) RELIG is a nominal variable. The best type of graph to view this variable is a _____ .

(10) AGE is measured at the _____ level of measurement.

(11) A _____ best graphs the data for AGE.

(12) The mean is a measure of _____ .

(13) The histogram gives the _____ , a measure of dispersion.

(14) The _____ is the most occurring response.

(15) The mean age of the respondents is _____ , and two-thirds of them are between _____ and _____ years old. [Round the numbers.]

(16) Collapsing categories in SPSS may be most easily achieved with the _____ command under the Transform menu.

(17) When you take a continuous variable like years of education and recode it into categories (those with high school education or less versus those with some college or more), the new variable's _____ changes.

(18) When recoding a variable, the cases that are missing should _____ .

INDEPENDENT PROJECT A

CHAPTER FOUR

NAME _____

INSTRUCTOR _____

DATE _____

Using GSS.SAV, recode the variable AGE into a new variable called AGE2 with categories for teens, twenties, thirties, and so on. Be sure to include the new value labels for the variable AGE2. Request a frequency chart for AGE2 and answer the following questions.

1. How many respondents are in their twenties?

2. What percentage are under forty?

3. Which category has the fewest cases?

Recode the variable EDUC into a new variable called EDCAT with new value labels that represent the categories: attended high school; graduated high school; attended college; graduated college; and graduate school (beyond college). Request a frequency chart for EDCAT and answer the following questions.

1. What percentage of respondents have more than a high school diploma?

2. How many respondents went beyond college and what percentage do they represent?

3. How many missing cases are there?

Recode the variable PRAY into PRAY2 with one category that represents people who attend religious services less than once per week and one category that represents people who attend religious services once per week or more. Be sure to include these new value labels. Request a frequency chart for PRAY2 and briefly describe your findings.

INDEPENDENT PROJECT B

CHAPTER FOUR

NAME _____

INSTRUCTOR _____

DATE _____

Request a histogram for the variable CHLDIDEL (ideal number of children) in the data set GSS.SAV. Fill in the following information.

The minimum response for ideal number of children is _____

The maximum response for ideal number of children is _____

The mode response for ideal number of children is _____.

_____ respondents answered this question.

The mean ideal number of children is _____.

The standard deviation for CHLDIDEL is _____.

Sixty-eight percent or two-thirds of the sample believe that between and _____ number of children is ideal.

Is the distribution of CHLDIDEL normal?

NAME _____

INSTRUCTOR _____

DATE _____

(1) When reducing the POLVIEWS seven (7) categories down to three (3) categories, you use the _____ → _____ sequence of commands.

(2) The frequency distribution for POLVIEWS shows that, out of the three categories, liberal, moderate, and conservative, the fewest respondents are _____ . _____

(3) To obtain a frequency distribution, you follow the sequence: STATISTICS → _____ → FREQUENCIES.

(4) The cumulative percent presented in frequency distributions is based on the _____ percent, which is out of only the total valid responses.

(5) _____ When recoding a variable to collapse categories, be sure to go into Variable View to enter the _____ for your newly created variable.

INDEPENDENT PROJECT A

CHAPTER FIVE

NAME _____

INSTRUCTOR _____

DATE _____

In the GSS.SAV file in SPSS, generate frequency distributions for CAPPUN, PREMARSX, HOMOSEX, and POSTLIFE.

What percentage of people (that answered the question) is in favor of capital punishment?

What percentage of people believe that premarital sex is always wrong?

How many people believe that homosexual relations are never wrong?

Do more or less than half of the sample believe in life after death?

Do any of the findings from the four frequency distributions surprise you? Why or why not?

NAME _____

INSTRUCTOR _____

DATE _____

(1) Composite measures are made up of _____.

(2) In SPSS, a table that examines the values of one variable for how contingent they are on the values of another variable is called a _____.

(3) Among the _____ respondents who favor abortion in the case where the woman can not afford any more children (ABPOOR), _____ oppose abortion in the case where the woman's health is seriously endangered (ABHLTH).

(4) _____ respondents oppose abortion in both the case of the woman being not married (ABSINGLE) and if there is a strong chance of a defect (ABDEFECT).

(5) To create a simple index measure based on two (2) variables, the _____ command under the TRANSFORM menu is best.

(6) When we first compute a new variable, we set it equal to _____.

(7) The two ways to create an index variable under the TRANSFORM menu in SPSS are _____ and _____.

(8) An easy way to delineate missing cases in the newly computed variable is to set them equal to _____. We then assign this value as _____.

(9) A more complex index variable is created using the _____ command.

(10) Our index only takes into consideration the respondents who answered _____ of the variables included in the composite measure.

INDEPENDENT PROJECT A

CHAPTER SIX

NAME _____

INSTRUCTOR _____

DATE _____

Using the GSS.SAV data file on your disk, request frequencies for the variables PREMARSX and HOMOSEX. Notice the value labels:

1 *always wrong*
2 *almost always wrong*
3 *sometimes wrong*
4 *not wrong at all*

Recode both variables to collapse the categories into 1 *"wrong"* and 2 *"not wrong."* Be sure to include values 1 through 3 as part of the new *"wrong"* category.

Generate a contingency table (crosstab) with your new recoded variables. Put your variable for attitudes toward premarital sex as your independent variable (the column variable) and attitudes toward homosexuality as your dependent variable (the row variable).

How many respondents feel both premarital sex and homosexuality are wrong?

How many think premarital sex is wrong but homosexuality is not wrong?

How many think homosexuality is wrong but premarital sex is not wrong?

How many think both premarital sex and homosexuality are not wrong? How many respondents answered both questions (valid N)?

Run the same crosstab table again, this time asking for the column percentage.

What percent of respondents who believe premarital sex is wrong also believe homosexuality is wrong?

What percent of respondents who believe premarital sex is not wrong also believe homosexuality is not wrong?

INDEPENDENT PROJECT B

CHAPTER SIX

NAME _____

INSTRUCTOR _____

DATE _____

Using the GSS.SAV data file on your disk, request frequencies for the variables PREMARSX and HOMOSEX. Notice the value labels:

1 *always wrong*
2 *almost always wrong*
3 *sometimes wrong*
4 *not wrong at all*

Recode both variables to collapse the categories into 1 *"wrong"* and 2 *"not wrong."* Be sure to include values 1 through 3 as part of the new *"wrong"* category.

Follow directions from Chapter 6 on how to use the COMPUTE command in SPSS to create a composite measure of "sexual attitudes" that combines your recoded variables for attitudes toward premarital sex and attitudes toward homosexuality.

Be sure to create value labels for your new variable. Print out a frequency and attach it below or recreate the frequency distribution by hand.

NAME _____

INSTRUCTOR _____

DATE _____

(1)   The three (3) criteria for testing causal hypotheses are *time order*, *co-variation*, and the ruling out of *non-spuriousness*.

(2)   In the hypothesis that states men are more likely to binge drink than women, gender is the *independent* variable, and binge drinking is the *dependent* variable.

(3)   A frequency distribution represents univariate analysis. A crosstabulation represents *bivariate* analysis.

(4)   In a crosstab, the independent variable is typically represented by the *columns* in the table, and the dependent variable is represented by the *rows*.

(5)   To test the hypothesis in question #2, when setting up the crosstabulation, you should request the *column* percentage.

(6)   The difference in percentages calculated from the distribution of attributes on the dependent variable between the extreme categories of the independent variable is called the *epsilon*.

(7)   The sequence to obtain a crosstabulation in SPSS is
Analyze → _____ → *Crosstabs*.

(8)   If you want to know the percentage of one attribute on the dependent variable, without concern for the influence of the independent variable, you look to the *row* total for your answer.

(9)   The conclusion that Republicans tend to be more conservative than Democrats was derived from the crosstabulation between _____ and
_____.

(10) The total number of respondents for a crosstabulation (valid N) is based on the number of people who answered *both* of the two questions.

INDEPENDENT PROJECT A

CHAPTER SEVEN

NAME _Tim Atwood_

INSTRUCTOR _Lozto_

DATE _3/21/06_

Construct a crosstabulation with the variables COLLBING and RELIGION from the BINGE.SAV data file. Remember to request column percentages.

Write a hypothesis about these two variables.

Students who say religion is very important are less likely to have binged than students who say religion is not important to them.

What is the epsilon comparing binge drinking between respondents who think religion is a very important activity and those respondents who think religion is not an important activity?

8.4% who binge thought religion was very important
40.3% who ~~b~~ thought religion was not important
~~40.3 -8.4 = 31.9 % points~~

46.8 - 19.4 = 27.4 % points

What percentage of respondents who report religion is very important report never binge drinking? *80.6%*

Is your hypothesis supported or not supported by this bivariate analysis?

Supported

Continuing to use the BINGE.SAV data file, recode AGE into a new age variable that distinguishes between 21 years old and over and under 21 years old. Crosstab this new age variable with COLLBING.

What is the epsilon between underage binge drinkers and 21-year-old and over binge drinkers? *42.6 - 40.4 = 2.2 % points*

Which group is more likely to binge drink? Is this what you expected?

Students under 21, yes but not by as large a margin as I would have thought

INDEPENDENT PROJECT B
CHAPTER SEVEN

NAME _____

INSTRUCTOR _____

DATE _____

Using the GSS.SAV data file, recode MARITAL into a new variable that compares married respondents and non-married respondents. Generate a crosstabulation with this new marital status variable and your recoded political party identification and political views variables. Remember to request the column percentage.

Write a hypothesis about martial status and political party identification.

Write a hypothesis about marital status and political views.

What percentage of married respondents are Democratic?

What percentage of married respondents are politically conservative?

What percentage of non-married respondents report moderate political views?

What is the epsilon when comparing married and non-married respondents on the measure of being Republican?

Are one or both of your hypotheses supported by the bivariate analyses? Explain.

REVIEW QUIZ

CHAPTER EIGHT

NAME _____

INSTRUCTOR _____

DATE _____

(1) If the independent variable is gender and the dependent variable is political party affiliation (Democrat, Republican, Independent, Other), the most appropriate measure of association is _____.

(2) A gamma reveals both the existence of an association between variables and the _____ of that relationship.

(3) A gamma of −.258 allows the researcher to conclude that, by knowing the independent variable, she reduced the number of errors in guessing her dependent variable by about _____ percent.

(4) Pearson's r correlation coefficient is appropriate for measuring the association between two variables with a(n) _____ level of measurement.

(5) When discussing measures of association, PRE stands for _____ _____.

(6) Lambda is calculated by comparing _____ and _____ errors.

(7) Gamma is calculated based on _____ and _____ pairs.

(8) Gamma is used with variables with a(n) _____ level of measurement, meaning the data can be _____.

(9) The measure of association between educational level (less than high school, high school, college and more) and receiving government assistance (no assistance, some assistance, entirely reliant on assistance) is a gamma equal to −.2345. This means that respondents with a higher level of education are, on average, receiving _____ government assistance.

(10) A sociologist found a −.40 Pearson r correlation between people's years of education and number of children. _____ percent of the variation in number of children can be explained by people's education. [You can use a calculator.]

(11) A regression line that starts from the lower left corner of a scatterplot and continues to the upper right tells us that, as the independent variable increases, the dependent variable _____.

(12) An instructor asked students how many hours they studied for a test. After the test, he calculated the following regression statistic for the number of hours students said they had studied and their test scores: alpha (intercept) = .30, beta (slope) = .10. The predicted score for a student who studied four (4) hours would be _____ percent. [Use a calculator if you wish.]

INDEPENDENT PROJECT A

CHAPTER EIGHT

NAME   _____

INSTRUCTOR   _____

DATE   _____

Using the BINGE.SAV data file, create a crosstabulation that measures the association between membership in a fraternity or sorority (FRATSORO) and binge drinking (COLLBING).

What measure of association did you ask for? What is the value of this measure of association?

What percentage of respondents who are not in a fraternity or sorority report binge drinking?

What percentage of respondents who are in a fraternity or sorority report binge drinking?

What is the epsilon?

Based on your analysis, is there an association between membership in a fraternity/sorority and binge drinking?

INDEPENDENT PROJECT B

CHAPTER EIGHT

NAME _____

INSTRUCTOR _____

DATE _____

Using the BINGE.SAV data file, create a crosstabulation that measures the association between year in school (CLASS) and importance of parties as a college activity (PARTIES).

What measure of association did you ask for?

What is the value of this measure of association?

What percentage of first year students believe parties are very important? What percentage of seniors believe parties are very important?

Based on your analysis, is there an association between year in school and the importance of parties?

What is the direction of the association? Explain what this means.

INDEPENDENT PROJECT C

CHAPTER EIGHT

NAME   _____

INSTRUCTOR   _____

DATE   _____

Using the BINGE.SAV data file, test the association between number of hours spent socializing (HRSSOCLZ) and number of hours spent participating in athletics (HRSSPORT)

What measure of association did you ask for? Square this value. What does this mean?

Is the relationship between hours spent socializing and hours spent participating in sports statistically significant?

Repeat the above exercise and add the third variable of hours spent studying (HRSSTUDY).

What is the coefficient value for the association between hours studying and hours spent participating in sports?

What is the coefficient value for the association between hours studying and hours socializing?

Are these relationships statistically significant?

NAME _____

INSTRUCTOR _____

DATE _____

Using the GSS.SAV data file from your disk, test the association between respondents' socio-economic status (SEI) and social class (CLASS). Use SEI as the dependent variable.

Fill in the following information:

$$\text{SEI} = \underline{\hspace{2cm}} + (\text{CLASS} + \underline{\hspace{2cm}})$$
$$\qquad\quad \textit{intercept} \qquad\qquad\qquad \textit{slope}$$

Calculate the predicted SEI for a lower-class respondent. Show your calculations.

Calculate the predicted SEI for an upper-class respondent. Show your calculations.

NAME _____

INSTRUCTOR _____

DATE _____

(1) A chi square tests to see if the relationship happened because of _bias_ or to assess the likelihood that the relationship could have occurred by chance.

(2) The variables best used with chi square have a _nominal_ or _ordinal_ level of measurement.

(3) Chi square is calculated by comparing the observed data with the _expected outcome,_ which is based on no relationship between the variables.

(4) By traditional social science standards, chi square has to have a probability level of ___.05___ or less to be considered significant.

(5) In SPSS the column under the heading "df" gives the _degree_ of _freedom_

(6) As values of chi square go up, the probability or "p" value goes _down_ .

(7) A researcher has used SPSS to find a lambda of .12 and a chi square with a probability of .001. This means he has found a relationship with a _12_ % proportionate reduction in error and a _significant_ chi square.

ratio, dichotomous...

(8) T-tests are best suited for dependent variables that have a _____ level of measurement.

(9) As in chi-sqaure, the "p" value in a t-test tells us if the relationship between the two variables is _significant_ or not.

(10) ANOVA extends the logic of the t-test and tests for a significant difference between a ratio dependent variable and an independent variable with _3_ or more attributes.

INDEPENDENT PROJECT A

CHAPTER NINE

NAME _____

INSTRUCTOR _____

DATE _____

Using the GSS.SAV data file, examine the bivariate relationship between a respondent's religious affiliation (RELIG recoded) and his or her opinion of homosexuality (HOMOSEX). Request a Chi-Square test.

What percentage of Catholics believe homosexuality is always wrong? What percentage of Protestants believe homosexuality is always wrong?

50% of Catholics   67% of Protestants

Which religious group has the largest percentage reporting that homosexuality is not wrong at all?

Jewish with 73%

Is there evidence of a relationship between religion and attitude toward homosexuality?

Yes, those at the Christian religions believe homosexual relation are wrong more then other religions or people at no religion.

What is the value of the chi-square? Does it indicate a significant association between religion and attitude toward homosexuality?

~~BA~~   p < .001   it indicates a significant relation between religion and attitudes toward homosexuality.

if p < .001 then 99.9% at general population

NAME _____

INSTRUCTOR _____

DATE _____

Using the GSS.SAV data file, compare the mean socio-economic score (SEI) *(ratio)* for males and for females (SEX). *run a T-test* *(nominal & dichotomous)*

What is the mean score on SEI for males? What is the mean score on SEI for females?   *51%*   *49%*

Request an independent samples t test to examine the relationship between socio-economic status and sex.

The average SEI score for males is ___*2.2*___ points (higher) or lower than females?

SPSS has calculated that ___*50*___ times in 1,000 samples, sampling error might produce a difference this great in either direction.

NAME _____

INSTRUCTOR _____

DATE _____

Using the GSS.SAV data file, request a simple, one-way ANOVA test for socio-economic status (SEI) for Whites, Blacks, and respondents from the "other" racial category. (RACE)

What is the sum of squares between groups?

What is the significance level?

REVIEW QUIZ

CHAPTER TEN

NAME _____

INSTRUCTOR _____

DATE _____

(1) The simultaneous analysis of three (3) or more variables that examines how two (2) or more variables cause a change in a single variable is called _____ analysis.

(2) The results from the GSS show that, while the relationship between age and attendance of religious services is the same for both men and women, _____ of all ages are more likely to attend services than _____.

(3) _____ theory suggests that people use religious activities to compensate for the lack of family, social prestige, or power.

(4) Dichotomous variables in regression analysis are sometimes called _____ variables.

(5) In multiple regression, the statistic that provides the comparable impact of independent variables on the dependent variable is the _____.

INDEPENDENT PROJECT A

CHAPTER TEN

NAME _____

INSTRUCTOR _____

DATE _____

Using the GSS.SAV data file, generate a crosstabulation to examine the relationship between having seen an X-rated movie (XMOVIE) and attitude toward homosexuality (HOMOSEX). Test this relationship while considering the respondents' gender (SEX) also. Request the chi-square statistics to check for statistical significance.

Fill in the information below.

PERCENTAGE OF RESPONDENTS
FEEL HOMOSEXUALITY IS ALWAYS WRONG

Seen X-Rated Movie

Yes   *No*

Males

Females

Is the relationship between having seen an X-rated movie and attitudes toward homosexuality statistically significant for males? For females?

Test this same relationship while considering religious preference (RELIG). Again, generate the chi-square statistics.

NAME _____

INSTRUCTOR _____

DATE _____

Fill in the information below.

**PERCENTAGE OF RESPONDENTS
FEEL HOMOSEXUALITY IS ALWAYS WRONG**

	Seen X-Rated Movie		**Significant (Y or N)**
	Yes	*No*	
Protestant			
Catholic			
Jewish			
No Religion			
Other Religion			

INDEPENDENT PROJECT B

CHAPTER TEN

NAME _____

INSTRUCTOR _____

DATE _____

Using the GSS.SAV data file, examine the influence of gender and race (simultaneously) on educational level. In SPSS, run a multivariate linear regression with education (EDUC) as the dependent variable. Recode gender (SEX) and race (RACE) into dummy variables. Be sure to include value labels in your recoded SEX2 and RACE2.

Fill in the following information:

$$EDUC = \underset{\textit{intercept}}{\underline{\hspace{2cm}}} + (SEX2 \times \underset{\textit{slope}}{\underline{\hspace{1.5cm}}}) + (RACE2 \times \underset{\textit{slope}}{\underline{\hspace{1.5cm}}})$$

Calculate the predicted education level for a white female. Show your calculations.

Calculate the predicted education level for a black male. Show your calculations.

Which variable, gender or race, has the most impact on educational level?

NAME _____

INSTRUCTOR _____

DATE _____

(1) A teacher looks at the relationship between the number of hours students studied for a test and their test scores and finds no relationship. She then looks at the relationship again for only those students who were below average on their SAT scores and finds a strong relationship between hours studied and test scores. This is an example of _____.

(2) In the GSS, the relationship between party and political philosophy is strongest for people who are _____.

(3) When performing a multivariate analysis, you can be relatively certain that gender is NOT the _____ variable.

(4) When social scientists speak of _____ for a third variable, they mean the relationship is examined for each category of the third variable.

(5) In SPSS, the crosstab window has a space for you to enter a third "layer" variable. This is the _____ variable you will examine for further influence on your dependent variable.

INDEPENDENT PROJECT A

CHAPTER ELEVEN

NAME _____

INSTRUCTOR _____

DATE _____

Using the GSS.SAV data file, examine the bivariate relationship between prejudice attitudes about why there are racial differences (RACDIF4) and religious affiliation (RELIG recoded). Consider the influence of gender (SEX), race (RACE), and education (EDUC). You will want to recode EDUC into a new variable that differentiates between respondents with high school or less and those with some college or more.

Complete the table below:

PERCENT REPORTING THEY BELIEVE A LACK OF WILL IS THE REASON FOR RACIAL INEQUALITY

	Religious Affiliation			
	Protestant	*Catholic*	*Jewish*	*None*

Sex
Male
Female

Race
White
Black
Other

Education
High school or less
Some college and more

Is there evidence of a relationship between religious affiliation and prejudice attitudes about racial inequality?

Is this relationship more evident among certain groups? Which groups?

NAME   _____

INSTRUCTOR   _____

DATE   _____

(1) Many dependent variables in criminal justice that are simple dichotomies or dummies can be analyzed with _____ regression.

(2) The _____ of something happening means the number of events compared to the number of nonevents,

(3) The odds ratio tells us the existence, _____ , and _____ of an association.

(4) A confidence interval around the odds ratio is used to assess statistical _____ .

(5) A single dichotomous dependent variable, several independent variables, and an estimation of conditional or adjusted odds ratio are all part of _____ .

INDEPENDENT PROJECT A
CHAPTER TWELVE

NAME _____

INSTRUCTOR _____

DATE _____

Using the GSS.SAV data file, examine the relationship between gender (SEX) and attitudes toward capital punishment (CAPPUN). Request the risk estimate and interpret the odds ratio.

Fill in the information below:

The odds of men supporting the death penalty is _____ times greater than the odds of women supporting the death penalty.

With about 95% confidence, you can predict that the population odds ratio for men's greater likelihood to support the death penalty will be between _____ and _____.

Name some other variables that might influence attitudes toward capital punishment.

Appendix D: Answers to Chapter Quizzes

Chapter 1 Quiz

1. Statistical Package for the Social Sciences
2. Basic; applied
3. Theory
4. variables
5. probabilistic
6. deductive
7. inductive
8. validity
9. reliability
10. multiple indicators
11. ratio
12. ordinal
13. true zero
14. cities

Chapter 2 Quiz

1. secondary
2. primary
3. data archive
4. multistage probability
5. missing

Chapter 3 Quiz

1. File → Open → Data
2. Variable View
3. Respondents (or cases); variables
4. File
5. Utilities

Chapter 4 Quiz

1. Variable label
2. 421
3. value labels
4. 41
5. valid percent; 1459
6. several times per year
7. 79.5; 20.5
8. 776
9. bar chart
10. ratio
11. histogram
12. central tendency
13. standard deviation
14. mode
15. 45; 28; 62
16. recode
17. level of measurement
18. stay missing

Chapter 5 Quiz

1. Transform → Recode
2. liberal
3. Descriptive Statistics
4. valid
5. value labels

Chapter 6 Quiz

1. multiple indicators
2. crosstab
3. 428; 4
4. 173
5. Compute
6. zero

7. Count; Compute

8. −1; missing

9. Count

10. all

Chapter 7 Quiz

1. time order; co-variation; rival causal factors

2. independent; dependent

3. bivariate

4. columns; rows

5. column

6. epsilon

7. Descriptive Statistics → Crosstab

8. row

9. POLVIEWS; PARTYID

10. both

Chapter 8 Quiz

1. lambda

2. direction

3. 26

4. ratio (or interval)

5. proportionate reduction in error

6. uneducated; educated

7. same; opposite

8. ordinal; rank ordered

9. less

10. 16%

11. increases

12. 70%

Chapter 9 Quiz

1. bias

2. nominal; ordinal

3. expected

4. .05

5. degrees; freedom

6. down

7. 12%; significant

8. ratio (or interval)

9. significant

10. 3

Chapter 10 Quiz

1. multivariate

2. women; men

3. Social deprivation

4. dummy (or indicator)

5. Beta

Chapter 11 Quiz

1. specification

2. highly educated

3. dependent

4. controlling

5. control

Chapter 12 Quiz

1. logistic

2. odds

3. direction; strength

4. significance

5. logistic

REFERENCES AND SUGGESTED READINGS

Alwin, Duane F. 1989. "Changes in Qualities Valued in Children in the United States, 1964 to 1984." *Social Science Research* 18: 195-236.

Archer, Dane, and Rosemary Gartner. 1984. *Violence and Crime in Cross-National Perspective.* New Haven, CT: Yale University Press.

Babbie, Earl, and Fred Halley. 1995. *Adventures in Social Research: Data Analysis Using SPSS for Windows.* Thousand Oaks, CA: Pine Forge.

Bailey, Carol A. 1996. *A Guide to Field Research.* Thousand Oaks, CA: Pine Forge.

Becker, Howard S. 1986. *Writing for Social Scientists.* Chicago: University of Chicago Press.

Blake, Judith. 1989. *Family Size and Achievement.* Berkeley: University of California Press.

Chamlin, Mitchell B. 1990. "Determinants of Police Expenditures in Chicago, 1904-1958." *Sociological Quarterly* 31:485-494.

Cohen, Laurence E., and Marcus Felson. 1979. "Social Change and Crime Rate Trends: A Routine Activity Approach." *American Sociological Review* 44: 588-608.

Cook, Elizabeth Adell, Ted G. Jelen, and Clyde Wilcox. 1992. *Between Two Absolutes: Public Opinion and the Politics of Abortion.* Boulder, CO: Westview Press.

Curran, Daniel J., and Claire M. Renzetti. 1994. *Theories of Crime.* Needham Heights, MA: Allyn & Bacon.

Czaja, Robert, and Johnny Blair. 1996. *Designing Surveys.* Thousand Oaks, CA: Pine Forge.

D'Antonio, William V., and Steven Stack. 1980. "Religion, Ideal Family Size, and Abortion: Extending Renzi's Hypotheses." *Journal for the Scientific Study of Religion* 19: 397-408.

Davis, James A., and Tom W. Smith. 1990. *General Social Surveys, 1972-1990: Cumulative Codebook.* Chicago: National Opinion Research Center.

Davis, James A., and Tom W. Smith. 1992. *The NORC General Social Survey: A User's Guide.* Thousand Oaks, CA: Sage.

Ennett, Susan T., Nancy S. Tobler, Christopher L. Ringwalt, and Robert L. Flewelling. 1994. "How Effective Is Drug Abuse Resistance Education? A Meta-analysis of Project DARE Outcome Evaluations." *American Journal of Public Health* 84: 1394-1401.

Felson, Marcus. 1994. *Crime and Everyday Life.* Thousand Oaks, CA: Pine Forge.

Glock, Charles Y., Benjamin B. Ringer, and Earl R. Babbie. 1967. *To Comfort and to Challenge.* Berkeley: University of California Press.

Hamilton, Lawrence. 1992. *Regression with Graphics*. Belmont, CA: Duxbury Press.

Hosmer, David W., and Stanley Lemeshow. 1989. *Applied Logistic Regression*. New York: John Wiley.

Lane, Roger. 1979. *Violent Death in the City: Suicide, Accident, and Murder in Nineteenth-Century Philadelphia*. Cambridge, MA: Harvard University Press.

Loftin, Colin, and David McDowall. 1982. "The Police, Crime, and Economic Theory: An Assessment." *American Sociological Review* 47: 393-401.

Lottes, Ilsa L., Marina A. Adler, and Alfred De Maris. 1996. "Using and Interpreting Logistic Regression: A Guide for Teachers and Students." *Teaching Sociology* 24: 284-298.

Maguire, Kathleen, and Ann L. Pastore (eds.). 1995. *Sourcebook of Criminal Justice Statistics*. Washington, DC: U.S. Bureau of Justice Statistics.

Maisel, Richard, and Caroline Hodges Persell. 1996. *How Sampling Works*. Thousand Oaks, CA: Pine Forge.

Maxfield, Michael G., and Earl Babbie. 1995. *Research Methods for Criminal Justice and Criminology*. Belmont, CA: Wadsworth.

Menard, Scott. 1995. *Applied Logistic Regression Analysis*. Thousand Oaks, CA: Sage.

Mullins, Carolyn J. 1977. *A Guide to Writing in the Social and Behavioral Sciences*. New York: John Wiley.

National Institute of Justice. 1994. *Data Resources of the National Institute of Justice*, 7th ed. Washington, DC: Government Printing Office.

Norusis, Marija J. 1995. *SPSS 6.1 Guide to Data Analysis*. Upper Saddle River, NJ: Prentice Hall.

Norusis, Marija J./SPSS, Inc. 1993. *SPSS for Windows Base System User's Guide, Release 6.0*. Chicago: SPSS.

Norusis, Marija J./SPSS, Inc. 1994. *SPSS Advanced Statistics 6.1*. Chicago: SPSS.

Pagano, Marcello, and Kimberlee Gauvreau. 1993. *Principles of Biostatistics*. Belmont, CA: Duxbury Press.

Reiss, Albert J., and Jeffrey A. Roth (eds.). 1993. *Understanding and Preventing Violence*. Washington, DC: National Academy Press.

Renzi, Mario. 1975. "Ideal Family Size as an Intervening Variable Between Religion and Attitudes Toward Abortion." *Journal for the Scientific Study of Religion* 14: 23-27.

Roe v. Wade, 410 U.S. 113 (1973).

Schutt, Russell K. 2001. *Investigating the Social World: The Process and Practice of Research*, 3rd ed. Thousand Oaks, CA: Pine Forge.

Schwartz, Martin D., and Victoria L. Pitts. 1995. "Exploring a Feminist Routine Activities Approach to Explaining Sexual Assault." *Justice Quarterly* 12(1): 9-31.

Skogan, Wesley G. 1976. *Chicago Since 1840: A Time-Series Data Handbook.* Urbana: University of Illinois, Institute of Government and Public Affairs.

Smith, Tom W., and Bradley J. Arnold. 1990. *Annotated Bibliography of Papers Using the General Social Survey.* Chicago: National Opinion Research Center.

Snyder, Howard N., and Melissa Sickmund. 1995. *Juvenile Offenders and Victims: A National Report.* Washington, DC: Office of Juvenile Justice and Delinquency Prevention.

Snyder, Howard N., Melissa Sickmund, and Eileen Poe-Yamagata. 1996. *Juvenile Offenders and Victims: 1996 Update on Violence.* Washington, DC: Office of Juvenile Justice and Delinquency Prevention.

SPSS, Inc. 1994. *SPSS 6.1 Syntax Reference Guide.* Chicago: SPSS.

Strunk, William, Jr., and E. B. White. 1979. *The Elements of Style,* 3rd ed. New York: Macmillan.

Turabian, Kate L. 1967. *A Manual for Writers of Term Papers, Theses, and Dissertations,* 3rd ed., rev. Chicago: University of Chicago Press.

United Nations Development Programme. 1995. *Human Development Report, 1995.* New York: Oxford University Press.

Vogt, W. Paul. 1993. *Dictionary of Statistics and Methodology.* Thousand Oaks, CA: Sage.

Walsh, Anthony. 1987. "Teaching Understanding and Interpretation of Logit Regression." *Teaching Sociology* 15: 178-183.

Weber, Max. 1995. *The Protestant Ethic and the Spirit of Capitalism* (Talcott Parsons, trans.). New York: Scribner's. (Original work published 1905)

Wechsler, Henry, Andrea Davenport, George Dowdall, Barbara Moeykens, and Sonia Castillo. 1994. "Health and Behavioral Consequences of Binge Drinking in College: A National Survey of Students at 140 Colleges." *Journal of the American Medical Association* 272: 1672-1677.

Wechsler, Henry, Charles C. Deutsch, and George Dowdall. 1995. "Too Many Colleges Are Still in Denial About Alcohol Abuse." *Chronicle of Higher Education* 41 (April 14): B1-B2.

Wechsler, Henry, George Dowdall, Andrea Davenport, and Sonia Castillo. 1995. "Correlates of College Student Binge Drinking." *American Journal of Public Health* 85: 921-926.

Wechsler, Henry, George W. Dowdall, Andrea Davenport, and William DeJong. 1995. "Binge Drinking on Campus: Results of a National Study." *Bulletin Series. Alcohol and Other Drug Prevention.* Bethesda, MD: Higher Education Center for Alcohol and Other Drug Prevention.

Wechsler, Henry, George Dowdall, Andrea Davenport, and Eric Rimm. 1995. "A Gender-Specific Measure of Binge Drinking Among College Students." *American Journal of Public Health* 85: 982-985.

INDEX